MISTRESS BRADSTREET

MISTRESS BRADSTREET

The Untold Life of America's First Poet

CHARLOTTE GORDON

LITTLE, BROWN AND COMPANY

NEW YORK   BOSTON

To all those whose stories have gone untold
and to
Julie Miles Gordon

Little, Brown and Company
Time Warner Book Group
1271 Avenue of the Americas, New York, NY 10020
Visit our Web site at www.twbookmark.com

First Edition: March 2005

We are grateful to the Trustees of Stevens Memorial Library, North
Andover, Massachusetts, owner of the Anne Bradstreet manuscript, for
permission to reproduce the dedication page of *Meditations Divine
and morall* and the title page of "The Tenth Muse."

Library of Congress Cataloging-in-Publication Data

Gordon, Charlotte.
  Mistress Bradstreet : the untold life of America's first poet /
by Charlotte Gordon. — 1st ed.
    p. cm.
  Includes bibliographical references and index.
  ISBN 0-316-16904-8
  1. Bradstreet, Anne, 1612?–1672. 2. Women and literature — New
England — History — 17th century. 3. Poets, American — Colonial
period, ca. 1600–1775 — Biography. 4. Puritan women — New
England — Intellectual life. 5. Puritans — New England — Biography.
I. Title.
PS712.G67 2005
811'.1 — dc22   2004022702

10 9 8 7 6 5 4 3 2 1
Q-FF

Book designed by Brooke Koven

Printed in the United States of America

Slender in build,
A narrow, almond-eyed shade,

. . . .

she drifts up from the gaping gold,

. . . .

to the crown of the Now.

—PAUL CELAN, from "In Front of a Candle"

Contents

Preface

I AM SOMEONE WHO BECAME OBSESSED, passionately so, with a woman who lived nearly four hundred years ago, a woman who lived right down the street from me. Sometimes I wonder if our subjects choose us or if we choose them.

In 1991 I was twenty-eight years old and terrified because I had just gotten my first real teaching job. I had moved to Ipswich, Massachusetts, a small New England village a few miles from the sea. Now I had to get high school students excited about poetry and, at the same time, teach them something about American history and literature. It happened that Anne Bradstreet was the first author on the course syllabus. I did not know much about her, aside from the fact that she was the "first" American poet and always appeared on a few pages in the first chapter of American-literature anthologies. In my mind her only claim to recognition was good timing. None of my English teachers had ever mentioned her, and the cursory introduction in my old college textbook was no help. The editor said she wrote in "laboring and tedious couplets." Poor Bradstreet!

But then one of those coincidences happened that change your life. The day before my first class, while I was on my daily run, I noticed a plaque mounted on a stone. It was partially obscured by a large bush, and this made it seem all the more mysterious. Curious, I trotted up the path and read, "Near this spot was the house of Simon Bradstreet, Governor of Massachusetts Bay, 1679–1686 and 1689–1692. His wife, Ann [*sic*], daughter of Governor Dudley, was the first American poetess. They lived in Ipswich, 1635–44." Suddenly I wanted to know more about my long-dead neighbor. What was she doing in Ipswich? What was she doing in America in 1635? I had thought only the Pilgrims were here then.

I raced home and studied her poems with sharpened attention. The next day in class I read aloud some of my favorite lines. About being a woman, from "The Prologue": "I am obnoxious / to each carping tongue / Who says my hand a needle better fits." About loss, from "Upon the Burning of Our House": "Here stood my trunk, and there that chest, / There lay that store I counted best. / My pleasant things in ashes lie." About love, from "To My Dear and Loving Husband": "If ever two were one, then surely we. / If ever man were loved by wife, then thee; / If ever wife was happy in a man, / Compare with me ye women if you can." To my amazement, my students liked them. One even asked if we could spend more time on her.

Years have passed since that discovery, and I have read Bradstreet with class after class of students. They have been thrilled by her passion and slang, her formality and humor; and because of their eagerness to know more about her, I soon found myself wondering why she had not been part of my own education in American literature. Nestled right next to her poems in her collected works, there is an astonishingly powerful autobiography, as well as religious meditations, and some reflections in prose. Anne articulates important ideas about what it means to be an American, a mother, and a person of faith during bleak and despairing times. Her writing is unabashedly honest and offers sudden brave glimpses into her struggles and her private ideas.

At the very least she should have turned up as a prominent early-American woman pioneer. She sailed to New England in 1630 at age eighteen, hiked through the first-growth forests with pines as huge as California redwoods, bore eight children in the wilderness, and published the first book of poems from the New World. Yet when I looked her up in the library, few people had written about her. To date there have been only two biographies, the most recent of which was published in 1974, and only one book-length critical study. Lately, it seems, she has become a favorite of literary scholars, perhaps because the immediacy of her voice speaks to contemporary readers. But whatever the reason for this scholarly interest, in general, most people have barely heard of her. Was it really possible that such a likable poet, who lived life on such a magnificent scale, had been so neglected? After all, she had been a celebrity in her own lifetime and had left a substantial body of work, as much as any of our other major writers.

I embarked on a pilgrimage to find Anne. I've read countless journals and letters from the time, as well as many books on topics such as seventeenth-century gardening, baking, shipping, economics, weaving, child rearing, courtship practices, theology, and legal codes. As a result, this book has become as much a quest for a lost country as it is for her.

It is difficult to reconstruct the past. In fact, really, it is impossible. There is little physical evidence remaining. Even her house is gone, like most of the dwellings of the early settlers, burned, torn down, crumbled to ash. On their bones, our houses crowd together, huge, windowed, balconied. Cars roar by on the old paths, now paved. I live less than twenty miles from where Anne used to live, but often she feels as far away as the moon.

But one December night I had one of those moments in which she felt close enough to touch. The snow was falling fast — more than a foot that afternoon, and more was piling up. The drifts were as high as the roof of my car. The wind was boiling in off the ocean, and the house shook with each gust of heavy air. This was a real storm, the kind that makes you glad you don't live in one of the houses on the shore. The sea was gray and smoky, like a cauldron, breaking over the little stone walls of the summer houses.

After supper my family's lights flickered ominously and then went out. At first the darkness was like an unexpected intermission. We were not cold yet and wouldn't be for several more hours. Simply, it was dark, dark, dark. We fumbled for flashlights, candles, matches, and once we had found these things, the muted tones of the house, the deep shadows, seemed romantic, as though we were having an extended candlelit dinner. But the wind continued to bang against the walls, the windows rattled, and the inconveniences began. There was no hot water to give my son his nightly bath, no light to read to him by. I couldn't find his stuffed dog. Once he was tucked in, it was too dark to read my own book, and too cold and noisy. Before long my son was out of bed, crying. The wind would not stop and he could not go to sleep. "It's too loud, Mommy," he complained. "It's cold." And it *was* cold, unrelentingly so.

I climbed into bed next to my son, and as we lay there shivering, I knew that this, of course, was how winter was for Anne, but worse. Her house had thinner walls. No foam insulation or storm windows, just panels of wood with clay daubed between the cracks. She and her husband were rich, so they could afford to light a few candles if they chose to, but still they had to use them sparingly. Largely they depended on messy, unreliable lamps fashioned out of pine resin and tar. Their fire would have gone out in such a storm unless they stayed up all night to tend it, and the house would have gotten colder and colder. If I found one night like this almost impossible to bear, how did she find the strength and inspiration not only to survive the wilderness but to stand firm in her faith, and to write? How did she not despair?

THERE IS A JEWISH TRADITION of *midrash*, which is when the rabbis attempted "to fill in the gaps" of some of the more mystifying biblical stories, such as those of Job or Jonah and the whale, and in many ways that is what these pages have become. By retelling some of the history, the details, and the facts of her time, I have attempted to resurrect Anne and her home in early America. But I have also tried to piece together something more — what it felt like to be one of the first Europeans in America and what Anne, a gently bred, highly educated woman, might have thought, done, and experienced as she struggled through the ordeal of emigration and settling a new country. What was it like to live in a time before electric lights and high heels, before microwaves, blue jeans, and pollution, when the fastest thing around was a seagull or a galloping horse?

Of course, Anne had no idea that she lived "before" anything in particular, any more than we think that the twenty-first century is a time "before." To us it is always now, modern times. We are the latest thing. So thought Anne, once upon a time. She believed that she was the most modern of the moderns.

Still, the limitations of what we can know, no matter how obsessed we are, have, inevitably, become clear to me. She walks ahead of me and I don't get to see her face. Was her hair brown or pale? Was she slim? Did she get heavier as she bore her children? Or was she petite, like a bird? What did her voice sound like? Did she argue with her husband? Did she like to cook? Was she as ambitious as I think she was? Would she have approved of my writing about her? But the closer I have drawn, the more she has receded, her figure diminishing, no matter how I strain to catch up. Those shores of early America are irretrievable, as is Anne. I have tried to revive her here, but some of the most important things are bound to be left unknown.

MISTRESS BRADSTREET

CHAPTER ONE

❦

Arrival

AFTER SEVENTY-SEVEN DAYS AT SEA, one Captain Milbourne steered his ship, the *Arbella* — packed with more than three hundred hungry, exhausted souls — into Salem Harbor, shooting off the ship's cannon in elation. It was early in the morning of June 12, 1630, a date that would prove to be more fateful to America than the more-famous 1492, but if either the captain or his hapless passengers had expected any kind of fanfare from the New World itself, they were to be disappointed. Far from offering herself up for casual and easy delectation, America hunched like a dark animal, sleeping and black, offering no clues about her contours, let alone the miracles reported by the rumor mill of the 1620s: inland seas, dragons, Indians adorned in golden necklaces, fields sown with diamonds, and bears as tall as windmills.

To the bedraggled individuals who clung to the rails of this huge flagship, once a battleship in the Mediterranean wars against Turkish pirates and now the first vessel of its kind to have successfully limped across the ocean from England, it must have seemed cruel that they would have to wait until dawn before they could glimpse this world that still swam just out of their reach. Most of the passengers, however, were pious individuals and bowed their heads in acquiescence to the Lord's will. But the few rebellious souls, and there were some notable firebrands onboard the *Arbella*, could not help but find themselves feeling more discontented than ever.

One in particular, a young woman of about eighteen years, could not subdue her resentment. She wished that the new land would never appear before her eyes, that she had never been ripped away from her beloved England, even that she had perished in the waters they had just crossed rather than face what would come next. Not that she admitted her fears to any of the other passengers pacing on the deck that morning. Anne Dudley Bradstreet was the daughter of Deputy Governor Thomas Dudley, the second in command of the expedition, and was too acutely aware of her responsibilities to show her feelings of resentment.

To her, though, it seemed an outrageous venture to have undertaken. To most English people, it was a foolhardy one as well. With the exception of the notorious Pilgrims, who had arrived in Cape Cod in 1620, whom Captain Milbourne and his passengers regarded as crazed radicals with admirable ideals but little common sense, few Englishmen and even fewer women had braved this terrible journey to Massachusetts. For the weary passengers onboard the *Arbella*, the greatest challenge they had to stare down was not starvation, storms, plague, whales, or even Indians. Instead it was the astonishing mystery they faced: Where were they going? What would it be like when they set foot on land? America had seemed as impossible as a fairy tale, and yet suddenly, in the next few hours, it was about to become miraculously real.

It was difficult not to speculate. Maybe there would be wild vineyards laden with grapes. Maybe tigers would spring up out of the water. Maybe the settlers would die immediately of some New World fever or get eaten by giant creatures. Maybe, though, they had finally arrived in the land of milk and honey, which was what some of the preachers back home had hinted at. If England was a corrupt country, then America had every possibility of being a new chance, the promised land, a Canaan that offered not only respite but also fame, glory, and God's approval.

Anne remained unconvinced by such heady forecasts. But she had learned to hide her doubts from those who watched to see how the deputy governor's eldest daughter behaved. Only many years later did she admit how resistant she had been to coming to America. When "I found a new world and new manners," she wrote, "my heart rose," meaning not that she rejoiced but that she retched.[1] Certainly she had no idea of the fame that lay ahead for her. Indeed, only a seer, the kind of mystic that Anne would have dismissed as idly superstitious, or worse, as a sinister dabbler in witchcraft, could have prophesied that within twenty years this seemingly unremarkable young woman — intelligent and passionate as she may have been — would spearhead England's most dramatic venture, the creation of a thriving colony in America, and assume her place as one of the significant people in the English-speaking world.

But all of this excitement and good fortune lay hidden in the future, while the present consisted of a frightening new continent swathed in darkness. Nor did things improve as the sun grew stronger. The shadows gave way to forest and a beach, and finally, the growing light revealed a rocky, uneven-looking land, remarkable more for what was missing than for what was present.

Here there were no chimneys or steeples. No windmills, crenellated turrets, wheat fields, or cities. No orchards, hedgerows, cottages, or grazing sheep. No shops, carts, or roads to travel on. This was true emptiness. Anne had known this would be the case, but the shock was still overwhelming. Granted, there were also no bishops who hated them, and the merciless king who seemed intent on the destruction of Anne's people was thousands of miles away. But for this eighteen-year-old and many of her fellow travelers, the thrill of escaping those foes had long since dissipated in the face of the "great waters" they had just crossed. Now, staring at this hulking continent, it was clear to the faithful that only the hand of their God could protect them from the dangers ahead. The only other reassuring consideration was that here was plenty of land for the picking and enough timber for everyone to build a house and barn and keep warm all winter long — a refreshing difference from England, where wood was so scarce that stealing lumber was punishable by death.[2]

Despite the uncertainty they faced after their long days at sea, most of the travelers were understandably eager to feel solid earth beneath their feet. Before they could disembark, however, Governor John Winthrop, Deputy Governor Dudley, and Anne's husband, Simon Bradstreet, announced that a small group would go to inspect the settlement in Salem that had been, they hoped, successfully "planted" by the advance party they had sent the year before. This courageous band of men had been charged to clear land, erect homes, and plant crops to help support the *Arbella*'s passengers when they arrived. But Winthrop and Dudley had received only a few letters from these pioneers, and although they had been optimistic and full of good cheer, no word had been received for many months, triggering concerns that the little group had not survived the winter. Perhaps the new arrivals would find only a shattered village and the dismal remains of their comrades.

No one could discern the settlement's condition from the *Arbella*'s anchorage. The great ship had lowered its sails about a mile away from shore to avoid any mishaps with hidden rocks or shallow waters. As a result, they would have to row for nearly an hour to find out what had happened in Salem. Anne may have been one of the few to hope that she would *not* be on this first exploratory mission ashore. However, it soon became clear that her father expected her, her mother, and her three younger sisters to climb down into the tiny skiff that lay tossing up and down in the waves. None of them could swim. But in Anne's world, a good daughter was, by definition, someone who obeyed her parents without question, and so she had little choice but to sweep her sisters along and guide them over the rails of the ship.

Over the years, Anne had become accustomed to yielding to Dudley's outrageous commands, whether they were spurred by his Puritan piety or by his innate sense of adventure. Still, this particular challenge was worse than usual. The tiny boat, or "shallop," was frighteningly unsteady, and these smaller vessels were notorious for their frequent capsizing. In fact, in the months to come, as boat after boat arrived from England, a few unfortunate individuals who had survived the months at sea would suffer the indignity of drowning a few hundred feet from dry land when their shallops overturned en route to the shore.

The sharp, whitened rocks of New England's ragged coastline seemed inhospitable and foreign to Anne and her family, but in the years leading up to their migration, these travelers had been prepared by their ministers to view their arrival in the New World as a return of sorts. It was a leap in logic that made sense to a people who had been taught to compare their "bondage" in England to the Israelites' in Egypt, and who saw their journey to the New World as a reprise of the Jews' famous exodus to the promised land.

In fact, to seal their intimate relationship with God, some of the most devout Puritans suggested that everyone learn Hebrew, so that the only language spoken in New England would be the same as in Scripture.[3] This proposal soon faded away, probably because the non-Puritans onboard complained bitterly. At any rate, such an ambitious project was far too steep for a people who would have to till fields, saw boards, dig wells, slaughter pigs, and fend off diseases, wolves, and other wild creatures from the moment they stepped ashore.

As the water splashed over the bow of the flimsy boat and a strange land loomed ahead, Anne knew she was not supposed to be yearning for the Old World. But for someone who had loved her life in England as much as Anne had, this was a difficult proposition.[4] Even if the Old World had truly been the "Egypt" of her captivity, as they drew closer to the shore, America gave no evidence of being the biblical land of vineyards, honey, and olive trees that her father had promised her. Instead, it soon became clear that a disaster had occurred.

The tiny colony had all but collapsed during the winter. What remained was truly a pitiful sight: just a few acres of cleared land, littered with a motley collection of thatch-roofed huts and hovels. The surrounding forest contained the tallest, widest trees Anne had ever seen, and the two-hundred-foot pines seemed like gigantic monstrosities, terrible deviations that bore little resemblance to the slender poplars, willows, and ashes back home. If the size of the trees was any indication, what of the wild creatures that lurked in their shade?

The inhabitants of Salem who had come out onto the beach to greet them were even more dreadful to look at than the landscape. Many of them appeared to be weaker than the sickest passengers on the *Arbella*, with their bones visible through papery skin. The outpost, it turned out, had endured a brutal winter, losing eighty people to starvation and illness. The survivors seemed lethargic and defeated. Many were invalids or were disoriented, withdrawn, and sullen, as is often the case with people suffering from scurvy, one of the diseases responsible for the devastation. Some of these sad souls also exhibited an incoherence that suggested they were drunk, while others seemed strangely drugged from the strong Indian tobacco that they smoked incessantly.[5]

For once, Anne could take comfort from the fact that she was not alone in her misgivings. It was clear to Winthrop, and Dudley, too, that Salem was not Canaan. Despite the coolness of their sea-soaked clothes, the summer heat was oppressive. The stench given off by the little settlement was rancid and nauseating, its weak residents having resorted to emptying their bowels behind their own homesteads, covering the fecal matter with dirt. To the newcomers, it seemed that the Englishmen they had sent to improve the land had instead deteriorated into savages, and that the wilderness, instead of being subdued, had succeeded in toppling the forces of civilization.

Further proof lay in the fact that the settlers had been unable to create adequate shelter for themselves. The laziest had dug caves in the hillside. Others had erected flimsy wooden huts. At best these structures had a wattle-and-daub chimney, a wooden door if the denizens had been industrious, and sometimes one small paper window. The dirt floors of all these dwellings were lined with reeds and wild grasses in a futile attempt to ward off the rain, cold, and damp.

To the new arrivals, however, the structures that were most disturbing were the odd "English wigwams." These were made from "small poles prick't into the ground" that were "bended and fastened at the tops." Like tepees, they were "matted with boughs and covered with sedge and old mats." Copied as they were from Indian dwellings, these tiny hovels could only appear "little and homely" to the eyes of the English, since anything Indian was not worthy of Christians like themselves.[6]

With this array of miserable homesteads, no one was even slightly heartened by the majesty of the pine groves, the gloriously uneven headlands, or even the blue noontime sky. Instead the land seemed lifeless, full of death and waste. Of course, this was an astonishingly arrogant viewpoint. New England was far from being the "empty" land that the English proclaimed it to be in order to assert their rights. In fact, this "desert," as the Puritans called it, had been cleared for centuries by the Massachusetts, the tribe that dominated the bay region.

Though their numbers had been depleted by contact with the 1620 Pilgrims and their diseases, especially smallpox, the best estimations of Indian population suggest that as many as one hundred thousand Native Americans continued to make their living along the shores of the bay. It should have been obvious to the Puritan leaders that the land had been cleared before. The groves that the settlers had at first termed "untrackable" were in fact full of paths and almost entirely free of undergrowth thanks to the Indians' forestry skills. But most settlers, including Anne, saw the improvements that the Indians had made to the land as a divine gift rather than as a sign of Indian expertise.

Needing to rest after their long morning's journey, Anne, her husband, and the other leaders repaired to what the settlers called the "great house," where Governor John Endecott, the gruff old soldier who had headed the advance party, made his home. This simple wooden structure, which had only two rooms on the ground floor and two rooms above, had originally housed the first Englishmen who had attempted to make a living from fishing the Cape Ann waters. The house had been floated, intact, along the shore from Gloucester; no one in Salem had attempted to build such a structure. Although to Anne it seemed like the house of a poor peasant family, it was the height of technological achievement for the colonists. Its boards alone represented long hours of labor in a sawpit.

Once inside, there were not enough chairs and benches to go around. The two tiny rooms were dank and smelled of old smoke, sweat, and dirty linens. Yet despite their poverty, Endecott and his men used up the last of their provisions and prepared a delicious meal of "good venison pasty and good beer" — a supper fit for princes back home in England.[7] The tales they had to tell, however, were every bit as grim as Salem itself. The winter had been colder than anything they had ever experienced. The food supplies of the poorest settlers had run out. They had had to rely on help from the Indians and from the few scattered old planters, adventurous Englishmen who had come to New England a few years earlier. These men were generous with aid even though Endecott had asked them to leave their plots in Salem to make room for Winthrop's party. But this kind of scattered assistance could do little to ward off the disaster they faced, and even Endecott and his second in command, the minister Francis Higginson, had been weakened by their travails.

It was with dismay, then, that the Salem men discovered that Winthrop's people had actually looked forward to being fed by their struggling little community. Endecott had been counting on the arrival of fresh supplies from the Winthrop fleet; now a crisis seemed imminent. Somehow Dudley and Winthrop would have to solve the problem of food and shelter before the treacherous frosts brought them to their deaths, and they would have to do this without any help from the Salem party. In fact, the *Arbella*'s leaders felt that the frailty of the little settlement could easily demoralize the rest of the passengers.

Impelled no doubt by anxiety — it was already June, and everyone knew they had no time to plant crops, very little food left, and only a few months to erect homes — Winthrop and Dudley got right down to business, brusquely relieving Endecott of his command and asserting their own leadership. This is no more than Endecott expected, and he told the leaders about a deserted Indian settlement taken over by some of the Salemites who had been desperate for a fresh start and "champion land." The English had named the place Charlestown, and Endecott emphasized that not only was it just a short sail away but there was also plenty of tillage suitable for planting. He had even had his men build a simple house and temporary structures there for members of Winthrop's party to inhabit.[8]

Endecott's idea suited Winthrop and Dudley, who were eager to put some distance between their own party and the squalor of Salem. Although Anne must have been relieved as it gradually became clear that they would not have to stay in the depressing settlement, the idea of continuing their journey only raised more questions. What would they find farther south? Charlestown was a vague, shadowy place. While Winthrop and Dudley finalized their plans to go farther down the coast, Anne, her mother and sisters, and their friends soon discovered that peeking out of the undergrowth were wild strawberries. When they ventured a little way from the great house, they found that the ground was carpeted with the fruit and with the white flowers that promised more.

To the women, this bounty seemed to have sprung out of the earth unbidden. But here was another example of the industry of the Indians, who had followed an ingenious agricultural rotation of fields, clearing more land than they needed so that some of the earth could stand fallow. As a result, almost no soil erosion had occurred; the earth was rich with nutrients. Since the epidemic that had reduced their numbers, the Indians had left the ground untilled for a number of years, giving the wild fruits of the region the freedom to multiply.[9]

The women spent the rest of their afternoon in a paradise they had not anticipated. The weather was warm, the air was gentle, and as the daylight glimmered into evening, they rejoiced not only in the sweet fruit but also in the simple pleasure of being on shore. Maybe Eden was not so far off. But in case any of the berry pickers had forgotten they were not in the calm of the English countryside, as night fell, an unfamiliar pest began to swarm around their necks, ears, and eyes. Mosquitoes. There had been no such insects back in England. English gnats were small and persistent, but they were nowhere near as fierce as these American insects. No amount of swatting could clear away the ruthless clouds, so the women hastily headed back to shelter.

When they had reached the safety of Endecott's great house, however, Anne and the others encountered a group of strange-looking men standing near the fire inside the old governor's dwelling. The first Indians Anne had ever seen had come to investigate the arrival of the new English boat. Even from a safe distance, Anne could smell the bitter odor from the herbs they had painted on their skin to defend against insects, various diseases, and the white man. And they were almost completely bare. Their chests and legs were shiny, hairless, muscled, and lean. They wore their hair long and loose like a woman getting ready for bed; a few even had on ropes of shell necklaces.

Englishwomen were not allowed to gaze upon naked men — if indeed these Indians were entirely male. To the English, the Indians seemed a confusing mix of male and female, smooth and hard, warrior and girl, and such confusion was unacceptable. Indeed, English society was grounded in the distinctions between the sexes. Anne's own roles in life — dutiful daughter and loving wife — were predicated on these assumptions; the Indians' apparent disregard for everything that she had been trained to value was deeply disturbing.

After a series of awkward exchanges, characterized by the incomprehensible formality of the Indians and the short bursts of translation by one of the old planters who spoke a little of their language, it soon became clear that the Indians would like to examine the

Arbella. It was at this point that Anne, her sisters, and the other women appear to have made their first independent decision of the day. Winthrop reported that the ladies elected to stay on land and camp out with the colonists.[10]

Despite the welcome novelty of finally sleeping on land again, for Anne and her companions there was no escaping the fact that this new country was more unpleasant and far more strange than anyone had realized it would be. As she tried to go to sleep, the distant howls of wild animals shook the night air, and Anne wondered how long she would be able to endure this terrible new country.

Unfortunately, her fears were well founded. Between April and December of that first year, more than two hundred of the one thousand immigrants died. Two hundred more fled back to England on the first available boat. One colonist, Edward Johnson, reported that "almost in every family lamentation, mourning, and woe was heard."[11]

But good fortune lay ahead, too. Against all odds and in the midst of unthinkable hardships — privation, freezing cold and blistering heat, hunger, disease, loneliness, and self-doubt — Anne would raise eight children to adulthood, help found three different towns, and run the family's busy household. Even more remarkably, she would find the strength and the time to write verse, diligently and fiercely, until finally in 1650 she had compiled enough poems to publish a book, *The Tenth Muse Lately Sprung Up in America.* To her surprise, her words would catch fire and she would become the voice of an era and of a new country. Having composed the anthems of a faith, she would be famous.

Anne Bradstreet's work would challenge English politics, take on the steepest theological debates, and dissect the history of civilization. She would take each issue by the scruff of the neck and shake hard until the stuffing spilled out; no important topic of the day would be off-limits, from the beheading of the English king to the ascendancy of Puritanism, from the future of England to the question of women's intellectual powers. Furthermore, she would shock Londoners into enraged attention by predicting that America would one day save the English-speaking world from destruction. Hers would be the first poet's voice, male or female, to be heard from the wilderness of the New World.

What would draw people to her was not just the glitter of her words but the story that lay behind the poems, a story that began in England long before *The Tenth Muse*, and long before the day she set sail on the first boat of the Great Migration to America. Not that Anne could have imagined such an extraordinary future for herself when she was growing up back in England, a well-bred gentleman's daughter. If she wanted anything back then, it was to stay in one familiar place and learn to be a good Christian wife and mother.

CHAPTER TWO

✥

Lilies and Thorns

I N 1620 A TERRIFYING JOURNEY across the Atlantic would
have seemed impossible to eight-year-old Anne. The sort of
travel she was accustomed to was the fifteen-mile road to St.
Botolph's Church from her home at Sempringham Manor in Lincolnshire. This dirt wagon trail made its way through marshlands of
reed beds and scrub, the black earth damp from the frequent
drizzle, the sky teeming with waterbirds, warblers, and terns. Travel
here was almost always slow and difficult; depending on the condition of the horse, the wagon, and the road, it could take three hours
or longer, especially in foul weather, when the ground was slick with
layers of mud. Worst of all, with few trees on this vast, flat plain,
there was no barrier to protect travelers from the bitter winds that
swept across the low-lying county, even in the summer.

Naturally, none of these hardships bothered Dudley, and so it
was on this blustery path, which had become the most well-traveled
thoroughfare in the county, that Anne and her family began their
Saturday pilgrimages to hear the popular minister John Cotton
preach. For most young girls, such an uncomfortable journey might

have been unbearable, but for Anne it quickly became a hallowed routine. Their destination was well worth the unpleasantness of the trip, and the wearisome hours she spent in the open wagon gave her plenty of time to think. Bundled in her thickest wool cloak, she could lose herself in her ideas, huddling close with her mother and younger sisters for warmth, while her father and her brother, Samuel, sat in the high driving seat, prodding the horse on.

The proximity of St. Botolph's was one of the benefits of Dudley's move to this region of England in the first place. Anne's father had instilled a sense of Botolph's sacred importance in all of his children, so that all week long, Anne impatiently awaited sitting in the grand nave of the most beautiful church in the county. It was here that she listened to the sermons of her beloved minister, the man who was the pillar of the tightly knit Puritan community in Lincolnshire. In fact, from the windows of her new home at Sempringham Manor, Anne had a splendid view of the fens and of St. Botolph's in the distance, a comforting reminder of Cotton's steadfast presence in her life.

At 280 feet tall, the tower of the minister's church was impressive, with an octagonal lantern at the top, known as "the stump," dominating the landscape for thirty miles around and looming over the town of Boston, where the church was built in 1341. Sailors depended on St. Botolph's as their guide as they braved the voyage over the stormy North Sea from Holland. For Anne and her family, the yellow stone was also a reassuring beacon during the tumultuous years of the 1620s; it pointed them toward their wise minister and his vision of a redeemed England, a country that would finally be cleansed of what Cotton called "great blasphemies" and "desperate deceit and wickedness."[1]

Cotton invoked Botolph's dramatic architecture frequently in his sermons, pointing up to "the stump" and telling his parishioners to "let the name of the Lord be your strong Tower."[2] They must steer their lives in the direction of the true God, he said, just as they directed their journeys by the sighting of his church. Anne took her minister's lessons so seriously that she "could not be at rest 'till by prayer I had confessed [my sins] unto God."[3] Riding to Boston along-side her prattling younger sisters, Patience, Sarah, and Mercy, who in Anne's opinion were remarkably untroubled by the significance of what lay ahead, she was often overcome with anxiety. As they drew nearer to the church, she grew increasingly "beclouded . . . with fear," certain that she had fallen short of her spiritual ambitions yet again. With each jounce of the wagon, she silently counted her various misdeeds — "lying disobedience to parents" — feeling she was in what she called "a great trouble" and had been "overtaken with evils."[4]

It was not that Anne was a morbid child by nature, but Dudley had taught her that "doubts and feares" could be gratifying evidence of what her family considered a "true faith" in God. Anne was already an exceptionally bright, perceptive girl who had begun "to make conscience" of her ways at age six.[5] She was used to hearing her parents and their friends lament their wickedness, a practice the Puritans paradoxically saw as virtuous. One family friend, the minister Thomas Shepard, reflected, "I saw my evils and resolved with more care to walk with [God]."[6] Consequently, Anne understood that it was her duty to know precisely what behavior was sinful and what was not. Her parents, Thomas and Dorothy, were two of Cotton's most devout followers and among the most respected Puritans in the county. Indeed, there was nothing Anne desired more than to measure up to their rigid if slightly contradictory expectations of her, particularly her father's.

Anne admired Dudley more than anyone else on earth, but her father was an imperious man and could be intimidating. Born in the quiet backwater village of Yardley Hastings in 1576, Dudley had been orphaned at age twelve and taken in by a fellowship of Puritan "brethren." Attracted to the staunch conviction of the ministers and their warm, affectionate community, he was converted to their faith before he was twenty.

These Protestants based their lives on the close study of Scripture and were dedicated to evoking a passion for God in their followers. They held that God had already predetermined who was chosen for heaven and who would suffer the torments of hell. But the paradox of Puritanism was that, damned or not — God's choices were inscrutable — one still had to strive to fulfill His commandments. Without any certain hope of reward, one had to try to rid oneself of sin and follow Him with a pure and lively heart. To Dudley the challenge of serving God with all of his being, when he might in fact be doomed, was strangely appealing; he spent his life pursuing seemingly unattainable goals. It also suited his ambitious nature to join a group whose members sought to triumph over "the dead, heartless, blind works" of most congregations and instill emotion and idealism in the Church of England as a whole.[7]

Thomas Dudley's unbridled enthusiasm for Puritan theology, which emphasized the scholarly tools of reading and writing for the study of the Bible, only served to deepen his innate love for literature. Intelligent and widely read, Dudley had taught himself Latin, wrote learned poetry, and pored over the Elizabethan poets Sidney and Spenser, as well as Raleigh's *History of the World*; Burton's philosophical text, *Anatomy of Melancholy*; and Bacon's exploration of the new scientific methods in his *Essays*.

Among the most educated men of his milieu, by all accounts Dudley was arrogant and used to getting his own way. Socially ambitious, he loved the well-mannered company and educated conversation of the highly born. As an astute financial manager, he also had to reconcile his desire for earthly fortune and fame with the Puritan idea that his ambition, as his daughter wrote, "lay above."[8]

But Dudley, at least in his own mind, had little difficulty being true to his Puritan beliefs. He had been taught by his ministers that his task as a father was to ensure that his son and daughters understood their essential sinfulness and helplessness in the face of God's almighty will. If any of his children dared to forget a section of their daily catechism, neglected their study of Scripture, resisted scrutinizing their conscience, or simply appeared, as Anne wrote in later years, to scorn God and "too much . . . love" the world and all of its temptations, Dudley did not hesitate to shame and chastise them. His punishments could be so severe that Anne called him "a whip and maul," but Dudley was convinced, and his children were supposed to understand, that this was the stern nature of true paternal love.[9] To feel the glory of God's might, the good Puritan needed to be aware of his own deficiencies. So, as a good father, it was Dudley's job to make sure his children knew how flawed they were.

Dudley fought his own fear of eternal damnation by striving for perfection. Driven by his compulsion for self-improvement and by his urge to create a better, more "godly" world sooner rather than later, he was prone to utopian visions, an inclination he shared with John Cotton. But Dudley was never content to let these visions remain unrealized. Eager to risk everything for the sake of his God, he saw himself as a kind of Puritan knight ready to do battle for his cause. An adventurer at heart, one of his first impulses as a young man was to dash off to France to captain troops in a fight against Catholic Spain.

Dudley held his children to the same high standards he demanded from himself. But he was also capable of being "mild and wise," as Anne once wrote. Having recognized in Anne a powerful intellect and a spiritual intensity that might one day match his own, Dudley had chosen her as his favorite from the beginning. He took a keen interest in her education, instructing her in English history and literature as well as in theology and the Scriptures. Anne, in turn, rewarded her father with her abiding love, declaring he was her "guide" and praying she would one day emulate his unshakable faith.[10]

Watching Anne brood over her conscience and strive to master her lessons, Dudley realized that his daughter had fallen heir to his heroic perfectionism. Although he had managed to channel his zeal into an energetic commitment to Puritanism, Anne would wrestle with this irrepressible legacy throughout her life. She yearned, as she wrote, to "tast[e] of that hidden manna that the world knows not . . . and have resolved with myself that against such a promise, such tastes of sweetness, the gates of hell shall never prevail; yet have I many times sinkings and droopings." But since Puritanism held that there was no possibility of ever attaining complete union with God — human beings were inherently sinful and God was a mystery — she knew that her desires for what she termed "the witness of His holy spirit" often came from insecurity and vanity.[11]

In a society where a woman was expected to be docile, humble, and quietly submissive, there was little opportunity for Anne to voice these doubts and ambitions. Her brother, Samuel, who was four years older, sat next to Dudley on the journeys to Boston and had the chance to engage their father in important theological discussions. As the eldest girl in the family, Anne had other tasks she had to perform.

For Anne's mother, Dorothy, the idle hours in the wagon offered the opportunity to teach her daughter how to be a good wife and mother. Descended from a "substantial yeoman," Dorothy was the embodiment of the virtuous Puritan woman.[12] She was, Anne wrote, "religious in all her words and ways," devoting "constant hours" to private meditation and prayer at the same time that she was "an obedient wife" and a "loving mother." She was also a stern taskmaster, ruled the household with an iron will, and was regarded by both her servants and her children as so "wisely aweful," or awe inspiring, that she merited their utmost obedience.[13]

Because Dorothy had no other ambition than to support her husband and provide her children with a good religious education, she took it upon herself to tame her precocious daughter's spirit, to teach her womanly virtues — restraint, modesty, and selflessness — that Anne would struggle with for the rest of her life.

On the long Saturday journeys toward Botolph's, the family could see windmills turning while sheep grazed on the low smooth hills and the clouds rolled by overhead. It was a vista not unlike those painted by the Dutch landscape painter Jacob van Ruisdael, and in fact, the fen country, wedged between East Anglia to the south and Yorkshire to the north, was so similar to the Netherlands that it was often called the Holland of England.

When Anne and her family moved to Lincolnshire, its rushes and swampy reed beds were being transformed into farmland, and the Dudleys could see the beginnings of rich, fertile pastures along their route, as well as innumerable church steeples.[14] Unlike St. Botolph's, which was the spiritual landmark of Lincolnshire and therefore the largest church in the county, these village churches were small, constructed of roughly hewn stone, with simple designs carved on the doors and on the columns inside. That the landscape was dotted with these abundant but unpretentious structures was gratifying to Anne and her family. The Dudleys did not have a particularly romantic view of nature and preferred to see signs of Christian civilization; each steeple that pointed up to the sky was a kind of triumph over the wilderness.

Eventually, the calm of the countryside gave way to the crowds, shouts, and smells of the boisterous city. As the center of the busy wool trade, Boston was the second-largest port in England, with a chaotic web of crisscrossing lanes and alleys, and redbrick buildings with brightly painted doors and windows.

To the Dudleys, however, Boston was much more than a bustling market town. It was a sacred location imbued with prophetic importance, starting with its name, which came from the phrase "Botolph's stone," after the Christian martyr who in the ninth century converted the savage Anglo-Saxons. Tradition had it that he had used one of the pale stones from the countryside to convince the locals of the truth of the Gospels. For those as steeped in Scripture as Anne and her family, this story was believable, since the chalky boulders that surrounded Boston did indeed seem to recall the white stone of the apocalypse described in the book of Revelation.

The town itself often seemed in danger of a watery disaster on a biblical scale. Boston was bordered by the Witham, an estuary too shallow to sustain the frequent surges of the tide; when the sea was high, the waves rolled in and out of the town with such frequency that most residents had built flood steps to protect their homes. The Dudley children had come to expect that they might be forced to wade to the church door, but a little floodwater could not deter them from their goal; wet feet were a small price to pay for the opportunity to hear Cotton speak.

Puritans from every corner of Lincolnshire joined Anne's family at St. Botolph's. When the Dudleys had moved to Sempringham, ministers like Cotton, who disagreed with many of the state's policies regarding the governance of the church, were just beginning to be persecuted. By the end of the decade, the king's bishops would sweep through the country, removing hundreds of these dissenting Puritan ministers from their pulpits and replacing them with their enemies, Anglican divines whom the dissenters called "Dumme Dogges," "Destroyeing Drones," or "Caterpillars of the Word."[15]

Handsome and charismatic, Cotton was the kind of man who was able to circumvent this royal system until 1633. Instead of challenging the bishops and the king directly, he quietly protested the ecclesiastical dictates of the Stuart kings — first James, who was crowned in 1603, and later Charles, who acceded in 1625. He refused to read from the newly issued Book of Common Prayer, kneel at Communion, use the sign of the cross, wear surplices, or allow the unsanctified to participate in the rites of the church.

Fortunately for Cotton, he was somewhat insulated from the Anglican authorities, because Lincolnshire was geographically secluded from the rest of England.[16] Surrounded by the fens and a great watery inlet known as the Wash, this protected enclave had long been a refuge for renegades; the conquered Britons retreated here after the Saxons invaded in the fifth century, and later the Saxons themselves fled to the fen country after the Normans invaded England in 1066. The earls of London had been remarkably sympathetic to the Puritan cause ever since the early sixteenth century, when King Henry VIII dissolved Lincoln's monasteries and granted the monastic lands to the first earl. By 1620 the county had a Puritan community fifteen thousand strong, and Boston, its central gathering place, was a cauldron of dissent.

Dudley made sure all of his children, especially Anne, understood the bracing history of their new home; because of its isolation,

Lincolnshire had long fostered independent thinkers. Reputedly, Henry VIII had once complained that the people of Lincoln were "presumptuous" and "the most brute and beastly of the whole realm," though this was probably due to the fact that it was here that he discovered his wife Catherine Howard's adulterous affair. The county seems to have bred unorthodox souls — Captain John Smith, the famous explorer; John Wesley, the Methodist evangelist; Sir Isaac Newton, the eccentric mathematician and theologian; and most important to Dudley, John Foxe, the Protestant author of *The Book of Martyrs*, from which Anne could probably recite by heart.

Thus, while dissenters in other counties faced increasing discrimination and persecution, Cotton was protected by Lincolnshire's politically astute Puritans. He managed to remain on the pulpit of Botolph's throughout this dangerous decade, much to the relief and gratitude of Anne and her family, who looked to him for guidance as England seemed to crumble around them.

AFTER THE DUDLEYS ARRIVED in Boston on Saturday evenings, they often spent a festive night eating "ribs of beef and many a pie" or "hot sheeps feet and mackerel" and drinking ale and hard cider in the earl's town residence.[17] These were lively evenings, but in the mornings there was church to face. Each Sunday Anne waited outside St. Botolph's, alongside her family, Cotton, and the other like-minded parishioners, sometimes for hours, until the town's new Anglican chaplain, Edward Wright, had performed the rites that Cotton and his followers deemed blasphemous. John Cotton was calmly insistent about not going inside because even being in the same room with Wright, who genuflected, wore elaborate vestments, made the sign of the cross, bowed toward the altar, and altogether behaved like a Catholic priest, was dangerous for the souls of "true believers." He had handpicked the members of Botolph's whom he considered the elect, including Anne and her family. This "tighter inner group [of] saints" excluded the individuals Cotton deemed unworthy, such as

Anglicans, so that his special souls would not learn any bad habits. To reinforce this point, he preached that his chosen ones, the Puritans, were as "a lily among thorns," the thorns being the "notorious wicked ones" among whom the faithful were forced to live.[18] Over time, as more Puritan preachers were "ferrited" out of their pulpits and Botolph's became one of the few places left where one could go to hear a true dissenter preach, Cotton's fame increased, as did the prestige of his followers, at least in Puritan circles.[19]

But it was not easy to be one of Cotton's saints. Anne was not always sure she deserved such an honor. Insecurity and self-doubt besieged her; she wondered if she could ever live up to her father's ideals or abide by the kind of humble resignation her mother required of her. All too often she was tempted to "neglect [her] . . . duties," though she was sure that if she failed in any of her responsibilities, a terrible fate awaited her, and she feared she would be visited by Satan. At night, when her parents instructed her to review her spiritual condition and to make her peace with God in case she died before waking, Anne felt profoundly discouraged by her moral weaknesses. The blessings most Puritan children had to learn by heart had little solace to offer: "At night, lye down prepar'd to have / Thy sleep, thy death, thy bed, thy grave" or "From Death's arrest no Age is free, Young children too may die."[20]

According to Puritan theology, desolation was evidence of God's great love; it kept one from the even graver sins of self-deception and hypocrisy and encouraged one to seek help from God. For her own protection, Dudley instructed his daughter that "inward peace" was always to be distrusted, as it might have been sent by Satan himself to tempt the poor Puritan into a slothful state.

Given this paradoxical theology and her parents' impossible strictures, John Cotton's words were indispensable salves. If Anne did confess her fears to her minister, he would have listened carefully and, instead of chastising her, would have selected appropriate passages to read from Scripture, such as "upon this rock Christ Jesus will I build my faith," a phrase that, she reported years later, never failed to quiet her "heart."[21]

Anne was fortunate to sit near the pulpit, where she could closely observe her beloved minister. As one of the more prominent Puritan families, the Dudleys were given pews up front. The women and children sat on one side, the men on the other, and the peasants crowded in back, three or four hundred people deep. One of the most famous orators of his generation, Cotton used what the Puritans called the "plaine style" of preaching, avoiding learned allusions and fanciful metaphors in order to reach the hearts of his listeners. His parishioners often felt that he entered their innermost thoughts, heard their fears, hopes, and jealousies. In his "melting way," he assured them that there was godliness in every one of their daily acts, from sweeping the house to carving meat for dinner.[22] Each quotidian moment of their seemingly unimportant lives was really a sacred drama in the battle between Satan and God, evil and good, chaos and order.

Sitting with her mother and sisters, Anne could also observe the other women, and there was one in particular whom she could not help but admire. Her name was Anne Hutchinson, and at age thirty-two, she was already a legend. Hutchinson was notable for her "nimble wit" and "active spirit," as well as for being warm and outgoing, with "a very voluble tongue."[23] Hutchinson's unconventional behavior contrasted sharply with that of Anne's mother. Like the Dudleys, Hutchinson was devoted to Cotton, and she and her wealthy merchant husband traveled many miles to attend St. Botolph's. Whether she was talking earnestly about Cotton's sermons or sitting quietly with a group of women discussing the state of their souls, Hutchinson had a dazzling presence that always placed her at the center of things. No one seemed to mind her confidence or her outspokenness. Instead, famously devout, she was held in high esteem by women for her midwifery skills and her spiritual counsel, and she was equally respected by the men. To the young Anne, whose own intellectual life was beginning to bloom, Hutchinson's accomplishments and intelligence must have been inspiring. Certainly, her forthright behavior suggested that there was more than one way to be a good Puritan woman.

Anne Dudley and Anne Hutchinson were likely both in Botolph's when they first heard Cotton's dream of a "City of God" populated only by saints. The promise of the New Testament was one of the unifying themes of Cotton's sermons; he taught his parishioners to yearn for a "new" England, one free from Rome's taint. The Anglican Church was failing, he said, and it must be restored to its scriptural purity, or else even the godly Puritans would suffer the Almighty's wrath.

Cotton's vision of a redeemed church and a fresh new world inspired many, but no one was more intrigued by the idea than Thomas Dudley. The wistful Cotton conceived of this new England in purely symbolic terms; he was not preaching emigration, and he never fully believed that such a world could come into being. But Dudley took Cotton's words literally, beginning to imagine how he might create a real "new" England, knowing it would have to be somewhere far away from the corruption of the old. Not surprisingly, when Dudley began to discuss utopian ventures overseas with other restless Puritans, Cotton argued that England must be reformed from the inside. "The Beast," or the Antichrist, must be driven out, Cotton said, and his flock must remain, resisting the temptation to sail away to nearby Holland, which had a thriving Puritan community, or to the faraway English colony in Barbados.

But these subtleties were lost on Thomas Dudley. Cotton's vision had, though inadvertently, laid the groundwork for the idea of a Puritan "remove." Ironically, Cotton himself would take far longer than his parishioners to be convinced that establishing a new England across the sea was the answer to their crisis. In fact, Cotton was so concerned that his flock might abandon England that he deepened his emphasis on compromise. He agreed with Thomas Shepard, a fellow minister, who wrote, "The Lord [makes] me feare . . . running too far in a way of separation from the mixt, [or England]."[24] For a time, Cotton's appeals succeeded in quelling any rash decisions that Dudley and his friends might make. These men respected Cotton's tempering words and loved England too much to launch themselves immediately into leaving their country behind.

For the young Anne, Cotton's moderate response to the political climate was probably more congenial than her father's more extremist position. But she was fortunate to be exposed to the ideas of both men, as well as those of her mother. When she came of age, her thinking would be tinged with her father's utopian politics, Cotton's gentle spiritual lessons, and her mother's pragmatic teachings about the humble place of women in this world and the next.

CHAPTER THREE

✣

Sempringham

NNE'S EDUCATION DID NOT only consist of her visits to
St. Botolph's. The medieval halls of her childhood home
were dark and forbidding, but it was in these cavernous
rooms that Anne received the extraordinary gift of a nobleman's
education. Her father's arrogance and ambition would turn out to
be a blessing for Anne's literary future.

She was eight years old when Dudley accepted an offer to serve
as steward to the Earl of Lincoln and moved his family to the young
lord's grand manor at Sempringham. The position, a combination
of business manager, lawyer, and secretary, was a plum situation for
Dudley, who had had to endure two years of unemployment before
finding this opportunity. Most employers regarded Puritans as
rabble-rousers intent on undermining the government's God-given
authority, not as individuals to depend on. But fortunately, the
twenty-year-old Earl of Lincoln, Theophilus Fiennes-Clinton, had
been raised as a Puritan and was sympathetic to Dudley's ideals.
Serving under one of the most highly placed noblemen in the country suited Anne's father's grandiose beliefs about his destiny and that

of his family. It was also in accordance with his view of Puritan theology: a pious father should enhance his wealth and status so his family could fulfill God's will on earth more effectively. In 1620, the year Dudley took the position at Sempringham, his four children — Samuel, Anne, Patience, and Sarah — were, respectively, twelve, eight, four, and two, and Dorothy was pregnant with a fifth baby. The rich benefits his son and daughters would receive from life on such a luxurious estate included an upper-class education as well as an assured knowledge of aristocratic manners.

Just how important these lessons were was self-evident to Dudley, as he had once worked as a page to the Earl of Northampton at the magnificent Castle Ashby. The world that he had found there was overwhelmingly sophisticated and urbane, and it brimmed with rules you had to learn fast if you wanted to survive. Social standing determined where you sat at banquets, what kind of overnight accommodations you merited, what sort of clothes you could wear, whom you could talk to, and which servants waited upon you. As a result, Dudley was a stickler for pristine etiquette and social distinctions, and he would pass on to his children a sense that the Dudley family was slightly more refined, and certainly more elegant, than others.

When Anne was first plunged into life at Sempringham, the contrast between her family's old home in Northamptonshire and the manor was overwhelming. For the first eight years of her life she had lived in a simple Puritan cottage. Now she had to learn to navigate the rambling corridors of a sprawling mansion. Instead of living a quiet life with her family and a few servants, she now lived in the midst of a bustling nobleman's estate. At least fifty servants staffed Sempringham, and famous visitors often came for extended stays. Theophilus's own family was huge. The earl had eight younger brothers and sisters, all of whom still lived at home when Anne took up residence in the manor.

Once they arrived, Dudley was far too busy to help his family get acclimated to their new environment. He was acutely aware of the young lord's dire financial situation — Theophilus owed creditors almost twenty thousand pounds, thanks to his dead father's excesses. Immediately, Dudley cut back on the laborers' pay and urged the earl to raise his tenants' rents as well as their annual contribution to the estate at harvesttime.[1] Naturally, those under his rule resented him, but Dudley did not seem to mind his unpopularity. He glared at people as though he would like to boss them around, or at least improve their manners. He held his chin up higher than was strictly necessary and stared as if he were boring a hole straight into the earth. His eyebrows were delicate and slightly arched, which lent his gaze an air of contempt or, perhaps, of inquiry. In keeping with his aristocratic leanings, he dressed in a far more elegant manner than most of his compatriots. In the one remaining portrait of him, he has on a creamy, silken tie, loosely knotted at his throat, rather than the enormous stiff collars of his colleagues. He made it clear that he was not a man to be trifled with and that his displeasure could harm his opponents in real and frightening ways. Dudley felt it was his job to improve the earl's estate, and he did this as directly and speedily as he could, producing extraordinary results. Within a few years, Theophilus was not only solvent but a wealthy young man.

Of course, there was another reason Dudley had no difficulty ignoring the complaints of the farmers. He saw harshness as his duty because he understood his role as steward in biblical terms. As Cotton Mather, the Puritan apologist of the next generation, would write many years later, Dudley would be as "Joseph was to Pharaoh in Egypt."[2] From the Puritan perspective, it was Dudley's "calling" to increase Theophilus's wealth.

As Dudley's oldest daughter, Anne soon became aware of her father's notoriety among the tenant farmers but fiercely defended him against his enemies, just as she would throughout her life whenever Dudley's firmness met with criticism. Later she would write:

> *Who is't can tax thee ought, but for thy zeal?*
> *Truth's friend thou wert, to errors still a foe,*
> *Which caused apostates to malign so.*[3]

Still, it was difficult to be a child of the unpopular steward, and it was with some relief that Anne encountered a new personage in her life — the powerful woman who ruled the household, Theophilus's mother, the dowager countess, Elizabeth. Never before had Anne met such an impressive female. Here was a woman who was completely unafraid of Dudley and who was actually his social superior. For Anne it must have been a complicated and liberating experience to see the man she thought ruled the world bow to the will of another — a noble, of course, but a woman all the same. Stickler that he was for elegant manners, Dudley always addressed Elizabeth by her full title, effectively demonstrating his own perfect breeding but also his own capacity for deference — a new side of his character as far as Anne was concerned.

Aristocrats had rarely crossed her path before. Now, thrown into the midst of the earl's family with the eccentric Elizabeth in charge, Anne entered a wholly new world of complicated manners, politics, and intrigue. She was used to her mother's quiet simplicity, while Elizabeth was famous for her outspokenness. The dowager believed that women were capable of far more than most people believed, and she made no bones about it. A deeply literate, redoubtable lady of not much beauty, who was famous for her own excellent education, Elizabeth was dedicated to the intellectual advancement of other noblewomen. She had even written a learned treatise on child rearing that promoted breast-feeding, a novel idea for most ladies, as they had been taught that they were too frail to feed their own babies and should employ wet nurses.[4] As the mother of five daughters, the soon-to-be mother-in-law of one young bride, and the potential grandmother of many granddaughters, Elizabeth had ample opportunity to exercise her ideas.

In 1620, the year Anne joined the throng at Sempringham, the dowager was still raising her younger children, and this important job involved instruction in the social intelligence they would need to launch themselves into the troubled and complicated world of Jacobean England. Tutors had to be hired, influential acquaintances had to be struck up, a thorough understanding of their responsibilities as lords and ladies of the manor had to be passed on, marriage contracts needed to be drawn, knowledge of the court and court politics had to be instilled, and ministers and vicars needed to be consulted on a regular basis to ensure the proper religious education for these noble young Puritans. In general, if children failed to live up to the expectations of their class in their adult lives, either through a disastrous marriage, sinful behavior, or the profligate management of their estates, the mother was almost always blamed.

Elizabeth seems to have believed that classical history and literature were vital to the education of women — an unusual viewpoint at a time when it was rare for females to be able to read much more than rudimentary passages from Scripture. For her daughters, she hired an outstanding instructor whose sole job was to teach them reading, writing, and ancient history. Dedicated as she was to the education of young women, it seems likely that the countess allowed Anne and her younger sisters to receive the same education as her noble daughters. Certainly the enormous breadth of Anne's reading and the refinement of her skills suggest that she had an early education that far surpassed the simplistic training of most gentlewomen: the ability to "reade plainly and distinctly, write faire and swiftly." Nor did she have to be content with "a Bible . . . and a good plaine cattichism." Instead she could eagerly read translations of the Latin historians and philosophers Josephus and Seneca, as well as medical texts such as Helkiah Crooke's *Microcosmographia, or a Description of the Body of Man*, truly extraordinary reading for a child — male or female — from any class background.[5]

Anne would have greatly admired Theophilus's younger sisters — Frances, Arbella, Susan, Dorcas, and Sara — who had their mother's confidence and zeal, knew the ropes of the manor, had exquisite manners, and could not only sew but read and write with far more grace and intelligence than Anne imagined possible. Although Sara was around the same age as Anne, it is likely that Anne's favorite of the five girls was nineteen-year-old Arbella, who was the particular beneficiary of the dowager's strength of mind and fortitude and who seemed to share Anne's fervor for religion and study.

As she spent the majority of her day with her mother and sisters, Anne could never forget the difference in rank between herself and the noble girls who were her fellow students. At times the gap that separated her from the others was uncomfortable: They dressed in silks; she dressed in linen and wool. They were conversant with luxuries and books and had met many of the era's most famous personages, whereas Anne had lived a quietly sheltered life until Sempringham. But Anne could take comfort from the fact that she shone as a student. The poetry she would write as an adult reveals that she was able to retain copious amounts of information, make probing political arguments, and master the details and overarching themes of history, science, religion, and medicine with more depth and complexity than most of her peers — male or female. Thus even Theophilus's younger brothers, Charles, Knyvet, and John, were undoubtedly soon surpassed in learning by this young middle-class aspirant.

Not surprisingly, Anne was particularly receptive to verse, which was esteemed as one of the most important arts of the age. She could scan difficult lines, marking the accented feet with speed and clarity. One of her favorite poets was the long-winded French Protestant, Guillaume de Salluste Du Bartas (1544–90), who had leaped into superstardom with his attempt to capture, in copious detail, each moment of God's Creation in verse.[6] This famous work, *The Divine Weekes and Workes*, unfortunately bogged down somewhere in day three. Creation was too gigantic an event for even this literary heavyweight to manage; snowed under by the enormity of God's handicraft, he could never bring himself to complete the poem. Nonetheless, Puritans everywhere loved this unfinished work, and Anne was no exception.

In later years she would remember that when she read his poetry, it was as though she were gazing at "glittering plate and Jewels," a "brave wealth" that she wanted to possess. This poet made her hunger to write poetry herself. She yearned for "some part (at least)" of his store of technique and knowledge. And she was not alone. Du Bartas so thrilled John Milton that the young poet attempted to imitate him in his own heroic undertaking, explaining the ways of God to men in *Paradise Lost*. But Anne knew that such literary dreams were "empty wishes" for a "silly prattler" like herself, since intellectual ambition was an inadmissible desire for a young woman of her time and place.[7] Females could not be poets, the experts said; their brains and constitutions were not strong enough, and too much learning might distract them from their proper station in life. The day would come when Anne would ignore these warnings, and then it would be Du Bartas's example that would spark her into action, leading her to hammer out her own poem about Creation, *The Quaternions*.

This brave act, however, would take place many years in the future on the distant shores of America. In the 1620s writing such grand verse would have been unthinkable for the young Anne. There was her own humility to contend with, as well as the societal taboo against intellectual women. Even worse, her frail health seemed to confirm the critics' feeling that learning weakened the female constitution.

A year or so after the Dudleys arrived at Sempringham, Anne had her first painful experience with illness, an indeterminate fever that confined her to bed for many tedious weeks. At least, she wrote, she had the opportunity to "commun[e] with my heart."[8] Unable to perform the domestic duties so prized by her mother, Anne could take part only in quiet activities while she convalesced. Encouraged by her minister and parents to reflect on her sins and to view her illness as a "correction" from God, Anne suffered spiritually as well as physically. Because she was separated from the flurry of everyday life as well as from the lively chatter of her younger sisters, Anne's misery became even more pronounced, until her father began to bring her books from the earl's well-stocked library and from his own. At last Anne had found consolation in her loneliness.

This was an extraordinary act for a Puritan father, not only to allow his daughter such weighty reading, but to promote her encounter with these writers. But to Dudley, history was a devotional tool, and so it makes sense that he would choose this time to bestow heavy tomes about this serious subject on his frail, bedridden daughter. Perhaps the thought that she might be facing death prompted him to overlook conventions. Before long, behind her heavy linen bed curtains, the nine-year-old could venture forth into realms of learning far beyond those of her sisters, mother, and even her older brother, Samuel. She devoured John Speed's *Historie of Greate Britaine*, William Camden's *Britannia*, Richard Knolle's *Generall Historie of the Turkes*, and Raleigh's *History of the World*, while, of course, never neglecting the study of her beloved Bible.[9]

Anne was fortunate that her father's unbridled passion for Puritan theology, which emphasized reading and writing, had allowed him to overlook his culture's prejudice against women and learning. Now, in the unlikely person of a sickly young girl, he had discovered an intellectual companion blessed with an inquisitive nature like his own, a voracious appetite for knowledge, and a capacity to immerse herself in her studies with ever-increasing determination. For a serious-minded Puritan child like Anne, history was a dramatic recital of the ways God moved in the world. He left His footprints everywhere, and because her father tended to dwell on periods of terror and woe, Anne became a kind of expert in disasters. Later, her history poems would sweep from one catastrophe to the next as she would attempt, in print, to wage her father's war against the enemies of Puritanism.

As Anne approached adolescence, it was impossible not to see her preternatural aptitude for poetry. Dudley had long held that he was related to the sixteenth-century poet Sir Philip Sidney, whose famous words "Look into thy heart and write" had inspired a raft of writers from Spenser to Raleigh.[10] Whether or not they were actually connected to Sidney by blood is arguable, but because Dudley believed so, he exploited the significance of this relationship to the fullest, telling his daughter of her family's poetic birthright. Anne was born to write poetry, Dudley seems to have thought, although it would take many years and an ocean voyage to the New World before his dreams for her were fully realized.

Anne, however, was a young girl during an era when her most important teacher was supposed to be her mother. Naturally, Dorothy

found it difficult to comprehend her daughter's obsession with literature. Although she supported Anne's studies because they had her
husband's sanction, she emphasized that household duties must come
first. Still, when Anne had fully recovered her strength, Dorothy
seems to have allowed her to spend a few hours a day away from
domestic chores, not only to study with the noble family's tutor, but
also to read with her father. By the time Anne was ten or eleven
years old, it had become clear that Dudley had anointed his eldest
daughter as his favorite, even over Samuel. As the years passed,
father and daughter established an intimate bond that excluded the
rest of the family. Together they moved beyond the English historians and tackled the classics available in translation: Homer, Aristotle, Hesiod, Xenophon, Pliny, Virgil, Seneca, Ovid, Thucydides,
and Plutarch, while continuing to study Scripture and the religious
writings that were the more customary texts for literate Puritans.

Their closeness was accepted by everyone except Anne's younger
sister Sarah, who suffered from the loss of her father's attention.
Patience and Mercy were content to follow in their mother's footsteps, but Sarah, like Anne, resembled Dudley — too restless and
passionate to be confined exclusively to her feminine role and religious duties. The time would come when the entire family would
have to endure the results of Dudley's neglect of Sarah, but as it was,
Dudley always did exactly as he pleased no matter the cost to his
loved ones. Sarah would have to make do with the crumbs she
received from her father, and Anne would have to bear the brunt of
her younger sister's jealousy and anger throughout both their lives.

At some point during their long hours closeted in his study,
Dudley must have taken the revolutionary step of teaching his
gifted daughter to compose verse. But before she could even begin
to compose poetry, Anne would have to master the mechanical act
of writing, a rare undertaking for a ten-year-old girl of this time. In
fact, there were really two kinds of literacy during this period. Most
Puritan women could read, since everyone wanted them to be able
to study Scripture for themselves, but fewer could actually shape
their own letters.[11] Fiercely determined, Anne set herself the task

of learning to use a pen. Her father made the alphabet look deceptively easy. When he dipped his pen in the ink, *l*s and *r*s, entire sentences, even poems, appeared in rotund and stately splendor, as if by divine grace. But her first attempts with a quill were not as graceful, and this was a blow to her dignity. Eventually, though, the figures she traced would become elegant, accurate, and, best of all, easy to read.

Of course, Dudley had no interest in fomenting any sort of feminist rebellion on Anne's part. With the support of the dowager countess, an excellent example of a writing woman whose wits had not become addled through her intellectual exertions, Dudley told Anne that writing and Christianity went hand in hand, that the poet's job was not simply to invent a line of pentameter but to consider how best to serve God while reading and composing. In fact, too much concern for flourish and romance, he warned, would lead poet and reader astray; the temptation to overadorn one's verse must be avoided. One Puritan minister whom Dudley particularly admired wrote: "The task of true art is to conceal art."[12] Anne quickly learned, therefore, that poetry reading and writing should not be simple intellectual or emotional acts. Rather, they should be like ladders to God, like prayers.

CHAPTER FOUR

A Man of Exemplary Discretion and Fidelity

WHEN DUDLEY DECIDED to invite a young man named Simon Bradstreet to join his household in 1622, no one could anticipate the impact this would have on the family, and especially on ten-year-old Anne. Simon, who was fresh from Cambridge, was to serve as Dudley's new assistant, since after two years of managing the earl and his affairs on his own, Thomas Dudley was savvy enough to understand that he needed help. Although he was loath to give up control of the estate, he had found he had less and less time to spend on reading, studying the Bible, writing his own poetry, and educating his favored scholarly daughter. Theophilus's financial situation had improved steadily — thanks to Dudley's diligent efforts — and now he could afford to pay for more help managing his properties. Simon was hired, therefore, and the Dudley children began to count the days until his arrival. It was, after all, a momentous event: A young man, whom they had never met, would be arriving in their midst. He would lay claims on their father as his master and their mother as his own, and would even regard them as his surrogate sisters and brother.

This rather odd adoption process was fully in accordance with both English custom and Puritan theology, which held that it was the duty of the father of a household to guard the spiritual well-being as well as the physical health and safety of all of those who slept under his roof, including servants, friends, apprentices, and guests. A solid family unit was the most important building block for creating a Christian society, or so Cotton and the other ministers believed, and English law supported them. Dudley, therefore, became liable for Simon's behavior and responsible for all aspects of the young man's care the moment he walked in the door.

Of the Dudley children, Anne and Samuel would have been the most interested in Simon's arrival. Samuel hoped that he would soon be attending Emmanuel College, from which Simon had just graduated. As for Anne, it would be useful if this ready-made older brother turned out to be learned and wise. Perhaps he would join her father and Cotton in guiding her exploration of her faith.

Neither child was to be disappointed. When Simon arrived at Sempringham, the young Dudleys turned out to meet a relaxed, ruddy-cheeked fellow unlike any man they had ever encountered. Their own irascible father rarely laughed and was more likely to lose his temper than tell a joke. Simon, on the other hand, was affable and eager, loved good food, and found the world a generally pleasant place to live. His genial attitude made him easy to like, though, thankfully, from the Dudley parents' perspective, he never allowed his good-natured bonhomie to overreach the decorous standards of a good Puritan gentleman.

Simon had been well trained not only in proper manners — he never would have dreamed of disobeying the precepts of his new master — but in the political and theological concerns that preoccupied Puritan leaders. Most important, he had been taught to believe that the reformation of the English church was his duty as a God-fearing individual. A vicar and a devout man in his own right, Simon's father had died suddenly when the boy was only fifteen, but not before he had arranged for Simon to study with the premier reformed divines at Emmanuel College. With no siblings, and having lost his mother many years earlier, the young Simon was bereft, but the Puritan faith and community filled the chasm left in the boy's life, just as it had for Dudley many years earlier.

At Emmanuel, the center of Puritan foment in England, Simon quickly learned that English dissent was in more trouble than he had ever suspected. His tutors were under constant attack from the king's bishops, and Simon was instructed to believe that Anglicans and Catholics, who in Puritan eyes were practically the same entity, were not just misguided but were evil persecutors.

From a theological standpoint, the young man's mentors at Cambridge preached the same tenets as Anne had learned from Cotton. This was not a coincidence. Many of Simon's teachers had been taught by the famous minister when Cotton had been a tutor at Emmanuel. The older ones had attended college with the great man when he had been the most brilliant undergraduate of their generation. At their hands, Simon learned the Puritan premise that King James was leading the country toward destruction and that the king's officials were miscreants.

A position at Sempringham was a coup for Simon, since Thomas Dudley was regarded as one of the most virtuous Puritan civic leaders in Lincolnshire. But once he finally entered the doors of the manor, the young Puritan must have been overwhelmed by the sheer size of the burgeoning Dudley family. Dorothy had given birth to her last child, Mercy, soon after their arrival in Sempringham, and the child's name clearly expressed the beleaguered wife's sentiments on at last being able to settle into their new home. It had been a long road to the manor.

With three young daughters under the age of ten, the house was full of more activity and chatter than Simon had ever experienced, and certainly many more females. His old life had been rather spartan, having consisted largely of the companionship of men, and women were a phenomenon that must have taken him some time to get used to. From all accounts, however, the demands of the toddler, Mercy; the prattle of Sarah and Patience; and the bustling of female servants did not dismay Simon; instead the busy swarm of women and girls seems to have delighted him, since he would one day create just such a household for himself.

Even if he started off on the right foot with the children and Dorothy, Simon still had to pass the standards of the ramrod-straight Dudley. Since Dudley already approved of Simon's theology and politics, this was less of a challenge than it at first appeared. The older man could immediately see that he had gained a hardworking, admiring youth who would help ease the burdens of being the earl's overseer. Simon was thoughtful, smart, patient, and in contrast to Dudley, had a pleasant way with people. It also helped that Simon and Dudley were from the same class background. Both men were of the rising middle class, although Dudley may have thought of himself as possessing closer ties to the aristocracy. For Dudley, the similarity in their background made nineteen-year-old Simon a far more congenial and compliant student than Theophilus. Simon was well behaved, obedient, and reverential, while the impulsive Theophilus was arrogant, never listened to advice, and was always on the verge of trouble, since he "was wont to be very quick in his notions."[1]

After watching Dudley rein in the impulsive young nobleman, browbeat the tenant farmers into paying rent, and levy fines from those who strayed from manorial law, Simon started to absorb the basic tenets of good stewardship. Managing an estate like Sempringham was like running a small town. You were the magistrate, judge, tax collector, administrator, and financial planner all at once. Dudley even had the right to interfere in tenants' family matters: For example, those who allowed their daughters to marry someone outside the lord's estates or who sent their younger sons away from the earl's service were punished with a fine. None of the older man's hardheaded tactics bothered Simon. Instead he regarded Dudley's rigidity as integrity and admired his legal experience as well as his business acumen. As a result, it did not take long for the young man to become Dudley's devoted disciple. Like Anne, he would prove to be fervent in his loyalty for the rest of his life.

Once the two men had established their working relationship, Dudley, with his typical zeal, made it his business to ensure that Simon's soul was in good health. The young man should attend church, listen to the conversation and counsel of the leading Puritans who came frequently to Sempringham, and participate in the Dudley family's religious rituals, from daily prayers to theological discussions and meditations on readings from Scripture, whether they happened at the dinner table or late at night next to the fire.

Simon had little choice but to comply with this spiritual regimen, not that he minded. These sorts of "godly" activity must have reminded him of both his father and his college days. In the evening, after their work was completed, Dudley led the family's talk by analyzing sermons they had heard, reading from various psalms, and of course, condemning the wrongdoings of the king and his bishops. For example, the Puritans were shocked by the recent publication of the king's *Book of Sport* (1618), in which James dismissed the Puritans' sober observance of the Sabbath and instead touted revelry, games, and drinking. This was a slap in the face for dissenters everywhere, although the king argued that he simply wanted his subjects to enjoy themselves after a week of drudgery. To Anne and her family, the Sabbath was a crucial ordinance of their God and certainly not a time for dashing after bowls on the common or for drunken cavorting.

Although Samuel and Anne were encouraged by their father to contribute their thoughts, it was with the reverence proper in children. On the other hand, Simon, while always deferential to his master, never gave any evidence of being afraid of Dudley. He chimed in with his own ideas, and as they listened, Samuel must have gotten his first taste of what college would be like, while Anne learned to admire Simon's steadiness in the face of Dudley's impassioned arguments.

Unusual though it was to include a girl in such exchanges, the times were extraordinary, Dudley felt, and he wanted his exceptional daughter to sharpen her wits for the challenges he believed lay ahead. If the king continued to wage war on the Puritans, Anne must learn to strike back, even if the only weapon she could use was her mind.

Thus Anne found herself in a startling — and even thrilling — new situation. She had never spent so many hours with a young man who came from outside her immediate network of family and friends, and Simon was gentle, handsome, wise, and kind. As for Simon, it is unlikely he had ever known such an intelligent, sensitive young girl, let alone one so well versed in Scripture, politics, and history. And so, before long, a delicate bond grew between the two young people. Anne turned to Simon for guidance in her spiritual travails, and Simon talked to her about his worries and ambitions.[2]

When Simon first arrived at the manor, Anne was still considered a child, and this allowed their relationship to flourish without any apparent romantic complications or any danger of impropriety. For the truly devout Puritan like Anne and Simon, there were many daily events to discuss in order to dissect their possible divine meanings. Perhaps a sudden thunderstorm was God's rage, or slow-churning butter was evidence of the family's sinful condition, or a severe head cold was punishment for misdeeds.

The dark-paneled rooms of the estate lent themselves to the contemplation of darker thoughts as well. Despite her youth, Anne had been instructed by her mentors to cry out: "Lord search me and try me, see what ways of wickedness are in me, and lead me in the way everlasting."[3] She never complained about these spiritual exercises, but it was difficult to live with this insistent dread of damnation.

As the months passed, Anne would grow to feel that without Simon near, she was "oppressed" and plunged into "a Chaos blacker than the first." In the years to come, she would describe not only how much she suffered from bouts of paralyzing spiritual anguish but also how much she relied on Simon to comfort her. He was her "sun," the man who illuminated her darkness, which seemed to descend all too frequently.[4] To Simon the girl's battles with misery marked her as an especially saintly individual, since Puritans believed that "being cast down" signaled a deepening of convictions on the part of the sufferer.

Happily, Anne and Simon did not have the leisure to spend all of their time repining over their spiritual condition. Living together in such close quarters, the two young people had many opportunities for other kinds of conversation; whether they were reading, eating, chatting, praying, walking, journeying to Boston, or laughing over the antics of Sarah or baby Mercy, the two young people were often together.

Although during these early years, Simon probably regarded Anne as nothing more than a dear sister, it is certainly possible he also regarded her as a prospective marriage partner. But he did nothing to alarm her and, it seems, took no action to further this plan. Eleven-year-old Anne was still too young to think much about the attractions of the opposite sex. The year after Simon had arrived in Sempringham, however, she witnessed a romantic drama that played itself out in the halls of the estate, its urgency driving home how crucial it was to find the right husband, since one's future, and one's standing in the community and the church, all hinged upon this terrible decision. As Anne would reflect later in life, getting married "changed [a woman's] condition" entirely.[5]

IN 1620 OR SO, the earl's nineteen-year-old sister, Arbella, had become an enthusiastic follower of Cotton and other dissenting ministers. Like her mother, this young woman was a single-minded and courageous advocate for her beliefs, and what she desired was a drastic change for England and the English church. But no young woman, regardless of her determination or her aristocratic pedigree, could sway the royal authorities who stubbornly resisted all attempts to modify the Anglican Church. Even Arbella's brother and his prominent Puritan friends were failing to make any inroads on King James's policies.

The situation took a promising turn, however, when Arbella encountered a young man named Isaac Johnson, a prominent Puritan whom Dudley and Theophilus had invited to visit Sempringham in 1622. Johnson seemed to combine all the elements they needed to render the dream of departure a reality, should the political climate for Puritans continue to worsen. Johnson shared

Arbella's passion for cleansing the English church of corruption and was excited about the idea of establishing a colony with other like-minded souls. An intelligent, thoughtful clergyman, Johnson was extremely wealthy and had enough resources to help fund such an enterprise. Conveniently, he was also a bachelor on the lookout for an appropriate wife.

Clearly, this was the right man for the idealistic Arbella, but Johnson was a commoner and Arbella was noble. They should find partners from inside their own social class, according to most people's thinking. Both young persons, however, had an incentive to break the rules. Although Dudley had helped Theophilus clean up the debts his father had left behind, Arbella was far from being a rich woman, and a wealthy husband like Johnson would help her put all her plans into action. As for Johnson, his family stood to gain from a potential connection to nobility, and he seems to have been captivated by Arbella's adventurous spirit. And so the two immediately became engaged, apparently untroubled by the scandal this might cause.

Anne could not help but follow these proceedings with excitement. Arbella's mother promptly declared that the marriage was a grand idea, but the drama intensified when Isaac's father refused to countenance it. At last Elizabeth approached Isaac's grandfather to overrule the disapproving parent. To the delight of the Sempringham household, the old man was in favor of the union. In April 1623, Anne watched as Arbella and Isaac exchanged vows, an event that would be of great significance for the founding of New England.

A WEDDING IN THE HOUSE naturally turned the thoughts of the other young people at Sempringham to their own prospective marriages. In the next few years, as Anne turned thirteen and then fourteen, Simon could no longer hold her at a distance as a beloved younger sibling. She was growing into a young woman whom he could love and desire. Anne's status as the eldest daughter in the family made her seem more mature than her years — her next sister, Patience, was a full three years younger — and her piety and solemn dedication to prayer and books gave her the steady carriage and serious outlook of a much older person. Until his prospective bride had reached a more appropriate age for an engagement, however, twenty-three-year-old Simon was content to wait.

Anne, on the other hand, was jolted by the shock of what she called her "carnal" feelings. At age fourteen, she was neither delighted nor enlivened by falling in love, but instead was deeply troubled. She worried that she had allowed "the follies of youth" to "take hold of me." All too often, she would later remember, she found herself "sitting loose from God," forgetting to contemplate her spiritual state and focusing too much energy on worldly matters such as her appearance and fashion. It was not easy to be a Puritan girl and love a man.[6]

As a middle-aged wife, Anne would recall the sorry condition of her soul during this period in her life, describing how tempting it was to busy herself with being "fine" — "to curl, and pounce" her hair. Sadly, at the time of this spiritual crisis, Anne had no ability to stand back and gently take stock of her failings. It would take many years before she could invoke the uncontrollable feelings she had experienced by creating the allegorical figure of a young person in one of her most famous poems. "My lust doth hurry me to all that's ill," Youth declares in *The Quaternions*, "I know no law . . . but my will."[7]

In actuality, as long as Anne did not act on her impulses, she did not need to lash herself so strenuously. Sex within marriage was considered a pleasurable duty: "God has given us the pleasures of this world to enjoy. . . . We should therefore suck the sweet of them and so slake our thirst," the minister Joshua Moody summarized.[8] For the Puritans (unlike their descendants, the Victorians), sexuality was not really the issue. The more worrisome problem was the social disorder uncontrolled behavior could cause, particularly when it jeopardized inheritance proceedings or the social hierarchy of man over woman. An earthy people who enjoyed their ale and a good feast when the situation permitted, the Puritans sanctioned and even believed in the virtues of sex, even premarital sex, as long as the partners ended up in a married state. Bastards and unwed mothers, not pleasure, were to be avoided.[9]

Anne's difficulty, then, was that her desire for Simon was "wild," and Puritans treated any evidence of ungoverned sexuality with severity. In the New World, for example, where Puritans would rule the colonies in accordance with their theology, adultery — a transgression that disrupted the order of the family — was punishable by death, although this was rarely carried out.[10] Most Reformed ministers, like Cotton, relied on shame and public humiliation to enforce their moral code; in New England the entire community would become involved, as in Hawthorne's depiction (nearly two centuries later) of the punishment meted out to the adulterous Hester Prynne in *The Scarlet Letter.* Anne had been taught to judge herself and others according to these severe standards, and so when she first experienced the strength of her own appetites, she was tortured by guilt.[11]

Eventually Anne must have made her anguish known to her family, as Dudley abruptly announced that the family would move from Sempringham to Theophilus's property in Boston, while Simon would remain to manage affairs at the Sempringham estate. Though sad to be separated from Simon, Anne may well have been relieved. Dutiful Puritan that she was, she knew that if she allowed herself to roam down the path of licentiousness, "My wit evaporates in merriment," "my woeful parents' longing hopes are crossed," and "my education lost."[12]

For Simon's part, the Dudleys' move to Boston may have cost him some pain over losing Anne's companionship, but it allowed him to come into his own as a man. He brought all of his charm, skill, and energy to his role as manager. Within a year, he had caught the eye of another noble dissenter, the Countess of Warwick. In 1627, presumably with Dudley's support, as this was part of the progression everyone expected for Simon, he moved away from Sempringham to serve this difficult woman, who was so impossible she had supposedly driven her husband to "great perplexities" until he was "crased in braine"; in other words, she had driven him mad. That Simon "discharged" his duties for this forbidding woman with "an Exemplary discretion and Fidelity" was regarded by all as an extraordinary achievement.[13] He was truly an adult in the eyes of the world; all he needed was a wife. Although he now lived more than a day's journey from the Dudleys, Simon did not forget his love for Anne. He was at something of a disadvantage, though, for there were no clear courtship rituals for Puritan young people, and he had no one to act on his behalf. In fact, the most prominent paternal figure in his life was the father of his beloved.

Puritan marriages were usually arranged by the parents of the two young people, although based on the interest of their children. If there was an attraction, the matter had to be prayed over and discussed with spiritual advisers. As with Arbella and Isaac, there were no private affairs of the heart; marital unions were family mergers and often involved extensive financial negotiations. In addition, there was not usually much of a ceremony, and this made it difficult in some cases for young people to discern when it was legal for them to engage in the sexual activity of a man and wife. There were certainly no church weddings, since marriage was considered a civic act.[14]

With these kinds of dire pitfalls to avoid, even older people such as widowers and widows, who no longer had parents to guide them in their choices, did not heedlessly follow their "instincts" or, worse, their "passions."[15] To win the hand of a good Puritan woman, then, a suitor had to present evidence that his intentions were prompted by the Lord's will, good sense, and in the best cases, the young woman's father or family representative.

Simon knew that at age fifteen Anne was still too young for marriage. But whether or not he had decided to venture proposing a future engagement, any such plans were preempted when a terrible crisis struck. Soon after the Dudleys moved to Boston, "God laid his hand sore upon" Anne and she became ill, this time with the dreaded smallpox plague that was sweeping the countryside, killing thousands. Though Simon was living miles away, Anne still perceived her suffering as punishment for her passion. Later in life she wrote, "It hath been with me that no sooner felt my heart out of order, but I have expected correction for it," and in this case she connected the fact that she had allowed "the follies of youth [to] take hold of me" with her illness.[16]

Smallpox, not surprisingly, was the sort of ordeal that tended to induce spiritual agonies in its victims. The patient's suffering began with nausea, body aches, and a rocketing fever that induced delirium and disorientation. When she was older, Anne recalled how frightening these feverish hallucinations could be: "Sometimes the frenzy strangely mads my brain / That oft for it in bedlam I remain."[17] For pious individuals, these seizures were interpreted as either divine or satanic visitations, depending on the nature of the visions, and they left the victims feeling shaken and desperate for spiritual consolation.

The famous pink sores, or "pocks," only emerged gradually. At first they appeared as tiny discrete spots, or macules, on the mucous membranes of the mouth and then on the face and forearms. These macules slowly grew into tight, painful papules that after a few days filled with liquid and formed a tense blister embedded deep in the skin.

The more pocks you had, the more danger you were in of dying, and children were the most vulnerable. Indeed, most parents believed that smallpox was an inevitable curse that families had to bear. It would be more than one hundred years before the smallpox vaccination was invented. In the early seventeenth century no one knew why some people survived and some did not; fully one-quarter of the people who contracted the disease died. Most people thought of the pox as "the scourge" that killed without mercy, although Anne might well have taken heart from the fact that the famous queen of her father's generation, Elizabeth I, was reputed to have been stricken with the dread disease and survived.[18]

Though Anne's suffering was drawn out — probably several months — and acute, and there was no assurance that she would survive, she never gave way to despair. There was no treatment to stem the course of the disease, but Anne believed she was in God's hands. Her shattering fever led her toward an even deeper commitment to her religion; she coped with her fear through prayer, and looking back on this time, she wrote, "When I was in my affliction, I besought the Lord and confessed my pride and vanity, and He was entreated of me and again restored me."[19]

AT LAST THE PAINFUL POCKS all over Anne's body dried up into a hard lentil-like crust. She would survive. Although there is no concrete evidence that Anne suffered scars from her bout with the disease, the scabs of smallpox sufferers usually peeled away to reveal pigment-free skin, and most sufferers were left with these blemishes for the rest of their lives. Whether or not Anne's face was pitted with the scars of the illness, her pride in her youthful beauty had been delivered a severe blow; she wrote, "The pox me sore be-mars with outward marks and inward loathsome scars." The severity of her pain left her wiser and more reflective, albeit far weaker, than she had been before.[20]

John Cotton's proximity to the Dudley family meant he could lead Anne and her family in prayer and reflection during her prolonged battle with death. But Anne did not give him or her father much credit for helping stave off her despair. According to Anne, it was God Himself who came to her in the midst of her misfortune and comforted her when she felt so troubled by her own "follies." Her illness had served as a kind of test, allowing her to discover the depth of her own faith. As she recovered, she felt rescued from the uncertainty of her passions and reminded of the course she wanted to follow in life, that of the devout Puritan pilgrim. God had saved her for some reason, and now she would have to devote herself to uncovering His purpose. As a result, she began to focus more intensely on her personal relationship with God rather than on her relationship with human authorities. This was a dramatic turning point for someone who had always been instructed to put the dictates of her father and her ministers first.

Although there is no evidence that Simon came to visit the Dudleys during Anne's illness, he must have been in constant touch with the family and deeply concerned that Anne was near death's door. At some point during her recovery, he made it clear that he wanted to marry the young girl whose conscience had been so troubled by her desire for him. Dudley agreed, and Anne's enthusiasm for this idea was expressed by the speed with which she married Simon. Instead of keeping to her bed and enjoying a slow period of convalescence, she fled the sickroom and plunged straight into a union with her old friend. Within a few weeks, the couple had moved away from her family to live on the dowager countess of Warwick's estate. Anne was, one hopes, further along in her recovery than another contemporary smallpox victim, who married her husband "as soon as she was able to quit the chamber, when . . . all that saw her were affrighted to look upon her."[21]

Having just turned sixteen, Anne was relatively young to be a wife, even in that time, especially since her husband was ten years older. It must also have been difficult for her to be separated from her younger sisters and her parents. But the challenges of the situation paled beside the gains. After all, smallpox had tried Anne's spirit, and she had not been found wanting. Now it was her duty to share sexual pleasure with her husband and to flourish as a woman in the "garden" of her marriage. The legitimization of her desires could not help but be a powerful relief to this conscientious teenager. No longer did she need to consider herself "carnal" and "lustful"; instead she could think of herself as "dutiful" and "loving" — she was safely back inside the Puritan fold. Anne also knew that as a married woman, she could now order her household as she saw fit. She was an adult, and God's vocation lay waiting for her.

With a passionate bride thrilled to embrace the liberating joys of union, a gentle groom who understood that he had almost lost his love to the pox, and years of a steady, intelligent relationship already under their belt, it seems almost inevitable that Anne and Simon would enjoy a blissful start in the world.

The year was 1628, however, and the young pair's life together had begun at a forbidding juncture of events. One Puritan minister after another was being silenced or imprisoned, and rumor had it that anyone who protested these events would be severely punished. It was becoming increasingly difficult to observe the tenets of their religion, and like the Israelites, the Puritans felt marooned in a strange and corrupt land; England had turned into a terrible Egypt and would soon be destroyed for her sins. All omens pointed toward disaster for Anne's future with Simon, and for Puritans in general. The fact that her father, Arbella, and, for that matter, most of her friends and family were now eagerly focused on emigration to America did nothing to inspire Anne with confidence. It seemed that only more suffering lay ahead.

CHAPTER FIVE

ക്കൈ

God Is Leaving England

THE CRISIS OF 1628 had not happened overnight. Years of violence between religious extremists had left a trail of bloodshed that no one could forget. The world was a dangerous place for Puritans, or so Anne and Simon both believed. Having been raised on stories of murderous Catholics and treacherous Anglicans, they spent their lives perpetually on guard against the enemy, whether this meant the devil in human or inhuman form, in Europe or England. The important thing was to be vigilantly prepared for catastrophe.

During the years of Anne's childhood and adolescence, the medieval principle of *un roi, une foi, une loi* — one king, one faith, one law — still held sway in both Protestant England and Catholic Europe. There was little understanding of the idea of tolerance, since to most people, two different faiths in one country made as little sense as having two kings attempt to govern one people. Religious people of all stripes and banners strove against each other in scorching fights for survival, and to most Christians, this violence shimmered in a bloody glow of glory and honor, as a kind of gallant assertion of faith.

Puritans used the most bloodthirsty rhetoric of all. A tiny subset of the Protestant grab bag, whose name had been bestowed on them by their enemies, they were outnumbered in a largely Catholic and Anglican world. In fact, the word *puritan* was an umbrella term for all sorts of dissenters, who ranged from the Pilgrims to proponents of adult baptism, and their different viewpoints only served to make them feel more isolated and more defensive.[1]

What they had in common, though, was a belief that the Anglican-controlled English church had not gone far enough in its split from Rome. This was ironic, since the Anglicans had been the original party of dissent in England, splitting off from the Catholic Church in 1536 under the leadership of Henry VIII. But most Puritans felt that the Anglicans were far too Catholic, or papist, in their tastes and customs. In general they hated the hierarchical system of church governance, where bishops controlled the fates of dioceses. They wanted worship to be simple and heartfelt and believed that there should be no fancy vestments for the clergy, no ornamentation of churches, and no preplanned feast days like Christmas and Easter. Preachers should be learned yet filled with the passion of God's grace. Nothing was more deadly, not to mention boring, than the rote chanting of memorized prayers. Congregations should be transfixed by riveting sermons and the words of Scripture.

Families like the Dudleys who had chosen to stay in England during the 1620s taught their children that they were fighting for the survival of the true religion in a largely Catholic world and that attacks might come at any instant from any quarter. Because Puritans blurred the distinctions between Catholics and Anglicans, Puritan children grew up thinking that the Anglican bishops who controlled the English church were simply an insidious brand of English papist and that English Puritans were, therefore, essentially surrounded by the enemy. Thus Anne learned that she must be prepared to defend the cause of Reform with her life and that all around her, the international community of "true believers" was in crisis and might be obliterated by their enemies if Puritans were not fiercely prepared to do battle. Given the martial righteousness of this theological point of view, it was almost impossible not to envision yourself as a soldier, even if you were a female.

Puritan wrath was further inflamed by the many stories about the evil deeds of their enemies that parents passed down to children and that ministers invoked from the pulpit. It did not matter that many of the reports of butchery had happened long before Anne was born. In some ways this distance in time and place was helpful for Puritan propagandists because, as the years passed, the stories grew increasingly gruesome; facts slowly slid away and emotions took over. For the men and women of Dudley's generation who had lost their fathers in various struggles against religious enemies, it was almost impossible not to pass their anger on to their children. As a result, by the time she was a teenager, Anne had been taught to view Anglicans and Catholics as deluded heretics intent on destroying the world. If some Puritan warrior could have burned down the Vatican's stronghold or murdered the king's Anglican advisers, she would undoubtedly have rejoiced.[2]

To English Puritans, the most dreadful accounts of Protestant martyrdom featured England's own "Bloody Mary," the unfortunate nickname angry Protestants affixed to the daughter of Henry VIII and Catherine of Aragon. In 1553, when Mary first stomped onto the throne — she had a limp and was something of a hunchback — the first thing she did was slaughter hundreds of Protestants in an attempt to bludgeon England back into the Catholic religion that her father had abandoned. Mary believed her father had cruelly rejected her by embracing Protestantism, and she was right. When the pope had refused to issue Henry a divorce from Mary's mother, Catherine of Aragon, the only way Henry could rid himself of his wife was to assume leadership of the church and order Catherine into the Tower.

Having dispensed with both Catholicism and Catherine in one blow, Henry did in fact marry another woman, Anne Boleyn, and promptly lined his coffers with proceeds from the sales of monastic lands. His eldest daughter witnessed these acts with shame and remorse, blaming Protestantism for leading her father astray. By the time she had come of age, her hatred for the Anglican Church had grown deep rooted and neurotic. It was Protestantism that had almost destroyed her life, and that of others, Mary believed, and she set herself the task of ridding England of this canker.

In actuality, Mary executed no more people than her popular father, or even her successor, Elizabeth, but she managed to compress her actions into a highly efficient five-year killing plan that haunted the Protestants of Dudley's generation.[3] If they had any doubts about her crimes against Protestants, they could refer to one of the best-sellers of the time, Foxe's famous *Book of Martyrs* (1563). This scholarly Englishman had meticulously recorded the victims' shrieks and cries, concentrating especially on their last words, their joyful acceptance of their martyrdom, and their death agonies. Thus it was easy for anyone of Anne's generation to become an expert on the suffering of Protestants at the hands of their Catholic enemies.[4]

This project was helped along by the fact that the detailed woodcuts in *Martyrs* allowed children like Anne to study the experiences of these martyrs long before they could read. Both of Anne's parents, in accordance with Puritan thinking of the time, undoubtedly encouraged their children to identify with and imaginatively reconstruct the torture these men and women endured and even seemed to embrace. To Anne it must have been appealing that female martyrs could be just as brave as men. In one famous woodcut three women surrounded by flames gaze up at the sky. Out of one's pregnant womb an infant emerges, perfectly formed and beautiful. Although the baby hovers in the air in the woodcut, his escape is clearly short-lived, as the executioners stand poised to pitchfork him into the flames. His mother remains serene and untroubled, however, as do her companions. The flames themselves appear orderly and rather lovely, carrying little destructive force, as though the artist were suggesting that in martyrdom you could find peace, symmetry, and even happiness.[5]

Anne embraced this particular moral of Foxe's gory tome — that if you could remain connected to God, you could withstand any kind of pain. If faith could convert anguish into a mark of special fortune — evidence of being chosen by God — then this was one reason the martyrs not only seemed to relish their suffering but also, astonishingly, went out of their way to court it. "One good man bathed his hands [in the flames] so long, until such time as the sinews shrank, and the fat dropped away. . . . All this while, which was somewhat long, he cried with a loud voice, 'O Lord, receive my spirit!' until he could not open his mouth."[6]

Exhilarating though it may have been to dream of such brave feats, it must have been difficult for a Puritan child like Anne to sleep at night. Her father made sure she understood that the threat of flames could not be relegated to the barbaric past. The Dudleys did not believe in false comfort but felt that Anne needed to be prepared for her own potential confrontation with the stake. You needed to practice envisioning torture, this logic went, in order to develop the spiritual muscles necessary to withstand temptation. No responsible parents wanted the threat of earthly flames to terrify their children into renouncing their religion. Such a sin could only result in the eternal fire of damnation, and which fire, after all, was worse?[7]

The agony of being burned was common parlance in Anne's world. Preachers commonly employed the tortures of hellfire to inoculate their flocks against sin. Most men and women of her parents' generation had witnessed at least one stake burning and told family and friends what this was like. Once the first layer of the victim's skin was singed and the nerve endings were deadened, the epidermis would begin to ooze blood, then water, then it would pucker and char and pull so tightly that even the mouth would be sucked back into a terrible wide-open howl and the fingers would curl into claws. Although some of the lucky ones died of smoke inhalation, for most of the people Dudley and his friends watched burn, release came only once they had become so hypovolemic, or deprived of blood and water, that their hearts gradually shut down, pumping what little blood was left only to vital organs. It was, perhaps, the extremity of such anguish that led one famous Protestant preacher to strike a prophetic note, delivering a terrible metaphor as the flames overtook him: "We shall this day light such a candle, by God's grace, in England, as I trust shall never be put out."[8]

The contemplation of such a horrific death could only under-
line Anne's feelings of vulnerability as a Puritan in England, even
though such fears were overblown. In case any Puritan thought it
might be safer abroad, the propaganda mill made sure everyone
understood how dangerous it was for Protestants in Catholic
Europe. The Spanish Inquisition, for example, had turned the full
force of its fury against Protestants in the 1540s. Even though the
pope himself had tried to restrain the Inquisition's excesses, it was
notorious for its sadistic executioners who dedicated themselves to
inventing ghastly deaths, from dismemberment to yet more fires.
Anne would also have known that in 1578, many years before she
was born (and when her father was only two years old), these same
Spanish Catholics had set Protestant Antwerp alight and, in a three-
day killing spree, disemboweled, raped, and grotesquely butchered
at least seven thousand people. Four years earlier, French Catholics
had tricked Protestants into attending an August wedding feast in
Paris and then, in the famous St. Bartholomew's Day Massacre,
slaughtered them with such ruthless dedication that Protestant
corpses clogged the streets, bobbed in the Seine, and spilled out of
houses and windows until the city became a slippery, impassable
mess and the stench drove those who were left to flee or to lock
themselves indoors in the sweltering heat.[9]

These sorts of stories led most English Puritans to believe that if
you ever did have to escape from the tyranny of Anglican miscreants
and actually leave the island, it would be better to brave the wilderness of an uncharted world than endure torture at the hands of
papists. Europe seemed a poisonous continent that upstanding
Reformed English people should avoid at all costs.

Surprisingly, Anne was far from shocked at the degree of violence she heard in these stories. Puritans, too, were notorious for
their rough predilections. Angry dissenters broke cathedral windows and looted Catholics' houses. In Angoulême, France, extremist Protestants had starved Catholics and then roasted them at the
stake.[10] Puritans believed they needed to strike immediately and
mercilessly against those who rejected the truth of the Reformation.

Enemies could be anywhere. The history of Catholic "pollution" still littered the country. What Anne hated was the triumph of papists and the death of "true believers," not the idea of bloodshed itself. To her, murder for the sake of your religion seemed reasonable and eminently praiseworthy. Decades later she would call for Puritans to "sack proud Rome and all her vassals rout / . . . / And tear [the beast's] flesh and set your feet on's neck."[11]

Though she had no direct experience with warfare, her mindset was understandable; she had inherited the ideal of glorious vengeance from her father and his family. Her grandfather (Dudley's father) had raced off to fight the Spanish, never to return. In 1597, when her own father had galloped toward "godly" battle to drive the Spanish out of France, he had earned "a Commission" as a military captain in Elizabeth's army even though he was only twenty-three years old. Few honors could have made Dudley, Dorothy, and their children more proud.[12]

To Puritans, even Sempringham, located in the stronghold of a Puritan county, was not free of the papist taint. The manor had originally been the home of the only order of monks to have sprung up in England, the Gilbertines. Even worse, Gilbert, who was responsible for founding this Catholic order in 1131, had grown up right in the town of Sempringham and had worshiped at the little church that still faced the manor house. This squat Norman edifice with jagged dogs' teeth zigzagging inside the arches, although partially in ruins, was a disturbing reminder of the enduring presence of imported heresies.

As for the manor itself, it was not actually one grand structure but an ancient collection of tumbled-down monastic buildings. The whole busy household — the pages, cooks, grooms, ladies-in-waiting, menservants, and Theophilus's family — lived on top of the ruins of English papists. Before the Dudleys arrived, the monks' farm buildings had been converted into living quarters, but they were still inevitably Gilbertine; the manor house had been newly constructed, but out of stone quarried from the monastery. Although it is unclear whether the Dudley family lived in the manor or in the freshly built outbuildings, the fact remained that all of the structures of their new home were created from the relics of a shameful past.

Early in his tenure as steward, an uneasy Dudley had urged his new employer to stretch the estate's resources by renovating the house even further and purging it of any remnants of the monks. Dudley oversaw the project, masterminding the design in the hope that he could erase evidence of the manor's Catholic heritage. Fresh walls went up. Workers hammered down boards. But even these improvements could not hide the troubling evidence that for four hundred years the Gilbertines had sung their Latin rites, genuflected, and rattled through their rosary beads right on the grounds of this present-day Puritan stronghold.

If DUDLEY COULD NOT FULLY CLEANSE the manor, there was certainly nothing he could do about the overall condition of the English church or the country. In 1625, five years after the Dudleys had arrived at the earl's residence, the climate in England grew tense. King James had died, and his son, Charles, had ascended the throne. Although Charles was ostensibly a Protestant, there were ugly rumors about the new king's Catholic sympathies. He had spent much of his adolescence in Catholic France, marrying, to the horror of Puritans everywhere, the daughter of the papist French king, the princess Henrietta Maria. Anne and her family worried that the young ruler would prove to be another cruel tyrant like Mary. Perhaps stakes would be planted in the ground and Protestants would once again stream up to heaven in a black funnel of smoke.

Charles confirmed Puritan fears by leaning heavily on the advice of a cleric who was famously hostile to Puritans, Bishop Laud. Laud actually wanted *more* decoration in churches and greater formality during worship services. As the months passed and Charles fought with the Puritan-dominated House of Commons and pressed for greater tolerance of Catholics, Dudley and other Puritans became increasingly worried.

Puritan anxieties were further provoked by Protestant losses overseas. In Germany, Lutherans and Calvinists had succumbed to the Catholic House of Austria. Protestants in France, the Huguenots, had been vanquished in their last battle and were subject to a Roman cardinal. So, although John Cotton continued to preach his strain of Puritanism, maintaining that the "lilies" could continue to live among the "thorns," his congregants could not help but believe their days in England were numbered.

By 1627 widespread disease, political dissension, and famine caused by extreme weather combined to create a crisis, at least to Anne's father, Arbella, and Isaac, who stepped up their efforts to promote the idea of a massive Puritan migration. But seventeen-year-old Anne did not contribute to the planning process. In later years her only memory of this time period is how reluctant she was to leave England and how she would have to be "convinced" to accept life in "a new world."[13] Her reluctance to consider this idea may have been brave evidence of her capacity to form her own opinions, as her father and Arbella were among the people she admired most in the world. But such independent thinking did not make her life particularly comfortable when the political storm clouds of 1628–29 swept onto the horizon.

Laud declared that Puritan ministers who disagreed with the royal policy of inclusiveness were required to permit "mixed communion." For people like the Dudleys this principal was sheer anathema. Dudley did not want to drink from the same cup as a non-Puritan, nor did he want his family breaking bread with a sinner who had not professed a true, pure faith in God. Charles did nothing to ease the tension by appointing Bishop Laud first to the powerful position of Bishop of London and then to the elevated post of Archbishop of Canterbury, making him the head of the Church of England.

Even worse, many of the leading Puritan preachers whom Anne's family most admired were being forced out of their pulpits. Clearly the king had appointed Laud expressly for the purpose of rooting them out. A few years later, the minister Thomas Shepard would complain that Bishop Laud "threatened me if I preached anywhere." He, like many Puritan ministers, was forced to hide like a criminal from the authorities, scurrying about the country to avoid imprisonment, fines, and other forms of persecution.[14]

At last even the reluctant John Cotton began to be swayed, although he still preached that the "Godly" should not abandon their mission of reform even if they left the country. This marked a new development in Puritan thought that would eventually usher in the birth of the settlements in New England. In the past, men like Dudley and Simon had conceived of themselves as "the saving remnant" of the island; it was their duty to remain in England and reform the country and the church from the inside out. But now, for Dudley and his fellow dissenters, already well versed in the history of religious persecution and victimization, it seemed that Charles's hostility toward Puritans could only escalate. Short of deposing the king, which seemed impossible, the only chance for "true" English Protestantism to survive was to transport all of the "believers" away from harm. Unlike the Pilgrims, these men declared that they would remain a crucial part of the English church, but at a safe distance. Thus Anne's father and friends arrived at the hard-won decision that they would carry the pure church with them, away from Old World corruption, saving England by preserving her religious ideals from papism. After all, as Thomas Shepard said, looking back on these years and his own decision to leave the Old World, "It seemed that even God himself was emigrating."[15]

Of course, now that they had decided on migration, Anne knew that the main problem her father and Simon were debating was where they should go. Right across the North Sea, there was Holland, which allowed dissenters to practice their religion freely. But the Puritans who had fled there, including the original Pilgrims, had complained that English children ran the risk of losing their identity and becoming too much like the Dutch. Dudley and Simon had no intention of raising their children to be anything but proud English people, and so they would need to go somewhere that was still somehow English. Anne clung to her national culture with pride and would have resented living in another country and learning another language. Besides, the memory of Antwerp persisted; Holland was entirely too close to Catholic marauders.

The prospect of the wilderness loomed as Anne's father was drawn to the vast emptiness of America. Anne was aghast, but only in isolation, Puritan leaders believed, could they truly build a new, redeemed England, one far away from the king. The French explorers in Canada were a worrisome factor, but Dudley and his colleagues steeped themselves in propaganda citing the attractions of the continent, such as the explorer Captain John Smith's overheated cries of the potential riches New England had to offer. "Who would live at home idly . . . only to eat, drink, and sleep, and so die," Smith exhorted, when there was the possibility of

> planting and building a foundation for his posterity, got
> from the rude earth, by God's blessing and his own
> industry. . . . What pleasure can be more, than . . . in
> planting vines, fruits, or herbs, in contriving their own
> grounds, to the pleasure of their own minds, their fields,
> gardens, orchards, buildings, ships, and other works, etc.,
> to recreate themselves before their own doors, in their own
> boats upon the sea, where man, woman, and child with a
> small hook and line, by angling, may take diverse sorts of
> excellent fish, at their pleasure?[16]

How could Dudley not resonate with such stirring words? New England sounded more like a garden ready to be planted than a wilderness yet to be tamed.

A fifty-one-year-old war veteran by the time of Anne's marriage, Dudley was now a senior man in the Puritan community, and his words were heeded carefully by more than just his son-in-law. Isaac Johnson led the pack of younger, influential "brethren" who, with Dudley's support, readied themselves to embark on the greatest adventure they would ever experience, the "removal" to a new world that seemed promising, unknowable, and best of all, far beyond the reach of their enemies.

AN AMERICAN NEW ENGLAND was still a vague, mysterious place on the map, despite earlier attempts by explorers to make the savage New World seem like a mere extension of the Old. Even the name New England was loaded with symbolic power. It was Smith who had first used the term, in 1616; until then, those Englishmen who gave the matter any thought considered the land from Penobscot to Cape Cod as "the north part of Virginia." Smith, eager to promote colonization, quickly replaced all the Indian names that had figured so prominently on previous maps with the more familiar names of English towns and villages, and distributed this new map to the public.[17] Still, Smith must have known that he was treading on dangerous territory if he hoped to convince Puritans to come and settle in America. Puritans tended to regard anything termed "new" with suspicion. After all, it was the king's Anglican Church that embodied innovation and change, sponsoring the "new" Book of Common Prayer, instituting "new" rules of decoration and formality. Later, when Anne described how difficult her "remove" to New England had been, she would write that she had resisted "a new world" with "new manners," and her contemporaries would have understood these negative sentiments.[18]

But it seems that Anne only fully realized how near they were to leaving when, a few months after she and Simon had moved to the Countess of Warwick's estate, they received shocking news from Sempringham. Charles's persecution of Puritans had finally spread to Lincolnshire, and Theophilus had been thrown into the dreaded Tower of London for resisting the king's demands of additional tax money, or a "loan" to the royal coffers, as Charles called it. Dudley himself, as a close adviser of the earl's, was in danger of arrest.

To make the situation even more threatening, in the midst of the chaos of Theophilus's imprisonment, someone at Sempringham had published an abridged version of the English statutes on the people's rights, proving that the king's request for additional funds from his nobles was illegal. Although it is not known for sure who wrote this pamphlet, it might well have been the dowager countess or the strong-willed Thomas Dudley himself. Whoever it was, the household now faced almost certain retribution from the king for harboring the unknown culprit. And yet the defiant Puritan stronghold did not back down. Dudley himself resisted the royal demand for money, as one informer whispered to officials: "Mr. Dudlye beynge reported to have 300 per annum, some say 400, refused upon our earnest request to bear 30 shillings towards the loan." In fact, contemporary witnesses reported that all of Lincolnshire appeared to be in "open rebellion" against "the Royal Commissioners."[19]

Conversations at Sempringham and the Countess of Warwick's estate now centered on the earl's fate. What would become of Theophilus? What would happen to his properties and family? What actions would the king take against Theophilus's allies and servants? Although Anne heard about these events secondhand, she followed them closely and, young matron that she was, sympathized with the women close to the earl, especially the dowager and Arbella.

Knowing her father as she did, Anne was not surprised when he proclaimed that it was the moment for Puritans to act. By 1629 everyone at Sempringham and in the surrounding neighborhood agreed that with Theophilus in the king's grip, it was time to set things in motion, to forge a New England colony far away from the king's tyranny. Ministers stirred their flocks with pronouncements that the Puritans were the chosen people and must be as brave as the Israelites leaving Egypt.

It was during this crisis that Arbella's husband, Isaac, proving that he was indeed the worthy choice of his visionary bride, created as thorough a business plan as he could devise. In 1628 he and several associates had formed the New England Company on the basis of their Sempringham meetings, but now he created the wealthier, more powerful Massachusetts Bay Company in order to facilitate a hasty "remove." He and Dudley invited other distinguished Puritans to help plan their emigration, most notably the clergyman Roger Williams, whose passionate idealism would inspire others to flee England, and the solid, experienced solicitor, John Winthrop, who would become the most important political leader of the colony.

Williams was an eager and intelligent participant in these meetings and gave no evidence of the extremist zeal that would appall his friends in years to come. Winthrop, who came from Suffolk, had some difficulty making his way through the marshy countryside to the manor house in Sempringham. He recorded that "my horse fell under me in a bogge in the fennes, so as I was allmost to the waiste in water."[20] Perhaps the difficulty of his journey through Lincolnshire contributed to his initial resistance to the plan. But Johnson and Dudley persuaded him to give the matter some thought, and before long he, too, had decided to join the venture. After extensive meetings, the group easily procured the king's permission to settle a rocky swath of land along the northern New England coast. Why should Charles stand in the way of their departure? He must have been glad to see the first boatload of troublemaking Puritans take leave of England.

In 1629 Isaac and Arbella put up the cash for an advance expedition to the area of their claim. This hardy band of explorers arrived safely on the shores of America and established the flimsy settlement that would so dismay Anne and her family when at last they arrived in New England twelve months later. But none of the planners of the migration had any inkling of what was to come. In fact their hopes could only rise when Francis Higginson, the minister of this experimental journey, wrote home a thrilling letter of discovery that fired the Puritans' determination: "Both land and sea abound with a state of blessings for the comfortable sustenance of man's life in New England." He went on to declare that "a sup of New England's air is better than a whole draught of old England's ale."[21] The excitement generated by these words echoed throughout the

Dudley and Bradstreet homes, confirming Thomas Dudley's dreams of what the New World would be like. Now he knew he was embarking on the right adventure. The only problem was that as the months passed, they never heard from Higginson again.

With the notable exception of Anne, the enthusiasm of the Puritans mounted, and as preparations continued, they began to feel that they were stranded in England and far from their real and rightful home in the New World. As Edward Johnson wrote, "Oh yes! oh yes! oh yes! All you, the people of Christ that are here oppressed, imprisoned and scurrilously derided, gather yourselves together . . . for planting the united colonies of New England."[22]

Not that Anne was entirely alone in her reluctance. Many Reformers knew that the fascinating accounts of "Penobscot to Cape Cod" might be unreliable, as they were written by financiers to encourage investment in New World mercantile projects. Although Higginson's report sealed the matter as far as they were concerned, Puritan leaders still continued to seek out information about the condition of the Pilgrims, who had settled in Plymouth in 1620. Again, all seemed promising. Travelers to the fledgling colony noted the "healthfulness" of the settlers. One wrote, "I know of no place in the world that can match it," listing the plentiful bounty: "delicate plums," "five several sorts of grapes," as well as "much plenty both of fish and foul everyday in the year." As they readied for the voyage, the preparations for which would take almost a year, Dudley had plenty of opportunity to read these reports aloud to his family and send them on to Anne and Simon. Life would be delicious there, proponents for the journey argued, with lots of "good cheer" to go around.[23]

But there were also the less appealing reports, from rumors of French Catholics who attacked Puritan settlers to man-eating Indians. As early as 1607, an English settlement in Maine had failed miserably, prompting those who survived to describe New England as "a cold, barren, mountainous, rocky desert."[24] In 1623 a pioneering group of traders had tried to settle a colony on Cape Ann, but most of them had died of disease or starvation within a few years, though a few stragglers did remain in Salem, living as traders, fishermen, and hunters. In fact these were the old planters who would help the Puritans establish their initial colonies. Although Anne's father and his friends were aware of the struggles of these men, they still felt eager to voyage to a world "as gorgeously garnished with all . . . pregnant nature ravishing the sight with variety."[25]

This was not the life Anne had envisioned for herself when she left her sickroom for marriage to Simon. Not only had her father plunged her and her family into this New World expedition, but they were to become leaders of the venture. Dudley was voted deputy governor, second in command under Winthrop. Simon, who was always happy to follow in his father-in-law's footsteps, agreed to serve as secretary of the Massachusetts Bay Company. Anne, who was now eighteen, continued to resist her father's decision, but only in the privacy of her own heart. She had been well trained by her mother and knew better than to complain to either Simon or her father. Whether she liked it or not, Anne and her willing young husband were bound for New England. She was a daughter, not a father; a wife, not a husband. Hers was not the deciding voice.

CHAPTER SIX

⊗✳⊗

Preparedness

We must . . . wait all the days of our appointed time till our change shall come.
— ANNE BRADSTREET, "Meditation 53"

The certainty that that time will come, together with the uncertainty, how, where, and when, should make us so to number our days as to apply our hearts to wisdom, that when we are put out of these houses of clay we may be sure of an everlasting habitation that fades not away.
— ANNE BRADSTREET, "Meditation 70"

IN THE EARLY MONTHS OF 1629, no one, not even Anne's father, could predict exactly when the journey would begin, and so, as far as Anne was concerned, the voyage hung in the air like an impending storm. Preoccupied as she was with the idea of her own death, having already experienced two close calls, the expedition that lay ahead could only exacerbate the eighteen-year-old's anxieties.

No one would have thought to soothe Anne's fears. Instead most of the potential emigrants were instructed by their ministers to meditate on their own "destruction" before they even began the undertaking. This activity made sense to someone like Anne not only because of the dangers she would confront but also because the process of closing one's affairs and bidding farewell to England seemed a kind of rehearsal for permanent departure from earthly affairs. She must also have secretly wondered if she would be able to survive a journey about which a contemporary had said "the weak bodies of women . . . could never be able to endure."[1]

Few journeys of any magnitude actually start with departure, and the sailing of the first ship in the Great Migration to America would be no exception. It was not a simple proposition, this climactic break from civilization. More than seven hundred men, women, and children had signed on for the trip. Although the *Arbella* would carry around three hundred of these pioneers, ten other, smaller ships were necessary to carry the remaining passengers and to help transport livestock and supplies. Three of these vessels would depart with the *Arbella*, and seven more would follow. This venture to the New World would be on a scale unlike any other, not only in the lives of the Lincolnshire Puritans, but also in human history, and therefore there were few precedents to follow. Only fiercely devout men like Dudley and John Winthrop, who believed that God had ordained this plan — the passage of so many unweathered civilians across more than three thousand miles of ocean — would have dared embark on such a terrifying experiment. But these were pragmatic men as well as visionaries, and so they did not set forth impetuously.

Anne's father and his colleagues devoted themselves to planning their journey, not only because of the practical benefits of such careful measures, but also because this was one of the requirements of their spiritual notion of "preparedness." This ideal held that you should aspire toward a perpetual anticipation of Judgment Day — a daunting task. Getting ready for the voyage, however, was as difficult spiritually as it was physically, since it involved one sacrifice after another; Anne soon found that her willingness to submit to her father's dream was constantly put to the test. She would have to weed out unnecessary luxuries from her household and pack what they hadn't sold — blankets, linens, pewter, clothing, and smaller boxes of food — in large wooden chests that were so heavy many men would be needed to hoist them aloft when it was time to leave.

Before sailing, they had to complete what were essentially the tasks of a dying person — selling cattle, houses, and furniture and transferring beloved items to people who were staying behind — and each activity naturally assumed a funereal hue. In a kind of mute acceptance of their fate, most Puritans who had not yet done so wrote their wills in the months before they sailed for America.[2]

To make matters worse, non-Puritan neighbors often mocked what seemed to them a foolish venture. In a much later poem, "The Flesh and the Spirit," Anne would capture the scoffing voices whose jeers echoed her own doubts: "Dost [thou] dream of things beyond the moon, / And dost thou hope to dwell there soon?" and "Art fancy sick, or turned a sot / To catch at shadows which are not?"[3] Anne could triumph over these insults in her poems, declaring, "I'll stop mine ears" against all insults, but at the time, lonely, sad, and terrified of what lay ahead, she had little choice but to worry: What if her tormenters were right and her father was wrong? What if the voyage to the New World turned out to be a disaster?

Still, despite her reservations about the enterprise, Anne remained devoted to her father, and so when disapproving neighbors asked why she and her family were deserting England, she knew exactly what to say and how to promote his vision. The colony in New England would one day take care of England, Anne had been taught. In the years to come she would have New England actually speak in one of her poems, asking a disease-ridden Old England, "What medicine shall I seek to cure . . . [your] wound?"[4] Anne would also have been able to cite one of the famous arguments for the exodus articulated most forcefully by the minister Richard Mather: "It was right," he declared, "to remove from a corrupt church . . . because by staying voluntarily in places corrupt we endanger ourselves to be corrupted."[5]

But Anne remained uninspired by the prospect of the move, and even her mother's stalwart example did not help. While they sorted and packed or sold one possession after another — including, no doubt, the artifacts of her childhood: the cradle used by all of the Dudley children and their few toys — to friends who were staying behind or to strangers in the busy Boston marketplace, Dorothy remained steadfastly organized and calm. It was her duty to bend cheerfully to her husband's wishes, and she would have had little patience for Anne's anxieties.

There was no sympathy to be had from her father either. Dudley acknowledged that the journey to America was not to be undertaken by the fainthearted but remained firm in his decision to bring his children with him. Winthrop, on the other hand, reflected the more ordinary person's approach to the journey, leaving his wife and young child behind to save them from the dangers of the wilderness and the ocean voyage. They could join him later, he decided, once he had established a home where they could dwell in comfort and safety.

Still, Anne could not help but derive an odd confidence from her father's unflagging commitment to bring her and her siblings to New England. It was really a compliment of sorts: Dudley had singled his family out for a kind of noble odyssey. And so, in her attempt to live up to his ideals as well as to please her new husband, Anne seems to have decided that she would not be like one prospective emigrant's stubborn wife, who declared that she would rather be "a living wife in England than a dead one in the sea."[6] Only toward the end of her life, long after her father had died, did she acknowledge her misery, and even then, only briefly.

Still, despite his overall optimism, Dudley was well aware that if they made mistakes now, the entire venture was doomed. To begin with, it was enormously expensive to undertake such a mission, and so it was important to figure out exactly what supplies had to be purchased. Dudley, who was wealthier than most prospective colonists, was worth around three hundred to four hundred pounds a year, and Simon's income was probably somewhat less. According to best estimates, a carpenter's income was around forty-five pounds a year. A shoemaker might make eighty pounds. Clergy usually earned less than one hundred pounds.[7]

Gentlemen like Dudley, therefore, could afford the expenses of the journey with careful planning. But other working men often needed to have their passage paid for them. In general, it cost about five pounds for an individual to book passage, around twenty-five pounds to ferry a family across the ocean, fifty pounds for rudimentary household materials such as "ammunition . . . soap, candles, implements and utensils, beer, wine, and liquor . . . steel, iron, merchandise for trading with the Indians, clothing, shoes, house furnishings, sail cloth, hay for fodder, and cattle," and perhaps an additional one hundred pounds or more to ship over the requirements of wealthy, highly placed families like the Dudleys and the Bradstreets.[8] This meant that Dudley would have to shell out at least two-thirds of his yearly earnings to make the pilgrimage to America; Simon would be even more hard-pressed. For both families, the journey could only be undertaken after a complete overhaul of their holdings; luxuries such as Anne and her sisters' fine lace collars or pearl hair ornaments would have to be sold to help purchase supplies. It was fortunate, then, that their religion explained material loss as sacred gain and as a sign of devotion to God and His mission.

This process of parting with worldly goods was not only a trial all future New Englanders had to undergo, it was also a stumbling block that prevented many of the faithful from joining the expedition. Aside from the emotional toll of "preparedness," Anne and her family were hard-pressed to convert all of their holdings into the cash they needed to purchase their basic requirements: heavy woolen capes for the sea voyage and the freezing winters they had been warned of, as well as thick linen shirts, handkerchiefs, "Irish stockings," extra pairs of shoes, and leather for repairs. Dudley, Simon, and Samuel each needed an extra pair of boots and also many more tools than they were accustomed to using in England.

Contemporary lists cited spades, shovels, hatchets, axes, hoes, pitchforks, vises, brands for livestock, hammers, hand saws, grindstones, nails, locks, hooks and twists for doors, cod hooks for fishing and mackerel line, chains and locks for small boats, a bellows, scoops, pairs of wheels for carts, plows, ladders, and anything else the emigrants could afford and believed would be useful for their new lives as farmers. But the Dudleys and Bradstreets also had to assuage their fear of potential human enemies — pirates on the ocean, Indians, French Catholics in Canada — and so the men brought their armor, including helmets, shields, and swords; twenty pounds of powder each; sixty pounds of lead for bullets, pistols, muskets, and other arms. Anne and her mother prepared for their own kind of battle, as they were forewarned that to make beds they would require "ells of canvas," and that for a working kitchen, they would need at least "one iron pot, one great copper kettle, a small kettle, a lesser kettle, one large frying pan, a small frying pan, a brass mortar, a spit, one gridiron, two skillets, platters, dishes and spoons of wood." Then, for a family like Anne's, there were amenities to consider like "sugar, pepper, cloves, mace, cinnamon, nutmegs."[9]

The unsteadiness of the monetary rates underlined the financial ruin they might face. Anne and her family knew that if their mission failed and they had to return to England, they could never recoup what they had spent, and many of their supplies were useless except in America. Each purchase, then, further sealed their fate, and each possession they parted with deepened their commitment to the future. Ten years earlier, the Pilgrim leaders John Robinson and William Brewster had acknowledged, "We shall much prejudice both our arts and our means by our removal; who if we should be driven to return, we should not hope to recover our present helps and comforts, neither indeed look ever for ourselves to attain unto the like in any other place during our lives."[10] Despite these risks, no prudent person skimped on provisions. Francis Higginson, the minister who had been sent ahead to America in the advance party, wrote a letter home warning his friends to "be careful" and to pay attention to their needs

> before you come. . . . For when you are once parted from
> England, you shall meet neither with taverns nor alehouses,
> nor butchers, nor grocers, nor apothecaries' shops to help what
> things you need, in the midst of the great ocean nor when you
> come to land."[11]

This was one of the few letters they had received from the expedition, and so Higginson's words had particular weight.

During the last few months of preparation, Simon and Dudley were usually either in London ordering supplies, such as the ten thousand gallons of ale or the two hundred dried oxen tongues that they would store in the *Arbella*'s hold, or meeting with Winthrop and the other company leaders in Cambridge. Their absence during such an anxious time threw Anne wholly on the resources of the women in her family, a circumstance that was somewhat unfamiliar, as she had spent so much of her girlhood in the company of her father and Simon. Yet these weeks provided excellent training for another aspect of what lay ahead. Anne would have to learn to do without either her husband or her father for long stretches once she was in the New World, and so she and her sisters needed to weave strong relationships as they sorted, prayed, sewed, and worried, comparing notes with the other women bound for America.

In fact it was almost impossible to stop the deepening of intimacy that occurred among the prospective travelers. Their daily routines had been dismantled, while their old friends were still going about their accustomed business. Consequently, even someone like Anne Hutchinson, who fully supported them in their venture but who had not yet chosen to take apart her own home or to trade her extra woolen underskirts for cart wheels and cod hooks, must have sometimes seemed unconcerned, or at least on the other side of the fence from those who were about to plunge into the unknown. Fortunately for the flagging spirits of the Dudley women, the Lady Arbella was undoubtedly a frequent visitor.

However, even Arbella could not cheer them up when a strain of what was apparently the black plague struck that winter. The affliction was so virulent it wiped out two of Hutchinson's daughters in less than a week. When word spread of the rising death toll in Lincolnshire, tension escalated rapidly; it was increasingly urgent for the truly devout to flee England, as this scourge seemed a new sign of God's displeasure with the corruption of the Old World. Dudley, Simon, and the other leaders rushed through the company's business transactions in an effort to speed their departure. But no matter how hard they pushed, they could not control the slow pace of the captains they had hired. Eleven ships needed to be readied, and the sailors seemed intent on puttying every crack and polishing each brass fixture.

Businessmen as well as pious pilgrims, Dudley and the other men spent as much of their waiting time dreaming up new ventures for potential investments as praying. As a result, their official letters often dealt with projects for salt production, "planting vines, collecting furs, setting up iron mines and exploiting New England's vast timber reserves."[12] Even Higginson, in his famous letter home, had written urgently requesting more skilled workers instead of more preachers, arguing that "of all trades carpenters are most needful, therefore, bring as many as you can."[13]

Dudley and his fellow planners understood that piety was not the only requirement of their recruits. The settlers would also need to take care of themselves, and so Dudley called for voyagers who were "endued with grace and furnished with means." True believers should be able to "feed themselves and theirs for eighteen months." If his vision of an American "plantation" were to succeed, the colony would have to be productive as well as saintly, rich in goods as well as religion.[14]

That these two realms, economic and religious, were tangled in an uneasy but inevitable snarl created an odd mix of snobbery, humility, disdain for material possessions, and a high estimation of wealth that seemed logical only to Anne and her family. When Dudley discouraged "the poorer sort" from joining their mission, it was not only because he was convinced that indigent "godly" men without any skills could endanger the fledgling colony but also because in the Puritan mind, destitution was often a sign of divine disfavor. Those who possessed solid assets were more likely to be righteous individuals because they had clearly found a righteous calling, or vocation. Those who were poor, on the other hand, might well have done something to deserve God's disfavor.

Thus, although Anne's father never promoted the Puritan mission as a profit-gaining adventure, he had no intention of taking a vow of poverty in the New World. Indeed, Dudley strongly disapproved of any such notion, declaring that any pious man who wished to come to America with no "goods" should be dissuaded. However, the other extreme was just as bad. A year after he had arrived in New England, Dudley wrote, "If any come hither to plant for worldly ends, that can live well at home, he commits an error, of which he will soon repent him."[15]

At last February turned to March. Ideal sailing weather began in April and extended through the summer, and so the race was on to finalize their preparations. If they missed their chance to sail, they would have to wait another twelve months before they could begin their journey. By virtue of their important position in Puritan society, Anne and her family shouldered an undue load of responsibility when it came to the success of the journey. If Anne and her mother made the wrong decisions about their domestic needs in the New World, they could ruin not only their own family's chance of survival but that of other families who looked to them for guidance. And if Dudley miscalculated or gave assent to the wrong individual's request to join them, the whole enterprise could be endangered. Everyone understood that bringing in the wrong sort of person could pollute their endeavor and doom it to failure.

Just as the Puritans had hated the "mixed" congregations of the Church of England, they dreaded the idea of importing sinners to the New World. It had been up to Dudley and his colleagues to sift through the constant flow of applications, to sort the upstanding individuals from those who might wreak havoc. Of course, if they needed a surgeon, they needed a surgeon, Puritan or not. There was no way around it; some of the emigrants would have to be "thorns," although the uncompromising Dudley resented this idea. He yearned for a truly "pure" colony, made up only of the faithful. After all, the whole point of their exodus was to escape the taint of corruption, whether the source was irreligious individuals, the Church of England, or papists. It was painful to have to yield to the requirements of earthly life in the course of molding this long-envisioned utopian plantation.[16]

Given their importance, the decisions about who should come and who should stay behind were wrenching ones, and they must have triggered Anne's anxieties about her own candidacy. The men and women her father rejected for their exodus had at least wanted to partake in this "remove"; whereas she, who was supposed to be a true pilgrim, was reluctant to leave England behind. Again, she feared that she was not worthy to follow in her father's footsteps. When Simon was near, he could reassure his young wife, and his steady love and belief in her piety were a great comfort. But usually she had to stare down her ambivalence on her own.

Anne was not alone in her concerns, nor in her resistance to the idea of the journey. Prospective voyagers wrote urgent letters of fearful inquiry.[17] They also begged for help in making the final decision to join the emigrants. Would it be a betrayal to the good people in England whom they left behind? Would they be abandoning their duty to help improve the Church of England? One sympathetic critic of the journey wrote to Winthrop, "The church and common welthe heere at home, hath more neede of your best abylitie in these dangerous tymes, than any remote plantation."[18] Another close friend of the governor's declared, "All your kinfolks and most understanding friends will more rejoice at your staying at home, with any condition which God shall send, than to throw yourself upon vain hopes with many difficulties and uncertainties."[19] But Dudley, Simon, Winthrop, and their friends had spent years devising their plans and at this point had no difficulty defending their probity.

During these remaining days in Lincolnshire, last-minute lists were published to help people plan, save, and organize their materials, and Puritan ministers gave sermons promoting emigration. The Dudley women and their servants nailed down the lids of their boxes, paid final visits to friends who had chosen to stay behind, prepared and packed the salt fish and grains they would need for the first few days of the journey, and tried to find time for quiet prayer. There was little respite from their labors, however; they had to be ready whenever the summons for departure came.

Finally the long-anticipated message arrived. Their ships were anchored in Southampton, three hundred miles away, pulling at their anchors and riding high in the water. It was time to leave Boston, meet up with their fellow travelers in Southampton, the port town that would be their point of embarkation for America, and oversee the loading of the vessels.

They would have to travel rapidly to avoid the additional costs of anchorage. Although the distance by sea was almost double that of the overland route, English roads of the time were so poor that the most efficient way to reach the south coast was by water. Ships that sailed out of Boston were by necessity small and shallow keeled, since they had to navigate the perilous shallows of the Witham River.[20] But this waterway that had always brought the world to them would now lead them out of their familiar corner of England to a terrifying adventure.

Early in the morning of a blustery March day, Dudley locked the door of the earl's townhouse behind them with a decisive click and Anne and her mother clutched the hands of the younger girls, Mercy, Sarah, and Patience, as they made their way down to the quay. After saying good-bye, perhaps for good, to the people they loved most in the world besides each other, including the dowager countess, John Cotton, Anne Hutchinson, and other members of their congregation, Anne and her family climbed up the narrow plank and found themselves aboard the unsteady ship. The canvas sails filled, and they floated down the muddy river. With each queasy hump of the ship, the teeming city of Boston shrank, until it looked like a toy village settled on a miniature plain.

The misery of departure was compounded by the shock of being onboard a ship. Before long, the boat spilled out of the river's mouth and into the waters of the sea, tumbling over the first waves Anne had ever experienced, and the new sensation was sickening. Although the indented coastline broke the force of the open ocean and the swells were mild, many people suffered from nausea. Of all the Dudley girls, perhaps only Anne's sister Sarah embraced the challenge of the sea, as she would be the only one who would choose to repeat the transatlantic crossing several times.[21] In contrast, in a telling display of repugnance, once she reached New England, Anne would never set foot on a ship's deck again.

After at least three days of sailing, the little boat clipped through the Strait of Dover, where Anne could gaze up at the sharp chalk cliffs. The water was quieter in the channel, and when they came in sight of St. Catherine's Point jutting ruggedly out from the Isle of Wight, they knew that the first stage of their journey was almost over — Southampton and a safe harbor were close by.

Even as the first brief stage of their voyage ended, however, and Anne and the other passengers disembarked, no one could avoid anticipating the dangers that awaited them. They would rest in Southampton only as long as they had to. When the ships were loaded and the winds were right, they would set sail once again, and the challenges they would face on the Atlantic would be far more formidable than anything they had yet experienced. Nobody knew exactly when this moment would come. It was still early in the month of March and the weather was notoriously unpredictable.

CHAPTER SEVEN

ɜ)ƙɞ

Our Appointed Time

The spring is a lively emblem of the resurrection.
— ANNE BRADSTREET, "Meditation 40"

SOUTHAMPTON WAS CROWDED, rough, and noisy and did not in the least suit the sensibilities of people like Anne and her family. Still, the town was planted on reassuringly solid ground, complete with houses, lanterns, and fresh water — a pleasant change after their voyage. These amenities, however, did not compensate for the fact that, to Puritans, the townspeople seemed even more frightening than a sea storm.

Like the majority of the English, the locals scorned the dissenters, viewing them as dangerous traitors to the king, or at best as "busy bodies" who spent entirely too much time trying to tell other people how to live their lives.[1] Anne and her family would have appeared peculiar to the locals. Puritans refused to enter the raucous alehouses. They would not join in local revelries during the Sabbath or on holidays; in fact, they made it clear that they disapproved of holidays altogether and would outlaw Christmas and Easter the moment they arrived in America. To the amusement of their non-Puritan fellows, they even hated the names of the days of the week, derived as they were from Roman and Germanic deities — for instance, Monday was named for the god Mars, Thursday after Thor — and lobbied their countrymen to denote each day simply with a number: Sunday would be the First Day, Monday the Second Day, and so on. Again, this innovation would have to wait until the New World.

Whenever they "gadded," which meant walking to church or a prayer meeting, Puritans proudly sang psalms or quoted Scripture frequently and loudly, asserting their religiosity with what could only be an off-putting kind of ferocity to outsiders. They believed, as one minister put it, that "none shall ever please Christ till they appear odd, strange, and precise to men of the common sort."[2]

And yet appearing "strange" put you at great risk, as Anne well knew. In some counties Puritans had been dragged through the street or beaten in their homes, and so she and her family faced some danger as they made their way along the narrow, littered alleys of Southampton, past alehouses, gambling dens, and brothels. Through the windows came raucous shouts, bawdy singing, cursing, and laughter, and from time to time, there were shocking sights: men and women slouched together in the shadows, sailors stumbling about drunkenly, boys holding knives to an enemy's throat. Winthrop put his disgust into words:

> Cruelty and blood is in our streets, the land aboundeth
> with murders, slaughters, incests, adulteries, whoredom,
> drunkenness, oppression, and pride where well-doing is not
> maintained, or the godly cherished, but idolatry, popery and
> whatsoever is evil is countenanced; even the least of these is
> enough, and enough to make haste out of Babylon.[3]

With her own eyes Anne could finally see why their flight was essential. Outside the Puritan stronghold of Lincolnshire, there was a "multitude of irreligious, lascivious, and popish-affected persons

[that] spread the whole land like grasshoppers."[4] No degree of psalm singing could drown out the carnival, and though Dudley and Simon did their best to shield the women from the crowds of ne'er-do-wells, the task was an impossible one. Winthrop wrote to his wife, "I am veryly perswaded, God will bring some heavye Affliction upon this lande, and that speedylye."[5]

Dudley, Simon, and Winthrop spent each day in furious activity, overseeing the loading of supplies and meeting with the other Puritan leaders. Anne, her sisters, and the Lady Arbella must have often trekked down to the docks to marvel as chests and barrels were hoisted into the air and swung onboard their vessel, the men groaning and sweating as they leaned on the winches.

The leading ship of the enterprise was huge: 350 tons and approximately 150 feet long — about half the length of a modern football field. Originally called the *Eagle*, this old vessel had once been one of the most famous privateers in the Mediterranean, withstanding countless onslaughts from Catholic battleships. In the spirit of starting anew and perhaps in an attempt to reform even their boat, Dudley and his friends had decided to ignore the old nautical superstition never to change the name of a vessel and had bestowed a Puritan identity on the ship. It must have been a rather glorious surprise for Anne and her friends to come down to the docks one day and see the fresh paint on the vessel's side announcing that the *Eagle* was now the new and holier *Arbella*.

In keeping with the warlike fervor sweeping through many of their followers, Winthrop reported that he and Dudley had armed their ship with "twenty-eight pieces of ordnance." The tradition of the sea was to rank ships like a military chain of command. Naturally, their ship was "to be admiral" of their voyage and the other three ships that seemed closest to being ready to sail, the *Talbot*, the *Jewel*, and the *Ambrose*, would be the "vice-admiral," the "rear admiral," and the "captain."[6] Like an advancing army, they had settled upon the order of the fleet, and this hierarchy would extend not only to the sea voyage but ultimately to life in the New World.

Fortunately, Southampton was a deep-water port and so even the enormous *Arbella* could be brought right up to the quay, where it was hard labor filling the hold with enough supplies for three hundred people, both for the voyage and for their first months in New England: ten thousand gallons of beer, thirty-five hundred gallons of water, fifteen thousand biscuits "of the coarser sort," five thousand white biscuits made from "sweet and good wheat, well baked according to the patterns delivered," two hogsheads of rusks, and hundreds of barrels of salted cod, pork, and beef, and peas, oatmeal, and flour. To spice up this dull fare, there were eleven firkins of butter, one cask of salt, a bushel and a half of mustard seed, vinegar, and one hundred pounds of suet. Sadly, though everyone knew that scurvy was a real danger, it was too expensive to invest in limes and lemons, and none of these valuable citrus fruits were onboard. As a result, many of the emigrants had to rely on concoctions of their own to ward off this dread disease of sea travelers, though none of them worked. Many would arrive in the New World weakened by illness and would perish when they encountered the fresh privations of the wilderness.[7]

Although the *Arbella* was destined to carry mostly human passengers, the colonists were intent on bringing livestock to America, and so before long the noise at the dock was compounded by the squeal of pigs and the lowing of the cows, who gazed helplessly ahead as ropes were cinched around their bellies and they were swung onto the holding deck of the *Talbot*. There they munched through the fodder that the emigrants hoped would last the length of the journey. In addition, families like the Dudleys and the Bradstreets were rich enough to try to bring as much of their favorite furniture as possible; chests, bedsteads, writing desks, elaborately carved chairs, tables, and many boxes of books cluttered the docks before they, too, disappeared into the dark mouth of the ship's hold.

The bustle at the water's edge and the general disarray of the port alarmed many of the Puritans, who felt that such lack of organization did not bode well for their journey. "Godliness" lay in the details, according to their way of thinking, and one such traveler was dismayed to find "things very unready" and lying in disordered heaps here and there." On the other hand, some years later the famously devout minister Edward Taylor forgot to say morning prayers because he "found the sailors' activity with ropes and canvas so absorbing." Rapidly, it became clear to Anne and her family that no hasty departure would be possible. In fact, over the course of the Great Migration, some passengers experienced delays of three months or more before they were ready to sail. Not only were these periods of waiting difficult to endure, but they were also expensive. There were lodgings to pay for and the constant worry that the food supplies would spoil or get eaten up long before the pilgrims actually boarded the ship.[8]

Equally worrying were the shouts and curses of the sailors, since these were the uncouth individuals they would have to rely on for the next dangerous months. The ropes, hooks, and other equipment were also intimidating, causing the travelers to confront, for the first time, their own lack of expertise when it came to seafaring. Anne's father could navigate the courts in London, and he had bartered goods, raised funds, ordered supplies, bought materials, and come up with a sound business plan for colonization, but now it was clear that he and Winthrop were the naive ones. No Puritan leader could steer a boat, gauge a current, measure the depth of the water, or tell one star from another, and so the brethren would have to depend on the profane to ferry them across the ocean.

Surprisingly, their vulnerability failed to trouble either Winthrop or Dudley. From the Puritan point of view, a lack of nautical prowess gave them a fine opportunity to exercise their faith.[9] It would not be the sailors' knowledge that would transport them safely across the sea, Puritan ministers argued, but rather God's providence and their own vigilant prayers. When he finally made the decision to leave England, John Cotton would bravely assert that "the safety of mariners' and passengers' lives . . . lieth not on ropes and cables . . . but in the name and hand of the lord."[10]

Winthrop and Dudley's leadership would therefore remain unchallenged by the superior knowledge of any sea captain. This attitude was, to Anne, a disturbing reminder of the importance of piety. If arrival in America depended largely on faith, she would have to find a way to conquer what she saw as her spiritual weakness. Otherwise, like Jonah, she might be the ill-starred passenger who brought furious storms down upon their heads.

There was plenty of time to brood about honing her spiritual rectitude as the days in Southampton stretched into weeks, but fortunately for Anne's sanity, there were many distractions from her anxieties. At meals and during prayers, Anne began to get to know her compatriots from other parts of the country. There was a certain comfort in sizing up the strength of the Puritan community, for the gatherings of these men and women had both a festive and a momentous feel. Together at last, they spoke of their dreams for the New World. They had been selected by God for a special mission, and at times like these it was exhilarating to be a member of a blessed community.

In forging new friendships with men and women from Norfolk, London, and the west counties, however, it soon became clear, to Anne's consternation, that there was not just one brand of Puritanism. The "godly" from southeast Essex and the Stour Valley had different beliefs and customs from Anne's family's.[11] Some thought they should completely disavow the English church. Others were not so willing to jettison Anglican worship traditions.

Even worse, some of the roughnecks who milled about the port were non-Puritan artisans and skilled laborers whom Dudley and Winthrop had allowed to sign on for the voyage because they needed their services. Instead of bidding farewell to scoundrels forever, as Anne and her family had hoped, they would actually be importing many ruffians to the New World. These individuals were primarily men with technical expertise that would be useful to the colonists, but there was also a sizable group of unregenerates who had been hired at the last minute as servants. Hoping to escape unpleasant conditions at home — from debts to prison sentences — they had little use for their solemn, dream-filled fellow travelers and chose to devote their last nights in England to revelry, "wenching," and frequenting alehouses, before such opportunities were out of their reach, perhaps forever.[12]

Winthrop and Dudley took heed of this delinquency and began to debate a question that would ultimately divide the two men when they arrived in America. How would they manage these impious folk once they were under way? Dudley argued that they should wield a stern regulative hand. Winthrop held a more moderate viewpoint but seems to have been persuaded at first by Dudley's insistence that there was no room for disobedience, nor for the weak of heart, especially on shipboard.

During this time of uncertainty, pious travelers desperately turned to fasts, prayers, Bible study, and a careful examination of all the omens to try to predict when their journey would begin and how it would end. Anne and her family were careful not to fall in with the superstitious practices of the sailors, who, as Cotton Mather would report many years later, were "afraid of sailing on such or such a day because 'tis an unlucky day," or who were prone "to practice rites of sorcery."[13] Still it was tempting to search for answers in the sudden spoiling of milk, the entrails of a dead animal, or the appearance of magpies jostling each other in the trees, and some of the devout sought out astrologers before they boarded the ship. Even the Puritans could not completely shake their dependence on folk traditions and necromancy.[14]

At last, though, there came a great sign. It was mid-March, and their disapproval of holidays notwithstanding, the Puritans knew Easter week was fast approaching. Good Friday would dawn on the morning of March 26, and the thoughts of the travelers turned to Christ's suffering on the cross. While they were in the midst of such sober contemplations, John Cotton surprised his parishioners by riding into town. Anne, like all of her fellows, was overjoyed by his arrival. The charismatic minister must have suspected that the lilies' spirits were flagging and had come to speed them on their way.

This was an especially gallant gesture, as Cotton was actually struggling with the beginnings of a fever that would fell him for

more than a year and would ultimately strike his beloved wife, causing her to die an anguished, heartbreaking death. Yet he preached
as soon as he arrived, delivering a rousing sermon that energized
the emigrants.[15] He referred to those touchstones of Puritan faith,
the Protestant martyrs under Bloody Mary, comparing the journey
to New England with the flight of the faithful from England during Mary's reign of Catholic terror. He also cited a famous text,
"I will appoint a place for my people Israel, and will plant it, that
they may dwell in a place of their own, and move no more," declaring, in effect, that his flock was indeed a chosen people following
the commandment of the Lord and that America was destined to be
their land for eternity.[16]

Such language was both thrilling and reassuring to those like
Anne who were fearful. Cotton went on to remind them that they
must not forget old England when they arrived and should not surrender their English ways. Even if they never returned home, Cotton assured them, the emigrants would remain the offspring of the
Old World, comforting those who were worried that if they left
their native country behind, they might turn into savages.[17]

The idea that America had been designated by God for their use
was supported, in Puritan eyes, by compelling information that had
trickled back overseas from the Pilgrims and the scattered traders
north of Cape Cod. The coastal Indians, who had been plentiful
only ten years before, had been reduced to almost a third of their
original population and were still greatly weakened from the virulent diseases imported to America by the English. The Puritans
had their own interpretation of what the "miraculous" devastation
meant: Clearly, God had providentially wiped the shores of New
England clean to make room for them and for a new, reformed
England. As Cotton declared, the Lord had "given" the Puritans
"the land by promise."[18]

It was an easy next step, then, for the Puritan leaders to proclaim
that their arrival in America would be a blessing for the Indians, since
they brought with them the Gospel of the Lord. Cotton declared that
their duty was to make "the poor natives . . . partakers" of Puritanism

and even wondered if this was the reason God had "reared this whole plantation."[19] But the idea of converting the Indians remained an afterthought for most of the Puritans, although there were some notable exceptions, such as one of the original planners, Roger Williams, who would devote himself to bringing Jesus to the natives.

The last formal words of encouragement the passengers heard before they embarked were most likely Winthrop's.[20] The governor stood before the entire group (including those non-Puritans who could be corralled into attendance) and delivered what would become one of the most famous sermons of all time, "A Model of Christian Charity."[21]

Winthrop's address sounds as though he was somehow able to predict the complaints, laments, and quarrels that would soon ensue. There should be no "repining," no "grudging," and no "reproaching," he declared. The colonists had to love one another as true Christians and employ "cheerfulness in serving and suffering together." Only then could they avoid "shipwrack," for just as they were joined together by a covenant to support one another, they were also united to God through such an agreement. Like the lawyer he was, Winthrop argued that the emigrants needed to hold up their end of the bargain. Only then would God fulfill the terms of the contract:

> Now if the Lord shall . . . bring us in peace to the place we
> desire, then hath he ratified this covenant. . . . But if we shall
> fail to embrace this present world and prosecute our carnal
> intentions, seeking great things for ourselves and our posterity,
> the Lord will surely break out in wrath against us, be revenged
> of such a perjured people, and make us know the price of the
> breach of such a covenant.[22]

The world was watching them to see if they would take a misstep; in his most frequently quoted words, Winthrop declared that they were as visible "as a city upon a hill."[23] Although the lack of interest most English people had evinced over their departure suggested otherwise, Winthrop told his listeners that their collapse would be a notorious and famous event, one that would shame the international effort of all Reformers to change the church into a holier institution.

Anne had no difficulty understanding Winthrop's message. The pressure was on. If she fell, others would fall. If their mission failed, they would let the entire world down. Dudley and Winthrop were like Aaron and Moses — the two captains of the Jewish exodus from Egypt — and as Dudley's daughter, she would have to elevate her actions immediately to live up to this kind of biblical heroism.

After Cotton and Winthrop had delivered their sermons, Dudley received the happy news that at long last the *Arbella* was ready to sail as soon as the weather was in their favor. The *Talbot, Jewel,* and *Ambrose* were also standing at anchor, and Captain Milbourne felt that these were enough vessels to ensure a safe passage. It was important to travel in a convoy owing to piracy on the open seas, even though everyone knew it was inevitable that they would become separated at some point during the journey.

The moment seemed particularly propitious. While the town of Southampton plunged into the celebrations of Easter week, Arbella and Isaac joined the Dudleys and Bradstreets in rejoicing at the synchronicity of events. There was, after all, a remarkable parallel between the church calendar and the timing of their own departure. On the night before His crucifixion, Christ had celebrated Passover, the commemoration of the flight from the Pharaoh, and now they were waiting for a "wind fair to the north" to begin their own pilgrimage, one that they hoped would lead them toward redemption.[24] And so, with Simon, her sisters and brother, Dorothy, and the Lady Arbella and Isaac, Anne gathered up her baskets and blankets and sallied forth to the docks to board ship.

But the women's resolve was shaken when they ventured below to set up housekeeping. No one knew exactly how long they would have to consider the crowded ship their unsteady home, and the estimates were not promising: at least eight or nine weeks. Some later crossings would take as long as four months thanks to storms, variable winds, and navigation mistakes. The sight of their quarters was shocking, especially to these gently bred passengers, who were used to their own chambers and to the rambling halls of aristocratic homes. On the *Arbella*, they would be cramped together in an open, undefined space, rather like a large parish hall or a small barn. Anne, her mother and sisters, a few of the other "gentlewomen," and the Lady Arbella would have a private sleeping berth in a separate compartment, but such an accommodation would only have been large enough for the beds the ladies would have to share, and certainly the thin partition would not block out the noise and smells of the rest of the travelers, who would be sleeping, eating, cooking, talking, praying, vomiting, defecating, and even copulating in the crowded space beyond.

According to Winthrop's journal, during their first hours on-board, many of the women wept and prayed in scenes of "bowel-breaking affections."[25] Certainly, there were plenty of reasons for everyone to cry: They were leaving their homes; they might drown in the watery deep, be assaulted by pirates, or die of misery in New England. The devout onboard understood that they were delivering their lives into the hands of the "Lord of sea and land" and that the journey ahead was a test of their sinful natures. Under such circumstances, those who were not afraid were not truly God-fearing folk, or so Anne and her friends believed.

The idea that it was correct to weep and sigh upon departure was shared by most Puritan emigrants. For example, Thomas Shepard reported that he spent a good deal of time loudly "lamenting the loss of our native country."[26] Visible grief helped prove the point of the Puritans' self-sacrifice. Not that their tears were a ploy, but if they cried loudly and publicly enough, their virtue could be more easily established by all who witnessed their sadness. For Anne it must have been a relief to have a sanctioned time and place to vent her sorrow at leaving England.

Even Dudley, Winthrop, and the other leaders of the company who attempted to comfort their wives and daughters could not refrain from tears. Winthrop was heartbroken to be leaving his wife and small children behind and sobbed at the thought of never see-ing them again.[27]

When the sailors began to hoist the sails and haul up the anchor, notch by notch, the passengers barely noticed. It was not until the entry planks were thrown aboard and stacked onto the top deck, the great flap of the canvas began to fill with wind, and the shouts of the men drowned out their cries that Anne, her friends, and family realized what was happening. At last the *Arbella*, closely followed by her three companion vessels, was off, charting a course through Southampton Water, the river that emptied out into The Solent, and then unfurling her sails when she reached the wide channel that led to the open sea. In a matter of hours they arrived at the Isle of Wight. It was Easter Sunday, March 27, 1630, and their pilgrimage had begun.

CHAPTER EIGHT

❧

The Crossing

He that is to sail into a far country, although the ship, cabin, and
provision be all convenient and comfortable for him, yet he hath
no desire to make that his place of residence.
— ANNE BRADSTREET, "Meditation 53"

THE NEXT DAY SEEMED to bode well for the beginning of
this momentous voyage to America. The wind was from
the north, and the four ships enjoyed a brisk sail to Yarmouth with the lines stretched tight and the spray kicking up a fine
white trail behind them. As they neared the town, Dudley and the
others were surprised to catch sight of a weary-looking ship, the
Plantation, at anchor after limping home from Virginia. The safe
return of this vessel seemed like yet another good omen for their
own journey, and immediately they lowered their sails, came to a
rest, and "saluted" the other ship by firing a shot from their cannon.
The *Plantation* returned the signal, and to the great excitement of
Anne and her family, the vessel's captain, a Mr. Graves, rowed over
to the *Arbella* and stayed to talk for most of the afternoon.[1]

It was the first opportunity many of the Puritan leaders had had to meet and ask questions of a man who had been to America, and so they listened avidly to his reports of the weather, the conditions in the southern colonies, and the gales he encountered on the Atlantic. Anne did not get to hear him firsthand, but it was reassuring for all the passengers to see that after braving the Atlantic in both directions, the veteran captain seemed not only unscathed but eager to sail for the New World again. While Dudley, Winthrop, Simon, and Captain Milbourne crowded around Mr. Graves in the roundhouse, however, the winds were beginning to shift to the southwest, a bad sign.

That night the weather continued to spiral downward, and when Anne woke the next morning, the wind was still to the west. At first the sky glittered clear and bright, but as the day drew on, clouds began to crowd overhead. Wisely, Captain Milbourne steered the great ship closer to Yarmouth for shelter, and soon Anne and her sisters could see the famous castle that loomed square, squat, and gray up on the cliffs, a last reminder of everything they were leaving behind. Built by Henry VIII, this structure bared its teeth at the Catholic world and was armed with three huge cannons. All too soon there would be no more evidence of England's glorious history, and many of the passengers peered mournfully over the ship's sides at this last evidence of civilization.

During the afternoon and evening, the weather continued to worsen, and so Captain Milbourne ordered the sailors to batten down any loose boards and ropes and sailed the ship even nearer to shore. The other three ships in their party followed suit. Anne and the other women were uneasy. Although no one, except perhaps Winthrop and Dudley, was looking forward to an Atlantic crossing, delay frayed people's nerves, particularly after the tremendous effort of preparation.

Just as they slid into their new anchorage, the storm broke over their heads, and an awful sight greeted those passengers who still braved the pelting rain on the deck. The skeletal outline of a great ship loomed high and bony against the horizon. This Dutch vessel, which at one thousand tons was more than three times the size of their own, had come to grief attempting to thread its way through the treacherous rocky passage that was the next leg of the *Arbella*'s journey.

The Needles stood almost one hundred feet in the air and were visible from the harbor at Yarmouth. Formed out of chalky sediment, they were astonishingly white, like glaciers, and steepled up to viciously pointed tips. What was worse was what you could not see: Beneath the water hid a treacherous comb of teeth that routinely sliced open the hulls of big and small vessels alike. The tides were fierce here, and if the wind dropped, all hope was lost, since the current could suck even the largest ship onto the jagged rocks.[2]

As the winds grew stronger and their own ship was thrown up and down on the waves, Anne must have prayed that they would escape the Dutch ship's fate, or worse. Meanwhile, the Puritan leaders were concerned with the portent of the storm. Was God on their side or not? With this first taste of their frailty, it was hard to imagine that they would survive their ocean passage, although in actuality the voyage was far safer than it seemed. Only one ship, the *Angel Gabriel*, would come to grief during the 198 recorded crossings in the 1630s.[3]

Anne had little choice but to join the other women. It was her duty to help her mother and fourteen-year-old Patience oversee the younger girls, particularly twelve-year-old Sarah, who had never been as compliant as little Mercy, only ten. When left to her own devices, Sarah would probably have enjoyed poking her head into parts of the ship that gently raised, pious young girls should have shunned. For the next three days, storm fronts tore in and out of southern England, throwing the miserable passengers down if they attempted to walk or stand, pitching them to and fro in their rudimentary quarters, and drenching all aboard, especially the ill-tempered sailors, who swore bitterly while they thundered up and down the ladders, making sure all was fast.

Conditions down below were terrible, a foul and fetid world. Passengers from all walks of life were forced together. Sleeping hammocks hung in every available nook and cranny. The passengers were separated from their belongings, since their chests and trunks were stored in the bowels of the ship. Only wealthy individuals were allowed to have a small box of personal possessions, such as food and warm, dry clothes; poor people did without such conveniences. The stench was already nauseating, as the passengers, unused to the bucking of the ship, suffered immediately from the miseries of "spewing" — their term for vomiting — and it was impossible to wash away the heaps of human waste during a storm. People lived in danger of breaking a limb or suffering severe contusions thanks to the tossing of the ship. Like most of the women, Anne likely became, as one traveler said, "seasick and mazy and light in head, and so could scarce go out without falling."[4] Even the most resolute had to admit that to begin a voyage this way tested everyone's commitment to the expedition.

In desperation, the leaders called for a penitential fast, not that most of the passengers felt like eating. While the others prayed, sang psalms, and called out for forgiveness from their Lord, some of the devout caught hold of two of the sailors who had "prized a rundlet of strong water [rum], and stole some of it." This kind of sinful behavior was shocking, but here also lay some hope. Perhaps it was this crime that had brought the wrath of God down on their heads; if so, the violent punishment of the men's misdeeds might right things with the Lord. Immediately, Winthrop and Dudley decreed that the offending men be "laid . . . in bolts all the night" and in the morning be "openly whipped, and both kept with bread and water that day."[5] After the men had been punished, no one was surprised to see that the weather promptly changed for the better. God had clearly taken the storms away once they had cleansed the ship of crime.

Even though the sky had brightened, the sea continued to heave, and the passengers still had to cling to each other and the sides of the ship to keep their balance. It took four days before the water had quieted enough to walk and stand safely on deck, and the sailors used this time to repair the broken timbers and ripped sails. Dudley, Winthrop, Isaac Johnson, and the other leaders of the expedition spent these extra hours composing a letter that announced their intentions to the rest of England. Undeterred by the fact that most of their fellow countrymen were largely unaware of their departure, these Puritans felt that their exodus warranted the attention of all posterity.

The document they created is known to us as "A Humble Request." The emigrants wanted to defend their actions against the criticism of those Puritans who had chosen to stay in England and to right any rumors that might "misreport [their] intentions." For example, unlike the Pilgrims, Dudley and his friends declared that, far from abandoning the Anglican Church and rebelling against the king, it was their "honor to call the Church of England, from whence we rise, our dear mother." Their leave-taking, they proclaimed, was not therefore a joyous occasion but instead one that occasioned "much sadness of heart and many tears in our eyes."[6]

Such sacrifice surely required the sympathy, if not the admiration, of those who were left behind. Of course, this was where the missive was not so humble. It was painful to leave and had cost most of the emigrants their fortunes, but the hardships they expected to endure and had already undergone were forging them into better Christians. In fact, all humility aside, Anne's father and his friends felt they held a sort of righteous supremacy over the stay-at-homes in England. That afternoon they sent their letter ashore, where it would be copied and passed around from town to town, inspiring other like-minded men and women to join them in the New World.

Naturally, Anne and the other ladies did not get to participate in the heady experience of writing this document. Instead, shaken by the storm, and with Yarmouth so tantalizingly close, Anne, Arbella, and the other gentlewomen "went on shore," as Winthrop reported, "to refresh" themselves.[7] Safely on the soil of Yarmouth, surrounded by the green hills and rocky outcroppings of the island, they found the steadiness of the land a pleasure after the first few days on the vessel. The daffodils were in their full-belled glory, the apple and pear trees were about to blossom, and tucked here and there in the rocky crevices, the women could find tiny lavender forget-me-nots. It was too picturesque to seem real, and all the more poignant because they would soon be leaving it behind. The seamen had finished repairing the damage done to the *Arbella* from the storm and had declared the ship ready to make passage past The Needles, out of the English Channel, and into the vast Atlantic.

About six the next morning, "the wind being E and N and fair weather," the *Arbella* "weighed anchor and set sail." This time, the passengers hoped, there would be no more delays.[8] It was April 8 and the perfect time of year to be setting forth for America. The next day "a merry gale" brought the travelers as far as Portland, and as the Isle of Wight slipped away from view, the passengers began to settle into their new life aboard ship. When they emerged from the channel, however, their tentative feelings of comfort proved to be premature. Eight strange vessels suddenly loomed on the horizon. No one recognized their sails. Perhaps these were Spanish Catholics or ruthless Turkish pirates. The captain sent messengers off in longboats to alert the others in their fleet to the threat, while the crew scurried to prepare the *Arbella* for an attack. The "powder-chests and fireworks" were "made ready" and "the hammocks were taken down." Twenty-five of the "landsmen" were "appointed for muskets," and when it became clear that the menacing ships were advancing, Dudley, Winthrop, and the captain decided to turn and face their enemies. It was time, they declared, "to fight."[9]

As Anne and the other women watched, the sailors ripped down the makeshift cabins that the Puritans had constructed on the decks and cleared everything out of the way that could burn or trip up a soldier during battle. Soon even the ladies joined in the effort, and Winthrop reported that "out of every ship were thrown such bed matters as were subject to take fire."[10] For Anne and her sisters, it was probably difficult to part with the bolsters and spare blankets they had brought to protect against the cold and damp, but fling them overboard they did, the linens and canvas ballooning into the air and then sinking irretrievably.

In the midst of this flurry, the captain "for an experiment" decided to shoot "a ball of wild-fire fastened to an arrow out of a cross bow which burnt in the water a good time." Everyone hoped that the approaching strangers would take note of their firepower and their courage. The little fleet might be half the size of the pirates', but they were ready to defend themselves. Undeterred by Milbourne's show of force, however, the strange ships skated steadily forward. It seemed clear that the invaders were intent on engaging them in battle. The sailors stood ready at the sails, the men nervously shouldered their firearms, and the women were sent below. Arbella, Anne, and Dorothy said prayers and tried not to give way to weeping and desperation. Their brave example must have inspired the others, for Winthrop commented that "not a woman or child . . . showed fear."[11]

Despite his nervousness, Anne's father was likely thrilled that at last he would get to see "Godly" action. When the strange ships were "within a league, [the captain], because he would show he was not afraid of them . . . tacked about and stood to meet" the pirates.[12] This was just how Dudley enjoyed things, skimming along the icy edge of danger.

In the last few minutes adrenaline ran high. The men clutched their weapons. There was a hush onboard, the only sound the muttered prayers of the pious. The enemy ships drew closer and closer, and then, whether someone waved, shouted, or ran up a flag, or whether one of the sailors recognized a mate on one of the vessels, it was suddenly clear that these were not pirates. All apprehension vanished, and the passengers became giddy and lighthearted. It turned out that the fleet was friendly and mostly English. No one on the *Arbella* was going to die, at least not yet.

The women streamed up the ladders, and "mirth and friendly entertainment" ruled the afternoon. Suddenly it seemed a blessing just to be alive. The ship was safe, and the waves were gentle. Offshore fishermen sold the passengers fresh catch; that afternoon Anne and the other women built fires down below (that were carefully encased in boxes of sand) to roast the fish "of divers sorts" — a splurge for this rather tightfisted group.[13] As they ate heartily, the sun still lingering in the sky, they gave thanks for their delivery, and it seems not one person complained about the unnecessary loss of their blankets and bolsters.

This close brush with danger led Dudley and Winthrop to post lookouts each night in case they ran into any real armed sea bandits. There were certainly plenty around. "Dunkirk rovers, Dutch capers, Irish raiders, and French, Flemish and Spanish privateers" were all likely to be lurking in the waters ahead, and everyone had heard horrible stories about "the Islamic Sallee-men, 'Turkish' raiders from Algiers" who captured English people and sold them as slaves.[14]

Of course, even without the threat of piracy, on the ocean nothing could be counted on — a good theological lesson from the Puritan perspective. Still, it was tempting to try to discern patterns in the chaotic weather, and since most pious travelers believed that their success hung upon the state of their consciences, this meant that everyone's mind and soul had to be clear if they were going to have a smooth passage.

Soon after their pirate scare, a thick fog engulfed the boat; immediately, a fight broke out on deck between "two young men, falling at odds." Naturally, the two events seemed connected. As punishment, the quarreling fellows were forced "to walk upon the deck till night with their hands bound behind them." But when the fog still didn't lift, it was clear that something else was amiss. It was now up to Dudley and his team to scour the ship, like some kind of Puritan secret police. Within a few hours, he and Winthrop discovered another man, who used "contemptuous speeches in our presence." This errant soul was "laid in bolts till he submitted himself, and promised open confession of his offence." No sooner had they taken this action, Winthrop wrote, than the fog was blown away by "a fresh gale at N and by W, so we stood on our course merrily."[15] Once again the pious had evidence for the link between their progress and their souls.

As the days passed, Dudley and Winthrop became worried about the passengers' weakness and growing despondency and came up with a plan for bolstering their spirits.

> Our children and others, that were sick, and lay groaning in
> the cabins, we fetched out, and having stretched a rope from
> the steerage to the mainmast, we made them stand, some of
> one side and some of the other, and sway it up and down till
> they were warm, and by this means they soon grew well and
> merry.[16]

When there were storms, however, there was little Winthrop and Dudley could do to cheer their flock. Even if they prayed publicly for deliverance, no one could hear them. The wind howled. The water slammed against the hull. Anything that was not fastened down flew through the air or skidded across the floor. These were desperate times, when each pious individual had to lean heavily on faith in order not to panic.

Even when the weather was calm, however, not all passengers on these overseas expeditions could be shaken out of their depression. A few years later onboard the *Champion*, a man named Peter Fitchew succumbed to despair and attempted to hurl himself over the side in front of the horrified eyes of his fellow passengers.[17]

AS THE DAYS STRETCHED INTO WEEKS, the hours alternated between terror and tedium. When gales swept upon them, or when they found themselves becalmed in the middle of the "great waters," it was impossible to find a rhythm for eating and sleeping. By the third week of the ordeal, most people were exhausted and dispirited, although Winthrop was the miraculous exception; somehow he managed to retain his optimistic outlook in the face of their difficulties.

His fellow emigrants, however, had fallen into bad habits right from the start. Captain Milbourne, outraged at their sloth, declared that the passengers "were very nasty and slovenly, and that the gun deck where they lodged was so beastly and noisome with their victuals and beastliness as would much endanger the health of the ship." Winthrop responded by establishing teams of four men who would "keep that room clean for three days, and then four other [men] should succeed them."[18]

The shipboard diet did little to cheer anyone up, as it consisted of "dried bread and biscuits, oatmeal pottage and buttered peas, salted eggs, salted fish, bacon and cured meats, [calf] tongues in bran or meal, 'bag pudding' made with raisins and currants, and perhaps some fruit or cheese, all of it subject to spoilage." Every passenger was entitled to basic rations, "included in the price of the passage," but those who had the resources, as Anne and her family did, brought extra supplies including meat, vegetables, ale, and, if they could find them, lemons to fight scurvy. There were some business opportunities here; one entrepreneur on a later voyage traveled with his cow and "sold the milk to the passengers for 2d. the quart" — a profiteering sort of activity that Winthrop would have promptly shut down on the *Arbella*.[19]

Cooking was rare. The only way to boil, fry, or stew anything was over an open flame, and since everyone was deathly afraid of a fire breaking out onboard, most meals were eaten cold. Passengers had water and beer, and sometimes wine and stronger spirits, to wash down their unappetizing meals. But none of these beverages could be counted on to be palatable, or clean. One man grumbled, "Our supply of water stank very much and our beer was like mud because of the slovenly negligence of those who should have taken care of it." And another complained that the drink was "either very salt or as thick as pudding."[20]

In such tight quarters it was impossible to escape people you did not like. Frequently Anne was crammed down below with strangers, servants, or others she would never have had to consort with back in her old life. But despite the many weeks on the ship, she still would not have known the names of all the passengers, especially those who were not Puritans or were below her in rank. One passenger wrote that there were "about 140 persons out of the western parts from Plymouth, of which I conceive there were not six known either by face or fame to any of the rest." Most people stuck to those they already knew from home, though some new acquaintances did spring up.[21]

The voyage was turning out to be more than a test of physical limits. Spiritual and mental fortitude were essential and could only be had with the support of others. Those new relationships that did occur formed with an intensity not usually found in villages back home; existing friendships deepened, and marriages tightened. The opposite was also true. When fights broke out, they were fired by the pent-up frustrations of shipboard life.

For Anne, Simon was the man upon whom she had lavished her "longing hopes" and "doubting fears."[22] But now that their old home was far away, there was no privacy for long conversations between a husband and a wife and even less opportunity for marital pleasures. In many ways, Anne was right back to where she had started as a young girl, immersed in the company of women as though she had never married and left home. Fortunately, Arbella was there, and their shared years at Sempringham, their mutual commitment to piety, and the fact that both were married but did not yet have children must have rapidly overcome their differences in stature and rank. It was their duty, after all, to shore up each other's faith, courage, and strength, especially as the journey drew on and neither could ignore that many of the women were growing physically weaker, including Arbella herself.

The sailor's curses and rowdy songs were a shock for most of the gently bred Puritans, especially the women and children. Cotton Mather would describe this "obscene, smutty, bawdy talk" as "so much filthy bilge water."[23] Some measure of social hierarchy was preserved, since Anne and her family and friends all rated slightly better lodgings than the others, servants still obeyed masters, and richer people had more food to eat than their poorer brethren, but the differences in class were not as evident as on land; everyone suffered the same miseries during a storm and the same boredom when becalmed.

The only amusements for adults and children alike, aside from prayer, contemplation, and conversation, were occasional fantastical sights from the deep. To begin with, there were "strange fish" — "some with wings flying above the water, others with manes, ears and heads, and chasing one another with open mouths like stone horses in a park." The minister of the advance party, Francis Higginson, remembered the "bonitos, carvels, grampuses, sunfish and whales" that swam by the *Talbot*.[24]

Sometimes the passengers managed to catch one of these curiosities, and then it was like a carnival onboard — the thrashing, dying animal, the cries of the men intent on subduing it, the shrieks of the thrilled onlookers. One traveler, Richard Mather, remarked that spearing porpoises and swinging them up on deck was "marvelous delightful recreation." He also reflected that the dissection of these creatures "in view of all our company was wonderful to us all, and marvelous merry sport, and delightful to our women and children."[25] The fish they caught also provided a change in their diet, although not all of these creatures were such delicacies. Another traveler wrote that shark meat was "very rough grained, not worthy of wholesome preferment." He did not much like porpoise, either, declaring that it "tastes like rusty bacon or hung beef, if not worse, but the liver boiled and soused in vinegar is more grateful to the palate." A fellow passenger disagreed; he declared that he relished porpoise when it was fried "with salt, pepper, and vinegar."[26]

Early in May the passengers were startled by an apparition far more alarming than any they had yet encountered. On the morning of the eighth, the wind was strong, the rigging was whistling, and the ship was whisking along, when suddenly a fountain of water sprang up, at least thirty feet high, right in front of the bow. The lookouts shouted warning and the passengers rushed to see the biblical sight of "a whale, who lay just in our ship's way (the bunch of his back about a yard above water)." The captain shouted for the sailors to tack and pushed the wheel hard to windward, but the whale followed them, as though he were lonely and wanted to play. Despite the wonder of such an encounter, the enormous animal could do great damage even to a ship this size. Repeatedly the *Arbella* shifted course, lurching back and forth between starboard and portside tacks, but despite these evasive maneuvers, "He would not shun us," Winthrop wrote. Finally, for no apparent reason, the giant creature gave up and they passed "within a stone's cast of him." He did not follow but lay spouting up water, as though he had had his fill of the game.[27]

Although none of the other passengers recorded their interpretation of this episode, they could only have experienced the whale's presence as frightening, albeit in an exalted sort of way. A leviathan seemed incontrovertible evidence of God's great might, and such a miraculous appearance suggested that the psalmist's perspective was accurate: "They that go down to the sea in ships, and do business in great waters, these men see the works of the Lord and his wonders in the deep."[28] The travelers were now among the select few who had had the opportunity to behold the wonders of God's oceans.

EVERYONE HAD HOPED that May would usher in warmer weather, since the first month of the voyage had been glazed by an arctic cold. But as time drew on and the weather remained frigid, it was hard for the passengers not to worry that freezing temperatures lay in wait for them in America.[29] The loss of the blankets and bolsters they had thrown overboard weeks before must have made the chill even more difficult to bear.

Although they shivered, Anne and her family were learning the ways of the sea. Winthrop could now observe that the passengers were no longer "sick" or "troubled" by storms even when they were "tossed" for "forty eight hours together." Understandably, both he and Dudley took some pride in the staunch behavior of their people; it would be a weathered and toughened company that would land in America, and this boded well for their colony.[30]

But there was still the naturally sinful inclinations of the passengers that had to be kept in check. Dudley and Winthrop required all of the faithful, and as many of the sailors as they could persuade, to listen to the minister, the Reverend George Phillips, who preached most Thursdays and twice on Sundays. These gatherings tended to unite the people, reminding the faithful why they had signed on for this adventure in the first place, and even converting a few non-Puritans to the "true religion."

On May 24 two of the sister ships appeared on the horizon, and a welcome exchange of news took place, although not all of the tidings were good. No one had seen the *Talbot* for many weeks; on the *Ambrose*, two passengers and two cows had expired; and on the *Jewel*, "one of the seamen died." The *Talbot* was carrying many of the animals and extra supplies the settlers were counting on when they reached America. If she had been driven under by one of the storms they had encountered, the loss would be a serious one, and Anne and her family prayed anxiously for the ship's safety.[31]

From these reports, Anne and her family could see that the *Arbella* had fared well throughout these weeks of gales and cold. Their efforts at prayer, their careful scrutiny of their own consciences, and their attempts to eradicate sinful behavior from the ship must have helped God regard them with favor. And there was far more exciting news to come. The captains of all three ships had decided it was time to start checking the depths to see if the waters were growing shallow. They were approaching North America.

On May 26 the sailors took their first sounding, and although they "found no ground," the tenor of the voyage changed.[32] The end was now in sight. Every few days the sailors took more measurements, and with tense excitement, the people clung close to the rails to hear their findings. The soundings were a tricky procedure for Captain Milbourne, however, as he knew that they were approaching the dangerous sandy shoals of coastal New England. If he read the measurements incorrectly, they could easily founder off

Cape Cod; if they overshot their mark, however, they could end up in Canada.

It took almost a week of frequent soundings, and a penitential fast by the Puritan leaders, before the shore came within reach.[33] On June 6, which was, auspiciously, a Sunday, or the "Lord's day," the wind strengthened from the northeast, and everyone lined the decks to catch a glimpse of the New World. After four or five hours, the passengers were rewarded for their patience. With barely contained excitement, the governor wrote:

> About two in the afternoon we sounded and had ground at
> about eighty fathom, and the mist then breaking up, we saw
> the shore to the N about five or six leagues off, and were (as
> we supposed) to the SW of Cape Sable.[34]

This placed them at the southernmost tip of Nova Scotia, in the perfect location for a straight shot down the coast to Massachusetts. The next day the captain ordered a celebratory pause, the sailors furled the sails, and as it was "somewhat calm," the men went fishing. To their astonishment, they caught "in less than two hours, with a few hooks, sixty-seven codfish, most of them very great fish, some a yard and a half long, and a yard in compass." The catch was impressive, and this was a reason to rejoice. The *Arbella's* "salt fish was now spent" and the passengers feasted with joy. Their suffering might soon be coming to an end.[35]

But the speed of their arrival depended on the wind and the captain's ability to navigate the new hazards of rocks, shoals, and uncharted islands. It would be all too easy to come to grief along the treacherous coastline. The weather was still alarmingly frigid, but on June 8 it turned from "close and to[o] cold" to "fair sunshine," and to the joy of everyone onboard, "there came a smell off the shore like the smell of a garden: There came a wild pigeon into our ship, and another small land bird."[36] As the birds chirped and cooed, settling on the railings, it was impossible not to think of God's promise to Noah after the flood. The future seemed bright, and the past dim and far away, as though the ocean had truly severed them from the corruption of their ancient land.

Four days later, just before dawn, the sailors sighted the head-lands of modern-day Marblehead and the rocky islands that marked the waters of Salem. Sixty-six days after leaving Yarmouth, men and women alike wept in thanksgiving. The captain "shot off two pieces of ordnance" as they "passed through the narrow strait between Baker's Isle and Little Isle, and came to an anchor a little within the islands."[37] They had reached Salem's Plum Cove.

To all of the pious, arrival was a solemn occasion. With Win-throp's words in mind, Puritan passengers understood that their safe crossing sealed their contract with God. Now they must turn their hearts toward Him or forever suffer His wrath. Undoubtedly, the Lady Arbella, who had been anticipating this moment for almost ten years, drew a sharp breath of elation. At last they had come to what she conceived of as the new kingdom of Christ; unlike Anne, she appears to have had no qualms about a New World covenant.

But amid the grateful prayers of her fellow passengers, Anne found herself resentful, frightened, and perhaps even more unhappy than she had been during the journey. She was far from experienc-ing the pleasure she knew such a moment should have induced. Instead, she felt sick to her stomach.[38]

Anne had no interest in America.

CHAPTER NINE

❧❦❧

New World, New Manners

*I think that in the end if I live it must be by my leaving, for we do
not know how long this plantation will stand.*

— THE COLONIST JOHN POND,
IN A LETTER TO HIS FATHER, 1631

ANNE'S FIRST HOME in Massachusetts was huddled on a
shelf of land that ran out into Boston Harbor. Unpro-
tected and desolate, Charlestown was a miserable place to
live. During that first summer, most of the flimsy tents and huts
offered very little protection; the sun glared down and the wind tore
across the hills, ripping the drying laundry off the makeshift ropes
and occasionally knocking down the fragile English wigwams.

When the rest of the Winthrop fleet limped into the New
World harbors in the months that followed the *Arbella*'s arrival, the
Dudleys and the other leading families greeted each of the vessels,
hoping that the livestock they had sent over had survived the journey. The meat, milk, and cheese might deliver them from their desperate straits. But it soon became clear there would be no such

respite. Even when the *Talbot*, the ship they had thought was lost, sailed into Salem, there was no relief. As Dudley wrote, "[H]alf of our cows, and almost all our mares and goats, sent us out of England died at sea in their passage hither."[1]

Although the men in Anne's family understood that they were coping with a humanitarian crisis of enormous scale — one thousand people would arrive from England that year — there was little they could do to ease the hunger and disease that plagued the little community. The comfortable-looking homes of the original colonists were no longer beacons of hope but instead served to underscore the privation of the new arrivals. Tempers began to fray. Prayer did not seem to do any good, although everyone considered it a blessing that neither the governor nor his deputy fell ill.

By the end of July, after nearly two months of hard work and in the face of growing unhappiness among the emigrants, Dudley and Winthrop decided it was time to make a public stand of their commitment to America and create what they had come to New England for in the first place — a church based on their own religious principles. Perhaps this move would lift people's spirits and stop the emigrants from fleeing back to the Old World. Dudley and Winthrop's grand plan notwithstanding, no actual structure had yet been built — there had been no time. To the English, open-air praying was a little too close for comfort to the behavior of the Indians, who regularly worshiped under the sky, but — roof or no — it seemed the right moment to make a formal proclamation of their commitment to God and to each other. Maybe this would turn their luck around.

Anne did not greet this idea with enthusiasm. Good Puritans knew that you endangered your soul if you made a vow to God that you could not fully embrace, and Anne was still filled with doubt about their venture. Later in life, she wrote that it was hard to be "convinced [that coming to America] was the way of God."[2] People were succumbing to disease and the privations of life in the wilderness. As Dudley noted, "yea almost daily" someone met his end.[3] As one survivor recorded, "It was not accounted a strange thing in those days to drink water, and to eat samp or hominy without butter or milk." Clams, mussels, and smelt helped keep the people going. In times of desperation they foraged for nuts and acorns, but no English person of the time believed that he could live without "beef, bread, and beer," and the scanty diet took its toll.[4]

For Anne, the physical hardships were compounded by the loss of her aristocratic lifestyle in England. It was disturbing to have to live in such close quarters with people she would never have met back in England: uneducated workers, non-Puritans, and roughened artisans. These men and women seemed uncouth and irreligious, and she was unaccustomed to the rudeness of their speech and customs.

But Anne knew she would have to make up her mind that these challenges were actually part of God's plan. The glorification of the Protestant martyrs of earlier generations probably helped make this idea seem possible, but in the years to come she would remember that she had to be persuaded to take the oath, although she never revealed how her mother, her father, the minister, and her husband talked her into joining them.

At last, on the first day of August, Anne "submitted," as she put it, to the will of God, the pressure of her family, and the exigencies of her life. She stood in the little clearing of Charlestown with the other leaders of the expedition, gazing at the odd little shelters their people had contrived, and vowed

> to unite . . . into one Congregation, or Church, under the
> Lord Jesus Christ our Head . . . and bind our selves to walke in
> all our wayses according to the Rule of the Gospell, and in all
> sincere Conformity to His holy ordinaunces, and in mutuall
> love, and respect each to other, so neere as God shall give us
> grace.[5]

Although there was no mention of New England in this covenant, the implication was clear. The settlers were starting the process of shedding their loyalties to the Old World and vowing their allegiance to each other, a reformed church, and a fresh land. The summer sun burned their arms and faces. The pines rose sharply behind their backs. The earth was untilled and rocky. The men and women themselves were hungry, thirsty, sweaty, and tired, and yet these words were a crucial reminder of why they had voyaged to America; even Anne would be strengthened by this act. She was the thirteenth person to proclaim her faith, the second woman, right after her mother, Dorothy.[6]

Unfortunately, the solemn proclamation of this covenant did not allay any of the suffering of the first year, even if it bolstered the spirits of those who participated. For Anne, the first test of her commitment to the colony was the illness of Arbella, who was battling a high fever back in Salem. The entire community waited anxiously as Arbella tossed and sweated on linen coverlets. This was the woman who had lent her name to their ship and who had provided the inspiration and monetary support to make emigration possible. But despite the many prayers said on her behalf, she died on a blistering day in August, never having witnessed the settlement in Charlestown.

This was a dispiriting loss for everyone, not just Anne. Arbella had been a person of the highest rank and importance, and her demise seemed like a bad omen. But while the death of her friend must have been devastating for Anne, she recorded no lament for Arbella, nor did she allow herself to voice her yearning for England. She had asserted her loyalty to the new colony and would not be swayed, at least not visibly. She was Dudley's daughter, after all, and her sorrows were not for outside eyes to see.

In something of a panic, Dudley and Winthrop sent a ship back to England for more supplies, hoping it would return in time for winter. They bought as much corn as they could from the Indians, but still the fragile settlement in Charlestown was beginning to look as though it might fail. The central problem was dehydration. The English distrusted water in general, relying largely on cider and beer to quench their thirst. If no ale was available, then they would drink water only when they could see its source. Thus, although

Charlestown had plenty of wells and ponds, it had only one spring, and this sole trickle was not enough to supply the needs of more than one hundred thirsty, dirty men and women.

Had it not been for the miraculous appearance of the eccentric William Blackstone, a pious dissenter who had come to New England in 1623, the settlers might never have survived. Blackstone was thirty-five and lived across the Charles River on a hilly peninsula named Shawmut, or Tri-mountain. When Dudley and Winthrop visited his house, they were astonished to find a large, roomy manor rather than a rudimentary pioneer structure. Unlike the other planters' homes they had visited, Blackstone's had even attained some degree of elegance. He had imported an impressive library of 186 books and had planted a thriving apple orchard, having meticulously saved the seeds from each of the English apples he had brought with him. Generously, he offered to share his resources with the Puritan settlers, although he must have known that the peace of his pristine hermitage would be ruined once he opened his doors.[7]

But Blackstone was a man of integrity and put the good of his fellow human beings before his own comfort. Believing the clear water that flowed abundantly in Shawmut would cure their ills, he soon convinced Winthrop that the group should move. Undoubtedly, the governor also liked the fact that Shawmut had three steep slopes, a symbol, perhaps, for the "city on a hill" that he had visualized in his sermon on Christian charity.

Dudley, however, balked. He did not think Charlestown should be their permanent home, but he would not budge simply because Winthrop wanted him to. He had settled in Charlestown and that was that. In the two months that his family had lived there, his servants had made substantial progress in constructing a house, and he saw no reason to start over again. At any rate, he believed that the further dispersal of the colonists was a bad idea; Simon, of course, sided with his father-in-law.

Winthrop ignored Dudley's protests, and by the beginning of September, all of the governor's supplies had been ferried across the Charles River. He was joined by many followers, including the group's minister, John Wilson. Having sworn their congregational oath to participate in the congregation's worship services, the Dudleys and Bradstreets would have to cross the Charles using Samuel Maverick's ferry service, which was not inexpensive. As a further blow, Winthrop and his friends decided to name their new settlement Boston in honor of Cotton and St. Botolph's. To a man of Dudley's temperament, it must have seemed like further effrontery on Winthrop's part to claim this name for his settlement. "Boston" had always felt like Dudley's town, and Botolph's had been his church, not Winthrop's.

Anne was not surprised by either her father's stubbornness or his resentment of Winthrop; she had been long aware of his simmering disagreements with the governor. Still, the squalor, disease, shortage of food, and lack of privacy in Charlestown made the settlement at Boston look increasingly appealing, although no one was having an easy time across the river either. Arbella's widower, Isaac Johnson, who had probably moved to be near Winthrop, had sickened. By the end of September, Dudley and his family received the bad news that he, too, had died.[8] As one of the leaders of the expedition, Johnson left behind a group of distraught settlers who felt rudderless without his guidance. One of the "yeomen" wrote to his father, "God hath taken away the cheifest stud in the land, Mr Johnson & the Lady Arabella his wife which was the cheiffeste man of estate in the land & one that would have done most good."[9]

As the fall days lengthened, conditions grew steadily worse. The poorer people suffered most, as their bark wigwams and cloth tents proved to be woefully inadequate against the frost. On Christmas Eve, a severe drop in temperature terrified everyone. Anne and her family were fortunate to have a fireplace in their "great house," and they huddled around it, praying for the weather to relent.

Although the daily "injuries" from "cold and wet" and hunger dominated everyone's thinking, there was another concern that prevented anyone from feeling, even momentarily, any sort of peace. Reports had come that the French were planning an attack on the tiny settlements.[10] Resentful of the English claims to New England, they had already allied themselves with a few of the neighboring Indian tribes and had issued warnings about the spread of English settlers. These threats deepened the Puritans' sense of being vulnerable. Both Dudley and Winthrop felt that they should be building a fort to which all of the colonists could retreat.[11] But such an ambitious goal was impossible owing to the weakened condition of the community. Instead the settlers would have to pray for deliverance not only from their physical privations but also from their foes.

During this first winter, even Dudley began to lose some of his optimism. He was ready to leave Charlestown and find a new place to live. Not that he ever would have considered giving up or returning to England, but life in Massachusetts was proving to be far more arduous than he had anticipated. Later he would complain that he had chosen to expose his family to the dangers of America because the advance party (Endecott, Higginson, and crew) had sent "too large commendations of the Country and the commodities thereof."[12]

For Anne it was something of a mixed blessing to witness her father's discouragement. On the one hand it might at last be possible for him to empathize with her unhappiness. On the other hand, without his sense of certainty, life in America must have felt even more desperate. Despite her summertime vow, she may have secretly desired to follow the coward's path back to England, since much of her early writing is saturated with her nostalgia for the Old World.

Anne was not alone in longing for England. More than two hundred members of their original group fled home that winter. Although they faced financial ruin upon return and, for some, religious persecution, anything must have appeared better than staying on in America, which seemed like a death warrant. As one desperate son wrote his father, "I think that in the end if I live it must be by my leaving, for we do not know how long this plantation will stand."[13]

Anne's father loudly sneered at those who had left. To the Puritans the fact that the voyage back to England was often more dangerous than the trip over proved that God was on their side and was intent on punishing deserters. Pirates attacked the *Charles*, the *Success*, and the *Whale*; the *Ambrose* was almost demolished in the same battle. A few years later, the *Mary and Jane* sank before she reached England. Winthrop took care to record that "of those that went back in the ships . . . many died by the way and after they were landed, and others fell very sick and low."[14]

Dudley helped institute hard measures to suit the hard times. Fearing that the mission was in danger, he resorted to his fail-proof method for survival: hunting out sinners and exacting retribution for any wrongdoings. He commanded people to report the misdeeds of their neighbors to the authorities, simultaneously urging Winthrop and the other leading men to take fast and cruel action against these culprits. In many ways this severity worked to hold the colony together. If you spoke against the authorities, you could face expulsion from the "plantations" — a punishment that could mean death by wolves, wild boars, Indians, starvation, or bitter storms. One hired servant named Ratcliffe was beaten and sent out into the wilderness for "foul, scandalous invectives against our church and government."[15] Needless to say, most people thought twice before they criticized their leaders.

There were not, however, many instances of this kind of harsh penalty during that first winter. Instead, criminals were locked into "cages" for their neighbors to gawk at; others were whipped, forced into hastily constructed stocks, or made to wear signs advertising their malfeasance. Exile was largely a last resort and still figured more as a threat than an actuality.

But even vigilant enforcement of the laws could not seem to stop the Puritans' God from hurling one storm after another onto the colony's crouching huts and wigwams. To a population already suffering from poor nutrition, the governor issued an order for "fasts." Perhaps a demonstration of heartfelt penance would appease the wrath of the Lord; it would also conserve their scarce food.

In the midst of these difficult times, while everyone battled hunger, cold, and the bleakness of the landscape, Anne wept over a hidden sorrow.[16] Despite the fact that she and Simon were at last able to share a bed again and could seek comfort from each other, she was not pregnant.

To Anne the thought that she might not bear a baby was more grievous than the prospect of starvation, illness, or being swept into the sea by a January storm. The inability to conceive or, for that matter, to produce a healthy child was to the Puritan mind a sure sign of God's displeasure. No matter how hard she had prayed or how strenuously she had scoured her conscience and tried to mend her ways, Anne had remained barren for two full years. Anne's lack of a baby brought shame to Simon as well. Neighbors might whisper that he was unable to perform his husbandly duties. In 1639, one childless woman would complain that a strange man "offered to put his hands under her coats [clothes] & sayd . . . because her husband was not able to give her a great belly he would help him."[17]

That Anne was undernourished, weak, and exhausted (and that many others were dying) didn't seem legitimate reasons for her lack of fertility. An empty womb could only be divine condemnation of her spiritual failings. Undoubtedly she eagerly entered into the frequent penitential fasts her father and Winthrop called for. Perhaps if she could degrade herself satisfactorily, God's wrath would melt away and she would find herself with child. Yet, by the end of January it was clear that Anne and all the other settlers were on the verge of collapse. As Dudley remarked, "The Lord would not yet be depricated," or satisfied.[18] Certainly Anne showed no sign of conceiving. She was barely alive.

By JANUARY OF 1631 illness, deprivation, and exhaustion had taken their toll on the settlers. At least two hundred people had died, Dudley exclaimed, "so low hath the Lord brought us!" And yet, in the midst of this kind of horror, where each death felt like a blow to the colony's chances of survival, when Dudley felt that they had "endur[d] much [and should] be pitied in the sickness and mortality of our people," still he rallied and declared that

> they who survived were not discouraged, but bearing God's corrections with humility and trusting in his mercies, and considering how after a greater ebb he had raised up our neighbors at Plymouth, we began again in December to consult about a fit place to build a town upon.

They referred to this as-yet imaginary settlement ("a mile East from Watertown, near Charles River") as New Towne, although later it would be renamed Cambridge.[19] During the hour of their anguish, it was inspiring to dream of a fresh start.

At the same time that he promoted the idea of a halcyon future, Dudley continued to tally problems, including a careful accounting of the financial losses of the "undertakers," the men who, like himself, had helped sponsor the emigration to America. Fortunately, Puritanism offered comfort here — fiscal disaster for the sake of the cause was a testimony to faith and courage.[20]

Weakened as they might feel by their sufferings, Dudley and his friends were rarely seen as such by their neighbors, whose transgressions they continued to monitor vigilantly. Indeed, one prominent disturber of the peace, Thomas Morton, a gunrunning fur trader, soon discovered how fierce they could be.

Morton had lived along the shores of New England for more than five years. He had built his home south of Shawmut, or Boston, midway between the Pilgrims and the newly arrived Puritans. Shockingly, he declared that he had come to America to get rich and have fun. He had no interest in the religious solemnities of his neighbors and found the country beautiful — a kind of playground for adventurous English gentlemen. He rejoiced in the "dainty fine round rising hillocks, delicate fair large plaines, sweet crystal fountains, and clear running streams." All in all, Morton declared, "the land to me seems paradise."[21]

Naturally, anyone who was unhappy with the strictness of either Puritan or Pilgrim rule raced to Morton's home on "Merry mount." At Morton's outrageous parties, young men, Indians, and truant servants — men and women — mingled happily together, drinking mug after mug of free ale and wine, shouting, dancing, copulating, and mocking the stiffness of their sober fellows to the north and south.

Long before Winthrop and Dudley had arrived, the Pilgrims had been horrified at what was going on so near the sanctity of their little settlement. Captain Miles Standish and a band of the faithful had set forth for Merry Mount with all the wrath of an advancing army. When they arrived, they found Morton and his comrades carousing half-naked in the grass and singing a little ditty: "Drink and be merry, merry, merry boys; / Let all your delight be in the Hymen's joys." After hearing a few lines of this chorus, Standish and his fellow Pilgrims could bear it no longer. They "stood at defiance" and waved their firearms, shouting that they would render Morton's home "a woeful mount and not a merry mount."[22]

This was exactly the sort of tumult that Morton relished, and when the Pilgrims mounted a charge, a rollicking slapstick affair ensued. Morton and his men were too drunk to put up much of a fight and staggered around as though their guns were too heavy to lift. The Pilgrims' historian, Governor Bradford, wrote that Captain Standish and his men "could get nothing but scoffs and scorns from [Morton]" although he did threaten Standish (whom Morton had nicknamed "Shrimp," for his short stature) with his carbine.[23]

Morton's devil-may-care attitude, however, could not protect him from the Pilgrims' determination to ship him out of America. They dumped him onto the next vessel back to England. Undaunted, he cropped up again the very next spring and in 1628 moved back into Merry Mount to renew his "mirthful" activities. Within months of his return, he had begun to sell guns to the Indians, alienating all the other settlers, Pilgrims or no, and then infuriating the Indians themselves by regularly cheating them.

Dudley and Winthrop could not tolerate such a character so near their settlements. Morton was "a proud insolent man," Dudley said, who had committed "injuries" against both the English and the Indians.[24] Clearly his immoral and chaotic behavior was corroding the purity they had hoped to achieve in America; maybe he was the reason God was dealing them a harsh winter. Far more determined than the Pilgrims, the Puritan leaders made sure to punish Morton within sight of both the offended Indians and the settlers, binding his hands, burning his house down, and "set[ting] his feet in bilboes [chains]." After they were through, they sent him back, once again, to the Old World, and this time he stayed put for ten years.[25]

The man's spirit was broken for good. When Morton did return to America, he was a feeble, half-mad old man. Ruthless to the end, Winthrop and Dudley did not relent; they threw him immediately into prison and showed no compunction when Morton complained that he was "laid in irons to the decaying of his limbs." When at last they released him, it was only after seizing all of his valuables and property. Morton retreated to Maine, where he died two years later, "poor and despised," according to a still-angry Winthrop.[26]

Their victory over Morton marked a turning point for the leaders of Massachusetts Bay. They had succeeded where the Pilgrims had failed and were now the most powerful governing force in New England. With Arbella dead, Anne and her mother were clearly the principal women in the land, and they had to endure all the pressure and scrutiny that came with this position. While in England there had always been countesses and duchesses, queens and baronesses, now there was no buffer at all. The Dudleys, Bradstreets, and Winthrops were at the top of the social ladder.

Accordingly, they had to learn quickly how to become a ruling class: how to make the decisions, set examples, provide for the poor, and inspire hope when almost everyone else despaired. Whatever hardship or grief she might feel, Anne still had to help support the other colonists whenever they faced setbacks.

Despite the importance of her position, Anne was in no danger of becoming arrogant; since she could not become pregnant, it seemed clear she was a wretched sinner. But like the other settlers who survived, she was also discovering an untapped ore of courage. They would later name this first winter "the starving time," calling those who did not die the "seasoned" ones. As with the sea voyage, these months of hardship became a rite of passage and a bond among those who had made it through.

That February the cold weather finally relented and the ship that Winthrop and Dudley had sent back to England, the *Lyon*, sailed into the harbor laden with fresh supplies from Bristol. Immediately, Anne's father regained his optimistic vigor. "If any godly men, out of religious ends, will come over to help us in the good work we are about," he crowed, "I think they cannot dispose of themselves nor of their estates more to God's glory, and the furtherance of their own reckoning."[27] Their supplies would last until the next harvest. It was time to turn their attention toward building New Towne.

New Towne's inland location was attractive to men like Dudley because of the Puritans' fear of European attack. Great capitals (and this is what they hoped New Towne was going to become) were always built along navigable rivers, well away from the ocean. Rome, Paris, London, and Antwerp were all good examples, and the Virginia colonists had followed the same logic in their choice of Jamestown. Accordingly, most people thought that Charlestown and Boston could only be "frontier towns." Better to dwell "further among the Indians" than be exposed to "the fury of malignant adversaries, who might pursue them" from across the Atlantic.

When New Towne became the seat of the Bay colony's government during the first four years of settlement, rather than Winthrop's Boston, this fact undoubtedly gave Dudley great pleasure. In 1636, when the magistrates of the General Court decided to move their meeting place from New Towne to Boston, the little settlement managed to retain its distinction, as it was honored over Roxbury, Dorchester, Watertown, and Salem to become the home of the country's first college. Harvard College would be hammered into place about a mile up from the river in the field directly across from Anne's neat little house.[28]

Still, there was little evidence of the glories in store for this narrow site when Anne and her family first arrived. New Towne was a poor younger sibling compared with the giant next door, Watertown. By the time Dudley and Simon had decided to claim lots along the Charles, the land had already been largely gobbled up by settlers in the summer of 1630. This left only one twenty-five-acre spot "pinched" between Watertown and Charlestown for the settlers to share. A thick woods bounded a flat greenish brown clearing, and it was here that Dudley and Simon planted their flags of ownership, on a patch of earth that was, at best, a kind of last resort.[29]

Undaunted, Dudley proudly declared that they had found "materials to build, fuel to burn, ground to plant, seas and rivers to fish in, a pure air to breathe in, good water to drink, till wine or beer can be made; which, together with the cows, hogs and goats brought hither already, may suffice for food."[30]

But despite the praise he had for the resources of New Towne, when he reported home to England on their situation, Dudley never allowed himself to write the kind of "hyperbolic" account he felt had led him astray. Instead, he reminded his English readers, "We yet enjoy little to be envied," resisting the urge to entice others with falsely glowing accounts of the riches of America.[31] In the New World there was no room, Dudley declared, for "profane and debauched persons." In fact, he argued, "their oversight in coming hither is wondered at, where they shall find nothing to content them." A true Massachusetts settler should be like a Christian martyr and fear "dishonor[ing] God" more than losing "his own life." According to this logic, Anne and her family were now living among heroes and were themselves valiant Protestant warriors.[32] At last Anne was becoming the kind of fearless soldier her father had always wanted her to be. She was certainly a braver, stronger person than ever before.

Encouraged and armed with a more complete knowledge of the exigencies of the country, Dudley and Simon set their minds to making New Towne the ideal village. The soft green land was a pleasant improvement after the desolation of Charlestown. Indeed, as spring drew into summer, "the spacious plain" of New Towne that the Indians had cleared years before seemed to the colonists "more like a bowling green then a Wilderness."[33] For Anne the meandering Charles must have been a reminder of the Witham back home. Even the low-lying marshes and the gentle hills on the horizon felt more familiar than the stark windy peninsula of Charlestown, with the ocean rumbling only yards away.

The small group huddled their homes as close to each other as possible and then created grazing lands for each family out of the land adjoining the town center. This was clearly the safest way to handle the threats of the wilderness, and it was a familiar arrangement imported directly from the Old World.

When Simon and Anne chose their house lot, they likely believed that this was where they would live out their mortal years. Their new home was about a mile away from the Charles, situated directly across from "Watchhouse Hill" on a site not far from the current Harvard Yard. Dudley built his own, larger home a little farther south, closer to the river. Although there are no records of what these early structures looked like, they were probably modeled after the "great house" in Salem, with two rooms on the first floor, where most of the events of daily living took place — cooking, eating, talking, and sleeping — and one large loft overhead for storage.

Anne's ambitious father had other plans as well. Having endured months of lugging crates and chests and bolsters up from the Charles, Dudley decided the Bay colony government should sponsor the dredging of the creek that ran right by his front door. Before long he had gotten his way. On June 14, 1631, the digging commenced, and by the time the men were done working, they had carved out a twelve-foot-wide canal that led straight from the river to Dudley's front door. Now a boat with a six-foot beam could float right into the settlement and deliver anything — lumber, corn, books, ale, cows, linens — practically on the settlers' doorsteps.

Civilization was beginning to conquer the wilderness, Dudley exclaimed, and when his daughter looked across the fields to the river, she could begin to feel a little optimistic. Perhaps they would survive. Perhaps God was truly smiling on them. Now all she wanted was proof that the Lord had taken her back into His favor, and so she begged Him for His mercy and for a baby — in her eyes, after all, the two were the same.

Chapter Ten

❧❦❧

Upon My Son

Thou heard'st me then and gav'st him me.
— Anne Bradstreet, "Upon My Son Samuel"

The second winter came upon the settlers almost imperceptibly. As the days drew bleaker, a sense of urgency overtook the scattered villages. Nobody wanted to endure another "starving time," and so most people plunged into preparations for the frightening months ahead.

To help ready her household for winter, Anne would have had the assistance of at least one, and probably more, female servants. Although these women would have done the bulk of the heavy chores — milking, tending the goats and pigs, getting water, collecting eggs, washing laundry, and other tasks that Anne set before them — this did not mean that Anne had an abundance of leisure time. In some ways, her position was like that of a schoolteacher or a mother: She was responsible for her servants' good behavior and their religious observance, even as she had to make sure their jobs were completed successfully.

This last responsibility was an enormous challenge for a gently raised woman like Anne, who knew very little about farm life before arriving in America. It seems likely that her servants knew more about livestock and managing a homestead in such rough conditions than she did, an embarrassing position for a "mistress" like Anne.

Worn down by the hard work and deprivation, by January 1632 she worried her family and felt further humiliated when she came down with "a lingering sickness like a consumption."[1] Incapacitated by fever and coughing, Anne had no choice but to leave her household wholly in the hands of her servants and her husband. Fortunately, her mother and sisters were nearby, as was her new sister-in-law, Mary Winthrop Dudley, the wife of her older brother Samuel and the daughter of the governor.

Having tended so many of the sick and dying during the first winter and having endured other hardships in the wilderness, Anne now felt "humbled" by her own "lamenesse." She suspected that this illness was yet another "correction" from God, and as such, it was a shameful public exposure of her spiritual frailty. Clearly He was punishing her for her initial resistance to America and her doubts about their mission.[2]

Anne's sense of shame could only deepen over time, since, when anyone fell ill in the little community, everyone else's labors became heavier. Her mother and sisters had to provide food and nursing care. Simon had to make sure the servants were fulfilling their duties, and the neighbors had to pitch in as well: doing the mending, the butter and cheese making, the brewing of small ale, the dangerous and constant work of keeping the fire going — while she lay uselessly in the big bed next to the fireplace.

Gradually the New Towne gardens and fields disappeared under a blur of snow, and the only traces left of the town were the muddled little houses. It seemed to be a time of winnowing away, of stripping bare, a stark fateful time in which only the essentials were left. This second winter, however, would be far easier for the settlers to endure. Most families had enough food to last until spring, and the death toll would be far lower than during the previous year.

Still, in such a climate it was easy to imagine one's own death. Anne, who always underestimated her physical strength, felt sure that she had come to the end of her days. "My race is run," she would write, "lo, here is fatal death."[3] And yet Anne did not despair but battled for many slow months until at last she emerged from the fever with a strengthened sense of confidence; God had allowed her to conquer yet another obstacle.

She did not recover her strength all at once, however, and during this time of convalescence, she began to realize that her illness had actually been a powerful spiritual aid. Later she would remember, "I saw the Lord sent [this sickness] to humble me and try me and do me good." God cared enough about her to single her out for spiritual improvement.[4] Smallpox had chastened her, but this latest affliction had brought her even closer to union with the divine.

Anne was not the sort of person to let this extraordinary experience pass. Without any fanfare, she turned to the discipline that her father had taught her back in the dim paneled halls of Sempringham — poetry. By counting out the beats for each line and searching diligently for beautiful rhymes, Anne found that she could fashion a tribute to God's glory and make order out of the chaotic fear of the last months. When she completed her first poem, she gave it the suitable title, "Upon a Fit of Sickness," including an additional note, "*Anno.* 1632. *Aetatis Suae*, 19."

Of course, needlework would have been the more ordinary occupation for a recovering young wife, but Anne found such activities tedious.[5] And she knew that composing a proficient poem could please others: Simon, her mother, Sarah, Patience, Mercy, and even the minister from the church in Boston, John Wilson, who had probably traveled to the Bradstreet's house to pray with Anne and Simon during her ordeal. A poem would be a fitting atonement for her many sins and a gift to all those who had had to shoulder her chores, mop her brow, tend her fire, and cook her food. But of all her readers, Anne would likely have been most conscious of Dudley's opinion. After all, he had undertaken her education all those years ago, and she longed to make him proud.

The first choice Anne had to make before she picked up her pen was what meter to use, since this was a crucial part of declaring her intentions as a Puritan and as a poet. Once she had decided, she could not waver. This was partly for practical reasons. Each page was precious to Anne. Although her wealthy father did have a larger supply of paper and vellum than most people and she herself had a small bound book to write in, once she had used up this writing material, it was expensive to get more, and it could take months to arrive from England. Mistakes were a costly luxury, therefore, and drafts were an impossibility. Anne would have to think out the lines first and memorize them before hazarding them onto paper.

Her virtue was also put to the test. Just as ink blots had seemed evidence of her sinful nature when she was a girl, so now would the wrong word or a false note. Each poem was meant as an offering to God and to her community and was far too crucial for her to take lightly.

The best choice for meter, she decided, was the one she was most familiar with, the ballad form. This popular kind of poetry, "the fourteener," was not sophisticated, but it was the kind used in the Sternhold and Hopkins translation of the Psalms to which her family was devoted, even though it featured stanzas such as this:

> My shepherd is the living Lord,
> Nothing therefore I need;
> In pastures fair with waters calm,
> He sets me forth to feed.[6]

The fourteener was also the meter employed by most Puritan writers, including the local minister. John Wilson had penned a long religious poem ("A Song, or Story, For the Lasting Remembrance of Diverse Famous Works, Which God Hath Done In Our Time"), and although it was neither beautiful nor particularly skillful, it was a comprehensive history of Protestantism and so was highly prized by Dudley and the pious colonists. If Anne could make it clear that she admired Wilson's work, she would be able to demonstrate her loyalty to the New England way of thinking, and to Massachusetts Bay Puritanism in particular. Because her literary efforts would be regarded as exclusively religious in nature, she could then work on developing her technique without raising eyebrows.

The poem succeeded. There was no greater honor than emulation, and Wilson was not immune to this kind of flattery. He would forever be one of Anne's fans. In addition, Anne's allusions illustrated that she knew Scripture and many poems of the "right" sort, according to the Reformed way of thinking. Better yet, she seemed well aware of the proper verse conventions for a pious writer. There were, however, some surprising elements in this modest composition. Despite her religious intentions, Anne introduced herself to her readers with an ambitious flourish that seemed to have nothing to do with Puritanism or proper feminine decorum.

When she penned the Latin words *"Anno. 1632. Aetatis Suae, 19"* after the title, Anne hinted that she was regarding this first poem far more seriously than she should have according to Puritan teachings. Although many devoted souls in New England wrote poetry, few were capable of using Latin, or even knew that *"aetatis suae"* meant "her age." Not that Anne herself was a Latin scholar; in fact, this would be the only such phrase she would use in her work. But this highly self-conscious literary manner gave the poem a "learned" feel; it also made it sound as if it were the first of many she planned to write, for an audience far larger than simply her family and friends.

Perhaps this was not so remarkable after all. Even though Anne had been taught to think of poetry as another form of prayer, Dudley's restless blood ran in her veins. Her father had trained her too well for Anne not to aspire to more than dutiful religious verse. Fame was on her mind, whether she realized it or not, despite the lectures she had heard about the vanity of such ideals and despite the propaganda against women — or men, for that matter — overreaching their bounds.[7]

If Anne was aware of her own aspirations, however, she kept them hidden; it was, after all, unthinkable for any Puritan to entertain dreams of worldly success, let alone a Puritan wife. Her duty was to be humble, not ambitious, to direct her attention toward heaven, not earth. It is astonishing, therefore, that she revealed any aspirations that were not purely religious in nature.

But perhaps Anne felt that the devout theme of her poem made up for any whiff of ambition in the title. "Twice ten years old, not fully told ... lo, here is fatal death" she began in a conventional way, emphasizing her youth in an attempt to capture not only her narrow escape but also, perhaps, the deaths of countless young people in the colonies. On she went, citing the supremacy of God's will and how death would usher in the good pilgrim's salvation and the blessing of eternal life. These sentiments were in accordance with her religion, as were her laments about her own suffering. "For what's this life but care and strife," she declared, quoting a Puritan truism about the earthly "vale of tears."[8]

Whatever Anne's intentions on composing this first poem, it does seem clear that the act of writing offered her a way of coping with the hardships she had to tolerate. She transformed her loneliness, disappointment, and profound disillusionment into verse, drawing on what she had learned not only from her most recent illness but also from the voyage and the first year in America. In so doing she discovered the tool that would allow her to endure and make sense of her experience in the wilderness. Only through "pain," she declared, did she stand a chance to grow.[9]

That summer, however, Anne's initial compositional experiments abruptly ended. At last she was pregnant. To her this turn of events did not seem coincidental. Later she would write that this baby was the result "of prayers, of vows, of tears"; she had no doubt that God had "heard'st me" and "gav'st him me."[10] Her illness had spurred her toward a spiritual awakening, which had inspired her to express her devotion to the Lord in a poem. Now her womb was filled with life. Clearly, poetry writing had ushered in a baby.

But children do not usually have the same effect on poems, at least not at first. For the next six years, Anne did not pen another word, although she did not complain about not being able to write. Nothing was more important than being able to bear Simon children. Many Puritan wives worried that if they were barren, their husbands would desert or abuse them, and everyone had heard such stories through the local rumor mill. Though it would have been entirely out of character for the genial and even-keeled Simon to distance himself from her, let alone cast her out of the house, in Anne's mind he would have had every right to spurn her if she could not provide him with a family.

It was a relief, then, to feel her stomach slowly begin to distend. It was even a pleasure to experience the telltale nausea of the early months, especially as the older women reassured her that the more sick she was, the healthier the baby would be. There were even those who whispered that if the mother was very ill, the baby was surely a boy. There were other odd bits of lore: If one had conceived on a certain day of the week or in a certain cycle of the moon, the infant would be born female, or strong, or with blue eyes. Above all, Anne prayed for a successful delivery and a healthy baby.

Practically speaking, she had some points in her favor. At twenty, she was stronger physically than when they had arrived in America. Thanks to the efforts of her father, brother, and husband, New Towne had grown into a recognizable little village with ample food and resources, and more homes were being built every day to house those fleeing the impositions of the king and his bishops.

Since Anne and Simon were among the richest of the settlers, they had managed to fortify themselves admirably for the approaching winter, but this also meant that Anne faced more than the average amount of work to keep track of their raw materials — a job that demanded the foresight of a general supplying an army. In October Anne had to have a sense of what her household would need in February and to regulate the family's use of corn, dried fruit, root vegetables, salted meat, and dairy supplies accordingly. If she were not careful, their food would go bad before it had gotten used. But if she allowed the servants to rush through their store, there would be nothing left to eat in early spring.

Simon had purchased large bags of English barley, oats, wheat, and rye, and they were stockpiled in their loft, where they had to be protected from rats, insects, damp, and mildew. Anne had to create a weekly regimen that included making bread and cakes from the wheat and rye, cooking the oats into porridge or "flummery" — a jellied dish spiced with herbs and dried fruit — and manufacturing malt out of the barley so they would not have to rely exclusively on the dark salty water of New Towne Creek.[11]

With the help of the women in her household, by early fall Anne would have preserved most of the fruit and vegetables from the summer, the berries boiled into jams and jellies, the vegetables that had not been eaten dried or pickled. The root vegetables had to be protected from rot and stored for eating that winter. Usually it was best to leave them in the ground as long as possible and dig them up as needed. Anne also had to make sure that the servants harvested and prepared her herbs correctly, drying them by hanging them in bunches from the ceiling ready to be pinched for cooking or for therapeutic uses. Rosemary could be used for a stew, burdock root for an aching shoulder. Once she was in labor, she might need chamomile, catnip, mint, feverfew, hyssop, tansy, or sage.[12]

Outdoors, some of the most important of the Bradstreets' "supplies" scratched for food in the gravelly dirt of New Towne and ranged around the commons. Their livestock was the family's insurance against hunger that winter. Fall was traditionally the slaughter season and, although Simon and the other men usually killed the cows and larger hogs themselves, it was typical for a woman to kill the smaller pigs, holding the "hinder parts between her legs, and taking the snout in her left hand" while she "stuck" the hog in his heart with a sharp, enormous blade.[13]

Naturally, Mistress Bradstreet would not have been expected to actually slaughter a pig, but she did have to make sure her servants did not make any dangerous mistakes. The first step was to choose the pig that should be killed, and then the strongest woman in the household would stab the animal and hold it until it stopped bleeding. Only then was it time to plunge the carcass into a kettle of boiling water.

Afterward the dead pig would be coated all over with rosin to strip off its bristles; then its belly was sliced open. No part of the animal could go to waste. The organ meats were pulled out and cooked immediately. The intestines, on the other hand, had to be cleaned carefully, making sure not to poke holes in the lining, since they would be stuffed with bits of meat and spices to create the highly prized delicacy of sausage "links."[14]

The meat itself needed to be sliced off in manageable hunks. Some of it could be roasted at once, but to Anne and her family, the specter of the winter dominated much of their thinking, and so they would probably have dunked a large portion of the pork into salt brine, where it would keep for months. The rest they turned into bacon, cutting the meat into "flitches" that they hung in the fireplace for smoking.[15]

All of these tasks were exhausting and messy, and yet there was no avoiding them; they were part of the seasonal toil for all new Americans. Anne was probably grateful that this year she was able to participate fully in her household duties rather than having to lie in bed while others slaved to complete her chores.

But as the fall days grew sharper and their third winter in the New World approached, Anne knew she faced a new reckoning. She was nearing the end of her pregnancy, and this was a dire time for a young woman. In fact, it was fortunate (although she would have disagreed) that she had not been pregnant when she was still weakened from the deprivations of the first year. It was best to be at the height of one's physical strength before undergoing the ordeal of pregnancy, labor, and delivery.

CHILDBIRTH WAS THE CENTRAL EVENT in a woman's life. No one knew whether the mother would survive. And if the child lived, it would likely die before it was two years old. In response to these early deaths, parents regularly named their new children after ones who had expired, not out of callous disregard, and certainly not for lack of names, but in an effort to overcome the dread facts of mortality. There was really no better way to commemorate the child who had died, these parents felt, than passing on his or her identity to the one who flourished.[16]

For the pregnant woman, the time before birth was a period for reflection as well as frantic industry. Food had to be stored and prepared for the lying-in period after the birth, and also to feed the many women who would come to attend the labor and help the new mother. After his wife's safe delivery, one colonist recorded, he served nineteen women a meal that featured "boiled pork, beef, and fowls; roast beef and turkey; and minc'd Pyes and cheese."[17]

Bonnets, hats, mittens, and smocks had to be knitted and sewed, and many prospective mothers put hours of labor into embroidering the new arrival's first clothing. Sadly, since the baby might die soon after being born, one of the most important creations in families like Anne's was the christening blanket.

To the Puritan mind it was crucial that the infant be baptized as soon as possible after birth so that it would have at least a chance of being among God's chosen. But although no Puritan theologian would have held with such an idea, the superstition remained among mothers that a glorious blanket could perhaps dissuade Death from taking the baby away prematurely. As a result, baptismal coverlets were often made of silk that pious women such as Anne embroidered with obsessive diligence; the Bradford family's blanket in Plymouth, for example, was covered with copiously cross-stitched pink flowers six inches apart. If Anne had not inherited such a coverlet from Dorothy, she would have devoted herself to making her own, bordering the silk edge with lace or silk fringe and choosing a suitable scriptural text to embroider on the front.[18]

Since she was already prone to the contemplation of her own mortality and had had three significant illnesses that induced such reflections, the time before labor was particularly potent for Anne.

Later in life she would take the time before the birth of one of her children to write a farewell poem to her husband, outlining her wishes in case she died. She was not alone. Other women also recorded testimonials and tearful good-byes to their families. Thus women entered their "travail" in the same spirit that men set off on long journeys or went to war.[19] The last month of pregnancy was not only a time of making "Pyes" but also a time of making peace with the idea of approaching death.

Although the exact date of her delivery is uncertain, it seems likely that early in the new year 1633 Anne felt her first labor pains. Fortunately, her mother, sisters, and sister-in-law lived close by, and before long the other New Towne women would have streamed into her house. This was the time to serve the "groaning cakes" and "groaning beer" that Anne had prepared in the preceding weeks.[20] Although there was not yet a midwife in New Towne, the combined experience at any birth was considerable. Most of the women present had had their own babies and had attended the births of their friends and sisters. In fact, this was a ritual ruled by women. The men of the house were usually relegated to the other room, or even to the house of a neighbor. Simon was banished from Anne's side, and she was thrown entirely on the resources of her female neighbors and her mother.

As much as she loved her husband, there was nothing Anne would have wanted more than the gentle, knowing ministrations of her women friends. During the early stages, the gathering had the feel of a party as everyone ate, sipped her ale, and told old war stories about her own childbirths or other travails she had witnessed. There was one tradition that during these early stages of labor the mother-to-be should start making bread, as some midwives believed the act of kneading the dough would calm the woman and move the contractions along at a brisker rate. Whether or not Anne actually began the process of feeding the yeast and mixing the sponge, it was important for her to stay relaxed and to eat in order to build her strength for what lay ahead. Her mother would have known to try to tempt her with food that was high in protein but easy to digest, such as broth or poached eggs.[21]

Conversation would have quieted, however, and jests and gaiety would have gradually subsided when it became clear that Anne's contractions were becoming hard to endure. This was the time for coaching the suffering woman through her pain, and everyone would have had her own techniques — calm words, cool damp cloths, sips of water, a back rub. Probably the most important assistance anyone could provide was the reassurance that her pain was normal and there was as yet no evidence that she was dying or that the baby was in danger. If a crisis did occur, however, no one would have thought to minimize the danger of the situation, as everyone knew of some friend or relative who had died in childbirth or had lost a baby in delivery or soon after.

When at last it was time to push the baby out, many arms were there to help Anne onto the birthing stool, which was low and open seated. During this, the most dangerous phase of delivery, the more experienced women stepped to the fore. A perfectly healthy baby could be lost if the women in charge missed the telltale signs of a cord wrapped around an infant's neck or if a shoulder got stuck in the birth canal. One of Anne's neighbors was probably a more skilled midwife than the others and used her experience and judgment to determine if the baby was beginning to struggle and had to come out sooner rather than later.

If Simon was still in the house, he could hear the cries of his wife, the murmurs of the women, and mysterious patches of silence. As the hours passed, he would have been forced to endure an unaccustomed helplessness.[22] As one anxious husband described this waiting time:

> After the Women had been some time assembled I went out to
> get a little Briony Water — upon my return my wife's mother
> came to me with tears in her eyes, O, says she, I don't know
> how it will fare with your poor wife, hinting withal her extreme
> danger.[23]

Despite his anxiety, Simon would have known better than to interrupt the crucial process in the other room; still it was hard to wait until the women came to him and reported on his wife's progress. Good Puritan that he was, and joined, no doubt, by Anne's devoted father and her younger sisters (although it is possible that they were allowed in the birthing room even though they were still unmarried), Simon would have used his time to say prayers and declare his willingness to submit to God's will.

For Anne it was reassuring to know that her family and friends were entreating God for her and her baby's safety. But she had been taught to believe that, like the illnesses she had endured, this pain was God's "corrective" tool. According to Puritan theology, each woman's suffering was her personal retribution for Eve's original trespass and was a kind of purification process meant to combat the dark lusts that were lodged in her heart. Someone like Anne might also have seen her agony in the redemptive terms of the New Testament. Christ, after all, had compared His crucifixion and miraculous return to a mother whose "time had come."[24] This meant that the anguish during labor was not only punishment for original sin but also an opportunity to join Christ and take up His cross. As one devout New England mother wrote after the birth of each of her children, "[T]he Lord apeard for me and maid me the living mother of another living Child."[25] For Anne, therefore, her labor was a passage far more important than her illnesses or her voyage to America.

When at last one of the women could see the baby's head, Anne must have hoped that her misery would soon be at an end. One traditional midwife's strategy was to have the mother touch the top of the baby's head, feel the damp tuft of hair and the warm miracle of the little being itself, so that the tired woman could get ready for the final push. When the baby finally spilled out between her legs and into the welcoming hands of one of the other women, she knew she had won an astonishing victory against her own physical weakness and against death itself. Or, more accurately, God had allowed her to triumph.

Anne's new baby was a healthy little boy. Nothing could have pleased this community of Puritans better than the arrival of a male child. If properly educated, he would be able to step into a leadership position in New England when he came of age. Despite the importance of women's contributions to the colony, men were still considered a more valuable asset to the future of Massachusetts than their wives and daughters. When Anne heard the pleased murmurs that her son was healthy and strong, she knew it was a wondrous event. Only two years before, she had almost died. Now she had a son.

After delivery, the other women flew into action, cleaning the infant and making sure the placenta and umbilical cord were not mishandled, as there was a host of traditions surrounding the ritual of cutting this emblematic connection to the mother's womb. If the cord fell on the floor, then the boy would not be able "to hold water." If it was cut too short, his penis would be too small and he would be "insufficient in encounters with Venus."[26]

While her attendants worried, cleaned, and prepared food for her, Anne could give herself up to the ecstasy of having borne a child. She had proved that she was not a spiritual outcast, she had pleased her father by helping swell the ranks of pious Puritans in America, and she had undoubtedly thrilled Simon by giving him an heir.

It was probably clear to everyone that she would name her baby Samuel. She had waited five long years for this child, and so it was only natural that she compare herself to the Old Testament Hannah, who had had to endure years of infertility before she gave birth to the famous prophet Samuel. Of course, it is also likely that Anne admired her older brother, Samuel, and wanted to link her little boy to his uncle. But above all, she had been taught to view her life on a biblical scale and so believed that the birth of her son connected her to a larger story.

There were many examples of this kind of exalted thinking among the Massachusetts Puritans. One prominent citizen, Judge Sewall, explained that he had named his son, Joseph, "in hopes of the accomplishment of the Prophecy of Ezekiel xxxvii." When his wife bore a little girl, he wrote, "I was struggling whether to call her Mehetable or Sarah. But when I saw Sarah's standing in the Scripture . . . I resolv'd on that suddenly."

Although traditional names such as Hannah, meaning "grace," and Abigail, meaning "father's joy," were frequently selected by Anne's friends and family because "the history of these two Hebrew women made their names honored," the length or oddity of a name was no impediment to such a single-minded people. Choices such as Zurishaddai, which meant "the Almighty is my rock," were not uncommon, and there were many instances of names that Puritan parents adopted to express their devotion to God or to declare their own earthly suffering, such as "Hoped For," "Return," "Believe," "Wait," "Thanks," "Unite," "Supply," or "Tremble." One recently widowed mother even saw fit to name her newborn "Fathergone."[27]

Although she had just undergone the most wearing experience of her life, Anne was now catapulted into the rigors of a new mother's schedule. She had been influenced by the Countess of Lincolnshire's opinions on this subject and breast-fed Samuel, nursing through the long night hours and attempting to soothe him when he wailed. It was a grueling regimen, and many years later she would write a poem from the perspective of an infant:

> *With tears into the world I did arrive,*
> *My mother still did waste as I did thrive,*
> *Who yet with love and all alacrity,*
> *Spending, was willing to be spent for me.*
> *With wayward cryes I did disturb her rest,*
> *Who sought still to appease me with the breast.*[28]

Anne could take comfort in the fact that since this boy had been born on the purer shores of New England, he would surely prove to be a finer man and a truer Puritan than those born in the corruption of the Old World. As one enthusiastic settler wrote:

The Christian children born here are generally well-favored and beautiful to behold. I never knew any to come into the world with the least blemish on any part of the body; being in the general observed to be better-natured, milder, and more tender-hearted than those born in England.[29]

To Anne her long-awaited baby must have seemed perfect in every way. But now that he was safely delivered, she could not help but grapple with a flood of new fears. Could she keep him safe, fight off his illnesses, tend him, keep him alive?

Infants in a pioneer settlement such as New Towne faced many obstacles to their survival, from diseases such as rickets, measles, whooping cough, diphtheria, and intestinal worms to hazards such as the canal that flowed past Samuel's grandparents' house, the gape of gigantic fireplaces, cauldrons of boiling water, unfenced and marauding livestock, and severe spells of both cold and hot weather. Babies were frequently referred to as "it," not because of any lack of maternal devotion, but because mothers were responsible for running an entire household and did not show their love through the sort of focused attention we now associate with maternity. In addition, childbirth was such a regular phenomenon in most families that the identity of the youngest changed from year to year.[30]

Sadly, there were often dire results to the many responsibilities a woman had to juggle, since it was impossible to keep an eye on the children at all times. One Puritan child "narrowly escaped drowning being fallen into a Kettle of Suds" and was only saved when he was "Seasonly Spyd and pulled out by the heels." Another little girl was scalded to death in a similar accident when her mother was still "lying in" from delivering a new baby. Since women often had to be out of the house to complete their chores, weeding their extensive vegetable gardens, gathering eggs, or fetching water, they often left their infants and toddlers under the care of servants or older children and had to count on their limited ability to supervise a curious small child. Often this simply did not work. One poor mother came home from hiking out to a distant field to deliver her husband his midday meal only to discover her baby had vanished. "It was here just now presently," an older daughter declared. But after a frantic search, the body of the toddler was found floating in an "unfenced water hole."[31]

Though Samuel was Anne's first and her house was not yet overrun with children, it was still hard to keep track of the baby, especially when he began to crawl and take his first steps. Nothing about life was safe. Anne had to be enough of an herbalist to know how to treat everything from bee stings and stomachaches to teething pains and head wounds. She had to be doctor enough to set broken bones or sprains and to stanch swelling and bring down virulent fevers. The other women in the village shared their lore and their extensive knowledge of healing plants and other practical remedies. But in a crisis, Anne would have to respond independently, quickly, and appropriately, or she might lose her child.

Miraculously, little Samuel managed to survive and even thrive. With each month that he grew stronger and bigger, Anne gained confidence in her skills as a mother and in her sense that God was now with her more than ever before. She knew that if she could raise her child to become a healthy Puritan adult, she would be giving an invaluable gift to New England. To many Puritan women motherhood assumed an overall weight that sometimes seemed unbearable. If her children flourished and devoted themselves to the true path of Reformed religion, a Puritan mother would have achieved the pinnacle of success and even fame in her community. One woman's gravestone in Newbury was twice as large as that of her husband's so that it could contain the lengthy epitaph written by her children:

To the memory of Mrs. Judith late virtuous wife of Deac[on] Tristram Coffin, Esqr. Who having lived to see 177 of her children and children's children to the 3d generation died Dec. 15, 1705 aged 80.

Grave, sober, faithful, fruitfull vine was she,
A rare example of true piety.

Widow'd awhile she wayted wisht for rest
With her dear husband in her Savior's breast.[32]

Anne aspired to this sort of glory, although she knew that parenthood on this scale entailed hard work, suffering, and then more hard work. Later in life she would reflect that a woman's tasks were both wearying and never ending, and she recalled her years of motherhood as ones of self-sacrifice:

I nursed them up with pain and care,
Nor cost, nor labour did I spare,
Till at the last they felt their wing,
Mounted the trees, and learned to sing.[33]

But to Anne and to most Puritan women, motherhood was the most important way to serve God. If she could help raise a new flock of the faithful, Anne would help ensure the future of the New England Puritan dream.

CHAPTER ELEVEN

ଅ୨୧ଓ

Enemies Within

Abstract yourselfe with a holy violence from the Dung heape of
this Earth.

— ROGER WILLIAMS

THE YEAR 1634 USHERED in a new set of problems for the colony, ones that came from inside the towns rather than from outside. Dissension, conflict, and arguments about the true path to take pitted old friends against each other and forced many prominent people into exile. It was dangerous in Massachusetts to stray too far from the accepted beliefs of the authorities. With both her husband and father serving on the governing board of the colony, Anne knew this all too well.

In the annual election that same year, when baby Samuel had just turned one, Dudley was voted governor of Massachusetts Bay in place of Winthrop for the first time since they had arrived. Immediately a flurry of crises landed on his desk. Rumor had it that King Charles wanted to revoke the colony's charter. In fact, people whispered that he was plotting an attack on Boston.[1] It was shocking to imagine that Charles might order their countrymen to fire upon them, brother against brother, Protestant against Protestant. The tense political environment the Puritans had worked so hard to leave behind seemed to be catching up to them.

Everyone prepared for the worst. Right before Dudley was installed as the new leader, Winthrop ordered a garrison of local men who had been trained as soldiers to occupy the fort on Castle Island in Boston Harbor. He also made a plan for the beacon on Beacon Hill to be lit if Charles's forces came sweeping into the bay.[2] Then, as if the threat of attack were not worrisome enough, another worry arose: Dudley's old friend, Roger Williams, was shaking the very roots of the community with a series of outrageous pronouncements.

Williams was one of the most popular champions of the migration to America. When he had met with Theophilus, Isaac Johnson, Dudley, Winthrop, and the others in Sempringham back in 1629, he had inspired them with the depth of his passionate faith. A visionary minister, he drew others to follow his ideas by virtue of his charm and profound convictions. But he was also one of the most stubborn, "God-intoxicated" individuals to come to America.[3]

From the moment he arrived in Massachusetts, Williams had been difficult. He refused to officiate at the church in Boston because he believed the membership was not "pure" enough, in effect denouncing many of the most pious settlers in the colony, such as his old friend John Winthrop.

But Williams did not care whom he alienated. Aghast at the tales that were crossing the ocean of the king's heresies and his continued harassment of Puritans, by 1634 Williams had lost patience with the colony's assertions of loyalty to the Crown and the Anglican Church. The king was a liar, he said, and worse, was in league with the devil. Such a terrible sinner did not have the right to grant land to the colonists; consequently, the royal charter had no basis, the settlers did not really own their acreages, the colony should be dissolved and everyone should return to England to confess that they had sinned by emigrating to America without any legitimate authority to back their claims.[4]

Winthrop, Dudley, and the other magistrates knew that if Williams's pronouncements came to the ears of the king, the Bay colony could be punished for treason and perhaps dismantled. Luckily, during the first months of Dudley's term, King Charles, who was distracted by the growing conflicts in England, turned his attention away from New England and let the matter of the charter drop. For Charles it seemed more important to contain Puritanism at home than to squander his limited resources on the remote and seemingly unimportant colony in America. To the colonists, the king's change of heart seemed astonishingly auspicious, but even as the threats from outside the colony diminished, the problem of Roger Williams only seemed to grow.

To the horror of Dudley; his deputy governor, Roger Ludlow; and the forty other magistrates who sat on the General Court, Williams began to attract new followers. He wanted the colonists to break off all communication with the Old World because he believed that only if New England Puritans were fully "separated" from the corruption of England could they achieve salvation. The king's recent sword rattling had made this seem appealing to some individuals, but Anne was not one of them. She saw herself as an Englishwoman and, therefore, as a member of the English church. After all, she and her family were among the "saving remnant" of the English people, the vanguard of the reform movement that would ultimately redeem England.[5]

But a zealot like Williams had no compassion for this lingering affection for the Old World. Rigid idealist that he was, he had lived briefly with the Pilgrims in 1633, hoping to discover in Plymouth a purer settlement than Massachusetts Bay. But he soon found that even holier-than-thou Plymouth had its pollutants. Reports trickled back to New Towne that he had refused to call his neighbors by the conventional "goodman" or "goodwife," because none of them were free enough from sin to deserve this title. This sort of prickly arrogance hurt his popularity, and before long he reappeared in Salem, where, his enemies believed, he had "bewitched" the towns-people into choosing him, unofficially, as their new minister.

Williams's absence from the center of government had given the colony's leaders a brief respite from anxiety, but now that Williams had access to the Salem pulpit, he could make real trouble. In his sermons, Williams harped on the visible imperfections of the colonists and their leaders. The minister's savage laments about the lack of virtue in New England often struck home. Dudley himself was sympathetic with the idea of correcting evildoers and separating oneself from those who would not repent. But as a government official, he would cope with this problem legislatively, cracking down hard on sin and sinners.

When he first took office, for example, Dudley led an effort to purify the community and remedy what he regarded as four lax years of Winthrop's leadership. He strengthened the magistrates' authority and passed a series of sumptuary laws, declaring a smoking ban not just in public places but also in the home. In addition, there could be no clothing adorned with gold, silver, or lace. Any fashion accessory that Dudley deemed excessive was banned, such as silver or gold belts, beaver hats, ruffs, and all "new fashions, long hair, or anything of the like nature."[6] But this was a slippery slope: After all, who was not a sinner? What litmus test could you use to test for purity?

Still, Dudley was a practical man, and he differed from Williams because he could see that compromises were sometimes necessary. Williams had gone too far in his attempt to separate himself and others from sin. There was no escaping the settlers' corruption; instead it was the job of ministers and government officials to curb their carnal inclinations. Williams could not accept such a position. In one of his Salem sermons, the passionate minister ruffled everyone's feathers by asserting that his church was "better" than the other New England congregations and therefore should secede from their sisterhood.[7] He could hardly have uttered more alienating words. The other ministers, who had hesitated to condemn him due to their respect for his piety and learning, promptly leagued themselves against him.

Like most of the settlers, Anne was shocked that her father's old friend had denounced the men she most admired, from Cotton to the New Towne minister, Thomas Hooker. But unlike other townspeople, especially the women, she was privy to confidential information about the colony's political goings-on, since Dudley and Simon probably used their time at home to discuss the issues that troubled them. From them, Anne would have absorbed the cautionary lesson that too much idealism could get you in trouble, that it was important to learn how to speak your mind in a way that did not cross the authorities.

As the months passed, Williams galloped on, declaring not only that England was corrupt but that the English flag with its prominent "Catholic" cross was a disgrace. He advised Massachusetts Bay residents to fly their own "corrected" flag — a lily-white banner that would eschew any such papist emblem.

Such a public assertion of New England's moral supremacy would surely strain relations with England even further, and there was nothing that Dudley, Winthrop, and the other magistrates feared more. What if the king remembered that he had wanted to revoke the colony's charter? But Winthrop, Dudley, Ludlow, Endecott, and the other magistrates were loath to take legal action against Williams, as everyone understood that the man had the right intentions. Perhaps his idealism was misguided, but the minister was a virtuous sort of sinner, an odd duck whom Dudley and Winthrop understood and even begrudgingly admired. No one wanted to see Williams condemned by the General Court.

The Great and General Court of Massachusetts was the only court in the land. It convened in the New Towne meetinghouse without any of the elegant trappings of the law as it had been practiced in England, although its members were the leading citizens of the era. The governor, deputy governor, and a minimum of six "assistants" were selected by "freemen," men who owned property and were members of a church. These officials were joined by elected representatives from every town. Without a king or parliament, the court needed to perform all the acts of government, from making laws and enforcing them, to the more traditional judicial role of hearing complaints and cases.

By the spring of 1635, when Dudley's one-year term as governor was over, the die was cast. Even Williams's few admirers saw that the minister had stretched the teachings of Puritanism to the brink and was now caught in the disease of "perfectionism," a spiritual ailment that led the sufferer to seek endlessly (and hopelessly) for the impossible goal of freedom from sin. Williams refused to back down from any of his statements and was called to the court in October 1635, where Dudley joined Winthrop as one of the assistants.

If the renegade minister hoped he would escape punishment, he showed no evidence of this. Instead he attacked the magistrates almost before they could charge him with misconduct. The compromises of the New England leaders, he declared, would destroy the sanctity of the Puritan mission, and he called for them to join him in his holy vision.[8] The other ministers of the colony, who had been invited to advise the magistrates on how to proceed, vowed that Williams had "run into heresy, apostasy," and even "tyranny." Unanimously, they called for the court to remove him from his pulpit and banish him.[9] And so John Haynes, the new governor, proclaimed that Williams would have to leave the Bay colony for good.

Although at first Dudley had felt they should be lenient with his old friend, there was no avoiding the truth: Over the last year Williams had grown increasingly intransigent. By the end of his term as governor, Dudley had joined forces with the other magistrates and lobbied for Williams's exile, even though he understood that in late October such a punishment could well be a death sentence. New England weather was brutal and the wild animals fierce. The colonists needed each other even more during the harshest season of the year.

At this inopportune moment, Williams became ill, and the magistrates delayed enforcing his sentence. But Dudley, who could not bear the fact that Williams was still at large, persuaded the court to seize the minister and set him on a ship to England. Winthrop, on the other hand, who had affection for Williams, intervened and secretly wrote to the fugitive, urging him to flee so that he could escape being returned to the Old World. When the agent of the court, Captain John Underhill, arrived in Salem, he found that Williams had disappeared into the wilderness.[10]

That winter the earnest "saint," who believed that he had been "unkindly and unchristianly . . . driven from my house and land and wife and children," surprised everyone by managing to survive. He turned up in Narragansett Bay, having traveled through snow and icy storms, and promptly set about establishing a new town, one where he could preach as he saw fit. Naturally, Williams took his safe journey as a sign that God was on his side and continued to chase after his visions for the rest of his long life. Ironically, however, he backed down from his pinnacle of separatism and instead began to preach congregational independence, a stance that would usher in a new kind of religious freedom. Soon the churches in what would become known as Rhode Island would offer safe harbor for all those who disagreed with the Massachusetts Bay authorities.

After Williams's departure, most colonists hoped to return to the relative peace of the settlement's first four years. Instead, to everyone's dismay, another prominent "heretic" began to stir up far more dissension than Williams ever had, although this second trouble-maker emerged from a most unexpected place.

In 1634, near the beginning of Dudley's tenure as governor, the pious residents of Boston and New Towne had been honored to witness the arrival of Anne's old heroine from Sempringham days, Mistress Anne Hutchinson. Hutchinson's reputation for wisdom and piety had preceded her, since many of her old neighbors and friends had already established themselves in the New World. For three years she had watched her friends sell their possessions, pack up their houses, and board their ships, but she had chosen to stay in England because she considered John Cotton the most important spiritual mentor in the country. As long as the minister was preaching at St. Botolph's, she wanted to be in attendance.

But when, in 1633, Cotton was silenced by the authorities and fled to Massachusetts, where he could preach freely, Hutchinson declared there were no other ministers in England that she "durst hear." Before long she felt in "great trouble" without Cotton as her guide.[11] When she recounted the story later, Hutchinson hinted that, at this point, it was as though the Lord spoke directly to her and told her what to do. "The 30th of Isaiah was brought to my mind," she later recalled. "Though the Lord give thee bread of adversity and water of affliction . . . thine eyes shall see thy teachers."[12] Immediately, she was convinced that God had directed her to chase Cotton across the Atlantic so that once again she could be steeped in her "teacher's" wisdom. Afterward, her enemies would point out that Hutchinson's message could have come from another, more sinister entity.

Once determined to go, Hutchinson prodded her husband and her eleven children to prepare in an astonishingly short time. In just a few months, their shoes, woolens, tools, grains, and bolsters were packed, their unnecessary possessions were sold, and the Hutchinsons set sail for America.[13]

Boston was four years old in 1634 and was undergoing some soul-searching of its own even before this powerful woman's splashy arrival. Having had a year to imbibe Cotton's lessons, the colonists were hungry for more religion. The minister had helped set the stage for Hutchinson's arrival by discussing her many talents and her piety, leading his parishioners and friends in prayer for the safe passage of her ship. This distinguished person's decision to sail to America seemed like an especially good omen for the colonies; the best and the brightest were choosing to join them.

"Bold of spirit" as she was, upon her arrival in early September, Anne Hutchinson was ready to take Boston by storm.[14] Accustomed to being leading members of their civic community and their church, the Hutchinsons immediately hired the best available carpenters to erect their new house directly across from Winthrop's on a central plot of Boston real estate. Anne's husband was almost automatically elected to the General Court, and she herself applied for membership in Cotton's church. He was, after all, the primary reason she had decided to come overseas.[15]

But in an ominous foreshadowing of what was to come, Hutchinson's application did not go as smoothly as anticipated. To become a member of a Massachusetts congregation, you had to prove your faith and adherence to Puritan tenets. Everyone had to go through this process, even if they were famously devout. Although she had the backing of Cotton, who not only celebrated her courage for coming to America "for conscience's sake" but also praised her abilities, declaring that "she was well respected and esteemed of me," it soon appeared that Hutchinson had some enemies in the New World.

The Reverend Zechariah Symmes had been among her comrades on the passage over and had become alarmed at her remarks (although he never recorded what they were), citing "the corruptness and narrowness of her opinions," and warning Governor Dudley that Hutchinson might harm the Massachusetts community's purity of faith. But when Dudley, Cotton, and Symmes himself examined Mrs. Hutchinson, it seemed that "she held nothing different from us," and at last she was granted membership in Cotton's church in November, a humiliating two months after her arrival.[16]

Now that Dudley had vouched for her sanctity, Mrs. Hutchinson was poised to assert her influence in Boston, New Towne, and the surrounding settlements. Not that this was necessarily her conscious aim, but her style was unhesitating and audacious. Immediately she plunged into what she knew best, the business of childbirth. The official town midwife was Mistress Jane Hawkins, but the need for skillful health care was boundless in the settlements. Hutchinson, who had extensive experience, soon fell into the habit of accompanying Hawkins on her visits to women in labor. Before long, Hutchinson herself was often summoned to deliver babies. If Hawkins was the more skilled medical technician, Hutchinson was a supremely talented religious counselor. This was important because ministers were unable to attend this exclusively feminine rite, and the women who were undergoing their travails needed spiritual sustenance as well as hands-on care.

In such a pious community, any woman who could assume the role of spiritual guide was regarded with reverence, and soon Hutchinson was known to most of the women in the settlements. Her fame was limited to female circles, however, since in matters pertaining to childbirth men bowed to women's opinions and were often unaware of the details of their wives' labors. Otherwise, Hutchinson seemed to hold herself aloof. Surprisingly, she refused to go to any of the informal discussion groups where pious individuals could study the Bible together or converse on topics such as the true tenets of faith. Such groups were not an official requirement in the colony, but most people went, and so Hutchinson's absence was conspicuous.

To those whom she appeared to shun, Hutchinson's refusals seemed to be a pointed rejection of local efforts to deepen piety. In scriptural expertise, she could keep up with the most learned of the men and was a devoted follower of Cotton. But she was asserting her difference from everyone else right from the beginning, and tongues wagged. Mistress Hutchinson was clearly full of "pride," her enemies said; she must think she was better than they were.[17]

This kind of vigilant acrimony when people were faced with anything out of the ordinary was common fare in both Boston and New Towne. Dudley had taught his daughters that it was their duty to report to him or to their husbands anything that seemed unusual or that contradicted the godly mission of the colonists. It was everyone's job to know what everyone else was doing. In Plymouth, for example, members of that settlement's governing board, "the grand jury," were required to scrutinize people's behavior on a daily basis, scouring the streets for "idleness and other evils occasioned thereby" and hauling any wrongdoers straight into court.[18] Sin was infectious, and unpunished bad behavior could bring about everyone's destruction. The state of your conscience was never solely a personal affair but was also a civic matter.

Ironically, though, it was because of the "aspersions" against her piety and the criticism she faced for not attending these meetings that Hutchinson began to hold gatherings for women in her house.

How else could she disprove the reports that she "did despise all" the rules and customs, the "ordinances," of Boston? Or so she would argue a few years later when called to account for her actions.[19]

At first Hutchinson's meetings were small — maybe five or six women — and were dedicated to studying the Bible and discussing Cotton's sermons. But they rapidly mushroomed into gatherings of sixty or more. In the few months she had been in the colonies, Hutchinson had helped deliver numerous infants and had buoyed their mothers with her stalwart faith. She had also proven herself to be a "fruitful vine" in her own right, having borne eleven children. Clearly she had important lessons to teach, and women of all ages flocked to her side.

But to her discomfited neighbor, John Winthrop, it seemed that "shee kept open house for all comers, and set up two Lecture dayses in the week, when they usually met at her house threescore or fourescore persons."[20] That winter the Boston men watched with growing concern as their wives trooped down the dirt lane and turned the corner to the Hutchinsons' homestead. No male could be certain what went on at these meetings that most people called "gossipings," the conventional term for such female gatherings. Each time a goodwife entered the dark cave of Mrs. Hutchinson's home, the door was effectively slammed in the face of her husband.[21]

The sort of female gossiping that the Bay colony men were beginning to suspect occurred in Hutchinson's house loomed as a danger because their settlement depended on "neighborliness." If women were prone to "wandering about from house to house," the men worried they would "spea[k] things which they ought not," as Paul wrote in a frequently quoted passage from the New Testament. Such female "scolds," their critics held, relished trouble because they wanted "to make debate abroad" and would never be able to resist the temptation to announce their husband's flaws for "all the Town" to hear. To speak in public like this — to "publish" — was to usurp the role of men and trespass into a world where a woman did not belong. Such "masculine women buried silence to revive slander." Women's "gossip," if uncontrolled and left unchecked, could render the speakers "deformed," "man-like," and even "monstrous."[22]

To the anxious male leaders in Boston and New Towne, this seemed the grotesque direction in which Mrs. Hutchinson and her followers were headed, and before many months had passed, their fears were confirmed. Hutchinson encouraged her pupils to revere Cotton's words but to despise the other Massachusetts ministers, especially the preacher John Wilson. As a result, whenever Wilson spoke, the women would get up and leave the meetinghouse or else direct insulting looks in his direction.

This behavior was an assault on one of the premier authorities of the colony and could not be left unchecked. But it was difficult to know how to stop Hutchinson and her followers. They were women and lived in a kind of strange legal netherworld, since they occupied no public positions in the colony. They could not be charged with sedition or treason. It was not illegal for a woman to leave the meetinghouse during a sermon. She could always cite female infirmities if accused of wrongdoing.[23]

As time went on, more reports against Hutchinson accumulated. Even though they were caught up in the Williams affair, the ministers and magistrates could not ignore that Hutchinson's enemies accused her of an important theological transgression: dismissing good deeds as an important element of the Christian's life. Such a stance could only result in the paralysis of the faithful, her opponents complained; if there were no benefit to be had in performing virtuous acts, then why would anyone bother with piety, sanctity, charity, or prayer? Her teachings would result in a licentious free-for-all; the self-discipline and upstanding ethical behavior the Puritans respected would be ignored and even flouted.

The logic of Hutchinson's enemies was based on the Reform paradox that although no person could depend on his or her own labors to achieve salvation, pious persons should still try to behave ethically and improve themselves, even if such a mission were doomed to failure. In other words, one's moral behavior was important and should not be dismissed, despite the teaching that God's will was incontrovertible.

Even if one were a dutiful Puritan, it was easy to slip to the wrong side of this delicate issue. Winthrop himself once confessed that he often fell into the torpor of believing that his own good actions could help him win God's grace.[24] However, Mrs. Hutchinson's emphasis on the individual's helplessness was too much for the authorities to tolerate. After months of misgivings, Dudley took back his endorsement of this accomplished woman and joined the other magistrates in voicing their pressing concerns, writing that "her strange opinions" — that Cotton was the only righteous minister in the colony and that the performance of good deeds was only meaningless busywork — were causing dissension and creating factions among the people.[25]

Consequently, when the weather grew hot and muggy in the summer of 1635 and Anne discovered that she was pregnant again, she knew that she would not be able to cross the river to Mrs. Hutchinson's house for spiritual counsel. Even had she wanted to, Anne could not have swayed her father from his stance. It was no longer possible for any of the Dudley women even to recognize Hutchinson if they passed her on the street.

Anne submitted to this policy without any evidence of resistance; however, it seems likely that her younger sister Sarah was not so amenable. Her volatile temperament made it far more challenging for her to obey her father's rules than for her more self-disciplined older sisters.

As soon as his term as governor had expired, Dudley decided it was time to flee the corruption of Boston, New Towne, and the simmering contention concerning Hutchinson. Anne, Samuel, and Patience were safely married and living squarely within the Puritan fold, but Sarah and Mercy were respectively fifteen and fourteen years old. He needed to protect them from the sin Hutchinson and Williams represented. As far as Sarah was concerned, however, he was probably too late. Her scandalous future actions would bear an uncanny resemblance to Hutchinson's, suggesting that she had done the unthinkable and succumbed to the dangerous woman's contagion.

Dudley himself must have been tired. While governor he had heard case after case of quarreling and corruption on top of the Hutchinson debacle and the Williams scandal. Neither Boston nor New Towne was the ideal city of God he had envisioned. Indeed, each now seemed dangerous to his family's spiritual health. And so immediately after the court had proclaimed Williams's exile, Dudley ordered his family to pack their bags. Like the restless saint he had vowed to stop, he, too, would flee the colony's impurities and embark on yet another strenuous pilgrimage. Once again Anne would have to follow in her father's pious footsteps, wherever they might lead.

CHAPTER TWELVE

❧❧

Ipswich

A NNE KNEW THAT HER FATHER was eager to shake the mud of government from his boots and that he was anxious about the religious well-being of his family, but even she must have been surprised at how readily he bade farewell to New Towne.[1] Driven by the impulse to breathe the clear, pure air of the frontier, at age fifty-nine Dudley was undeterred by the challenges that stopped most other settlers from venturing so far away from the established towns.

Ipswich, the site he had decided upon, lay on the edge of the wilderness, forty miles north of Boston — a two-day hike over largely uncharted ground. Salem, the closest village, was about eighteen miles away. Except for a few scattered huts on the site of modern-day Portsmouth, New Hampshire, there were no settlements beyond this frontier post.[2] Characteristically, Dudley seemed to find the idea of virgin soil appealing. Perhaps here he could have more control over shaping a godly community.

The Indian nomenclature for this bountiful and as yet unspoiled place was Agawam. With the goal of opening up fresh farming and grazing land for the waves of emigrants arriving from England, in 1633 Winthrop's son, John Winthrop Jr., had led twelve others in an expedition to this site that one visitor described as

> one of the most spacious for a plantation, being near the sea, it aboundeth with fish, and flesh of fowles and beasts, great meads and Marshes and plaine plowing grounds, many good rivers and harbors and no rattle snakes.[3]

The younger Winthrop was so enthusiastic about the possibilities of this land that he moved his new wife there almost immediately. Sadly, though, she did not last long in the wilderness, dying in childbirth in 1634.

Although Winthrop Jr. hastily fled the scene of his young wife's death, leaving the little settlement to develop on its own, Dudley was not discouraged by the young man's departure. He believed wholeheartedly in the enthusiastic accounts of Ipswich, just as he had swallowed the good news from the New World back in the 1620s. The new promised land seemed so close, they had better rush there quickly.

To Anne there was nothing remarkable about Dudley's behavior. She understood that it would be as hopeless to attempt to deter her father in his pursuit of a more ideal settlement as it had been for Dudley to try to stop Williams from seeking a pure kingdom of Christians. Even the fact that the little clearing in the wilderness was particularly vulnerable to Indian attacks could not prevent her father from chasing the mirage of perfection.

As usual, Dudley rolled through all obstacles to their move with the sense that he was merely doing his duty. It did not seem to cross his mind that his commitment to the spiritual health of his family might end up shortening their lives. As his children knew well, he deemed such worries beneath the notice of any truly religious person.

Anne helped the servants pack boxes and sort through clothing, repair the holes in their blankets, and heap grain into sacks, but she undoubtedly mourned the leave-taking that lay ahead. New Towne may have been tiny compared with the cities of the Old World, but the settlement had swollen to more than sixty families, and nearby Boston was even larger. Almost every month in the summer and fall a fresh boatload of immigrants arrived, many of them intent on seeking their salvation in the holy land of New England. The newly arrived settlers gave Anne news from home, and she and her family could easily order silks, spices, books, and other amenities from England.

Indeed, in the four years they had been there, Anne and her family had sown the seeds of a recognizably English life. Her brother and his wife, Mary, lived nearby, as did her sister Patience, who had married a military captain named Daniel Denison. Neighbors had become friends, and Anne had established bonds with the women in the little village since giving birth to a baby in their company. She could borrow soap or rosemary and ask anyone to watch two-year-old Samuel if she needed to go into the fields. And though, reportedly, there was a fine minister in Ipswich named Nathaniel Ward, it was always difficult to become accustomed to a new church and a new preacher.

This fresh departure could only remind Anne of the bitterness of their flight from England. To her, Dudley had never ceased to embody a kind of idealized self-denial and detachment from earthly comforts. Each time he pulled her away from what she cared about, she knew he was acting in her own best interest. But she sorrowed over the fact that she could not emulate him and felt unworthy of the blessings God had showered upon her.

The trek that lay in front of Anne and her family was forbidding enough to keep most settlers close to Boston and New Towne. But even the fact that Anne was in her second trimester of pregnancy and had a two-year-old in tow did not seem to give her or her family pause. Indeed, Anne's pregnancy was probably one of the reasons Dudley and his family were intent on leaving quickly. It was easier for a woman to travel while pregnant than after childbirth, and Dudley, impatient as always, had little interest in waiting the months it might take his daughter to recover from labor.

Even Anne's husband did not seem to raise any objections to his father-in-law's haste. An intelligent businessman, Simon could see that the resources of New Towne were becoming stretched. The earth was thin and gravelly and could not sustain the livestock of all the families who had settled there in the last three years. Farmland was limited, constrained by the town's tight boundaries. To Simon, Ipswich may have represented the utopian purity that his father-in-law craved, but it also offered him the chance to fulfill some of his chief responsibilities as a Puritan father by expanding his hold-ings. A few of his friends from college had also chosen to settle in Ipswich, and so the move would bring him into a far more conge-nial community than the one he was leaving behind in New Towne.

Although no one spoke about it, everyone knew that it was less overwhelming for the men to say good-bye to their old home than for the women. Dudley and Simon would still be able to make frequent trips back to Boston and New Towne for matters of busi-ness and government. In general, men were far more mobile than women, who were limited by the constraints of "breeding" — either they were far advanced in a pregnancy, had a new baby to nurse, or were recovering from the effects of labor or, in some cases, miscarriage. Anne and her sisters would be far more bound to Ipswich than their husbands and father — an alarming prospect given the town's remoteness.

But without complaint, the women joined the men on the path to the frontier, a track not yet wide enough for large wagons. As a result, they had had to leave behind much of their furniture — chests, tables, and their few chairs — and Anne could only hope that these reminders of her old home would soon be shipped down one of the local rivers to the new settlement. Everything else they had to carry, pack on the animals, or drag along in carts — pots, kettles, shovels, grain, dried meat and vegetables, bolsters, clothing, and books. As they walked, the young men were largely concerned with keeping the rangy cows, chickens, and pigs in order, for it would have been unthinkable to set up a new home in the wilder-ness without livestock.

Their servants traveled with them and did much of the heavy labor of the move, but there was not enough indentured help to go around. Consequently, New England servants could often be recalcitrant and were notoriously "insolent" if they felt overly taxed by their employers; no one could be sure how much one could ask of them.[4]

The Indian track rolled up and down large sloping hills the farther north they went. Fortunately, the forest that separated New Towne from Agawam was more like a park than the tangled English woods Anne and her family were used to. The undergrowth was negligible, thanks to centuries of controlled burning by the Indians. As one settler wrote, the natives' fire "consumes all the underwood and rubbish which otherwise would overgrow the country, making it unpassable, and spoil their much affected hunting. . . . In those places where the Indians inhabit, there is scarce a bush or bramble or any cumbersome underwood to be seen."[5] These repeated ground fires set by the Indians had discouraged the growth of some trees, allowing others to flourish. Hemlocks, beeches, and junipers tended to be almost absent in southern New England, whereas chestnuts, oaks, and hickories grew to enormous heights.

It must have been an extraordinary experience to walk through one of these cultivated woodlands. Even in late November, which is probably when they set out, the overall impression would have been one of imperial variety. There were long wide avenues of what Anne called "glistering" sunlight, and the soil was warm and dry. Later in life, Anne would write admiringly of the beauties of the New World trees, describing the "strength, and stature" of "a stately oak . . . whose ruffling top the clouds seemed to aspire." Even burdened as she was by her heavy unborn child and her bundles of possessions, she could not help but gaze up at the sun through "the leavie tree[s]" and confess that the more she "looked, the more [she] grew amazed."[6]

But it was dangerous to be alone in the forest. Few Englishmen had ever ventured so far into the wilderness. The path itself was barely discernible, and it was hard to trust that their Indian guides knew where they were taking them. Indeed, naive and inexperienced as she and her family were, it would have been easy for the Indians to betray them and to steal their goods, leaving them to die.

America still seemed treacherous, unknowable, and untamable to the English; it could fool you into taking a wrong turn. Winthrop often told a story about searching for firewood not far from his home and suddenly finding himself lost. He spent a terrifying night wandering in the forest, bewildered and turned around, before he found his way back in the morning. The newcomers believed that every moment they were away from a settlement they were in mortal danger, and they were not far from the mark. There were many tales of vanished explorers and settlers who had strayed too far from their villages only to encounter wolves, a sudden impenetrable snowstorm, or other dangers too awful to consider.

Anne must soon have been exhausted by the long trek. It is possible that the women had the opportunity to ride one of the few horses that had survived the journey from England, but even the respite from using their own legs would have ushered in other discomforts — stiffness, blisters, and cold. At times they walked through stands of enormous trees, at others they emerged into clearings and grassy meads, startling deer and geese that Dudley, Simon, and Anne's brother, Samuel, attempted to shoot for their dinner. When they were silent, the sounds of the land crowded in upon them. Odd birds cried, branches cracked, the wind tossed. Anne could not help but feel the enormity of the countryside around them, its vastness, its mystery, and its danger, as well as the presence of the Lord. Later she would write, "If so much excellence abide below, / How excellent is He that dwells on high?"[7]

On that first night as they built a fire and breathed in the comforting smell of smoke, Anne must have been grateful to be able to sink to the ground and hold Samuel in her lap while the servants busied themselves, clearing places on the ground to sleep and preparing the evening meal. As the night thickened and the dark closed in around them, the disconcerting howl of the wolves would have reminded everyone of their danger. The livestock was herded close to the fire, and the men posted a watch with their guns ready. Hard as it might have been to sleep under such conditions, it was important to rest. There were twenty more miles to cover.

The next day, the hills began to slope down into lower country and they began to encounter marshy lands that were reminiscent of the Sempringham fens. This meant they were drawing near the settlement, but the sun set early in late November. If they did not want to spend another night in the wilderness, they would have to push along briskly. At last, shimmers of lights, curls of smoke, and the sharp triangular pitch of well-roofed homes lay spread out before them. Thankfully, Ipswich was not another Salem. In the two years of their settlement, over fifty settlers had constructed sturdy cabins and a few "great houses." The homes were grouped together in a wide and pleasant-looking clearing that spilled down the side of one of the seven hills ringing the village.

As they strode into the town, footsore, thirsty, and weary, they were greeted by Simon's old Cambridge friends as well as by many of the General Court's officials. Surprisingly, this remote settlement was the home of eleven elected assistants, or magistrates, notably Richard Saltonstall, Nathaniel Ward, Richard Bellingham, and Samuel Symonds. All of them, like Simon and Dudley, had wanted more land and a certain distance from the politics and disturbances at the center of the colony. These men were wealthy, educated, and pious and, to Anne's delight, had substantial libraries. They prided themselves on staying in touch with the latest political and theological developments in England and the New World. No other frontier town in history had ever been populated by so many intellectuals and university colleagues. It might have taken longer than usual for roads to get built and fences erected, but the conversations and debates were undoubtedly lively. Perhaps life in Ipswich would not be as terrible as Anne had feared.

At the heart of the settlement, there was a simple meeting-house with two respected ministers installed: Nathaniel Rogers, yet another Emmanuel College alumnus, and more important, the distinguished Nathaniel Ward. Ward was famous among the Puritans because of the strength of his convictions. It was reassuring that he, too, had selected the frontier for his home. Anne and her family recognized a kindred soul in this eccentric old Elizabethan, a man with many of the same tastes and inclinations as Dudley. In fact, both men were in their fifties, elder statesmen in what was really a young man's world, since the bulk of emigrants were in their twenties and thirties.

Almost immediately, Ward warned the newcomers that despite the tidy new houses that had been constructed and the old friends they were glad to see again, they must "be carefull" whom they trusted in Ipswich. The settlement did not consist only of highly educated and wealthy colonists. There were plenty of other "ill and doubtfull persons" who spent the majority of their time "drinking and pilferinge." He complained bitterly about the "idle and profane young men, servants, and others" who seemed drawn to life on the edge of civilization.[8]

But Anne seems to have been untroubled by these ne'er-do-wells. Instead, it seems likely that she and her family took up temporary lodging in the largest house in Ipswich, since it was vacant when she and her entourage arrived. Built by John Winthrop Jr., the cottage had wind-tight walls and enough room to store their belongings until their new homes were constructed. The library alone contained hundreds of books. Certainly this young man's house would have been a far more agreeable shelter than any that Anne had enjoyed since they arrived in America.

It is likely that most of the extended Dudley clan — Dorothy, Dudley, Sarah, and Mercy; Samuel and Mary; Anne, Simon, and baby Samuel; Patience and Daniel; and their servants — spent at least part of their winter in this snug "great house." Despite the quarrels such tight lodgings might have caused, there was comfort to be had in close quarters. The gentle hills notwithstanding, Ipswich seemed forbidding when wintry nor'easters banged in from the ocean and battered the hopeful little town.

It is not clear when Anne went into her second travail, but it was probably early in the year 1636. She entered this trial without the benefit of Mrs. Hutchinson, but the attendance of the Ipswich women and her mother and sisters seems to have worked just as well. To her delight, she delivered another healthy baby — this time a little girl. In honor of her mother, Anne named the new infant Dorothy. The Dudley-Bradstreet clan must have seen the infant as an auspicious sign. Perhaps their future on the edge of both ocean and forest would be fertile and filled with joy. Of course, Anne viewed the birth in religious terms. Little Dorothy seemed evidence that God was yet again blessing her with His love.

The first months of Anne's sojourn in Ipswich were spent largely indoors, and although it was helpful to have her sisters and mother close at hand, the lack of privacy was probably challenging.[9] Her servants were helpful, but Anne had been taught that they were liable to get into trouble if not closely supervised. Although they could prepare food and draw water to wash the linen rags she used for Dorothy's diapers, many responsibilities were Anne's alone.

It was time for three-year-old Samuel to start reading his letters and to memorize the children's catechism, which was forty-five thousand words long.[10] Between household chores, therefore, Anne brought out the well-worn texts her father and mother had used to instruct her. While the kettles simmered and the women busied themselves sewing, knitting, and slicing turnips and onions, little Samuel began to mouth his letters and repeat the lessons of Puritanism:

> *A: In Adam's Fall*
> *We Sinned all.*

And

> *T: Time cuts down all*
> *Both great and small.*

And

> *X: Xerxes the great did die*
> *And so must you and I.*[11]

Somber though these words seem, they were recited by children throughout Massachusetts. Anne would have felt remiss if she had not required Samuel to memorize them and to focus on readying himself for God. Since she was also responsible for her servants' spiritual education, Anne might well have made them learn these verses, too.

AT LAST THE AIR became sweet smelling, and when the daylight hours stretched past dinner and into the evening, Anne and her sisters grew eager to move into their new homes. All winter long they must have heard the strike of axes as their husbands and hired carpenters built their houses out of white oak and pine. Generally speaking, it would have taken at least three or four months of good working weather for the new homes to be habitable.

Each house was constructed around a towering chimney. Without brick, stone, or other fireproof material, the settlers made enormous clay-daubed structures, hoping their width would help ward off the sparks that inevitably flew upward. The mouths were so wide that two young Ipswich pranksters once dropped a live calf down the tunnel of their unsuspecting neighbor's chimney, startling the man and no doubt horrifying the calf.

Most of these houses, like Anne's cottage in New Towne, had two rooms on the first floor. The hall was where most activities took place: cooking, chopping food, sewing, eating, visiting, and sleeping. There was a big four-posted bed near the fire, a cradle for the baby, and a little sleeping pallet for Samuel. Another slightly more private room might hold another bed for the servants, a spinning wheel, or stored sacks of grain for easy access. Two rooms on the second floor provided additional storage and extra sleeping quarters during the summer. In the winter, though, everyone needed to sleep near the fireplace downstairs.

The walls, floors, and ceilings were often daubed with clay to keep out the wind. Sometimes, as additional fire protection, they were whitewashed or even, as time went on, plastered. But generally the planks of new wood were left untreated, and as a result the rooms smelled bright and clean, the resin from the pine perfuming the air. Rugs and bolsters were too precious to be laid on the floor. They were saved for bed coverings and were essential for enduring the long winter nights. Some women "sanded" their floors, sprinkling a white layer of sawdust or sand from the nearby beach across the planks as yet another layer between themselves and the damp pest-ridden earth.

As Anne and her sisters' houses took shape, they started to plant their own vegetable and herb gardens, putting in the peas first and then the seedlings that they had grown indoors, near the warmth of the fire — carrots, rosemary, angelica, and lavender, to name just a few. A New England garden needed to contain not only squash, lettuces, and onions — as well as "pot herbs" (savory, sage, dill, mustard, and so on) for flavoring pasties, salads, soups, stews, and pottages — but also medicinal plants. There were no stores at which to buy the healing tinctures that might be needed and, in the earliest days of the settlements, no doctors to prescribe a treatment. Anne was responsible for the overall health of the garden and for properly selecting, harvesting, and storing each plant. If she could not find the varieties she needed in America, she would need to send for seeds from England. As one poet wrote: "Good huswives provide, ere an sickness do come."[12]

She would have known that adder's tongue was excellent for healing wounds and ground ivy for those struggling with a "ringing sound and humming noise" in their ears. Angelica could "abate the rage of lust in young persons" and was an antidote to poison, "all infections taken by evill and corrupt aire," toothache, sciatica, and gout. Anise quieted "belchings and upbraidings of the stomach" and also helped mothers produce "an abundance of milk." Artichokes eliminated "the rank smell of the arm-holes" because they produced such a "stinking urine" that the body was purged of all foul-smelling toxins. Basil was used by women in labor, as it "expelleth both birth and afterbirth." Cinquefoil treated toothache, "falling sickness," ulcers, liver disease, pleurisies and other lung complaints. There was cucumber for complexion; endive for "cool[ing]" the "heated" stomach; fennel for kidney, lung, and liver complaints; gentians for those who had fallen off a roof or to rub on the udders of cows that had been bitten by a snake.[13]

Herbs were also useful for emotional and spiritual complaints. Anne, who was prone to "droopings of the spirit," would also have been sure to plant feverfew, which was famous for "draw[ing] away . . . melancholy," but she would have known to avoid eating garlic, as this herb was considered harmful for those suffering from depression. Lavender could help when she was afflicted with too much "passion of the heart." Blessed thistle could help bolster her memory; marigolds were known to help shore up the fearful. Mint would have been especially important to Anne because it was said to stimulate the mind. Rosemary could make you feel more "lively" and lift up your heart with joy. Sage also "quickeneth the senses," enlivening those heavy in spirit, and Saint-John's-wort was useful against melancholy and madness in general.[14]

It was not enough simply to grow these plants and then harvest them. You had to know whether they should be taken raw or dried. Should they be made into a syrup or candied? Were they most effective on their own or mixed with other herbs? Did you use the root, the leaves, or the oils? How long should the tinctures rest before use? At the old manor house in Sempringham, Anne and her sisters would have learned from their mother the delicate arts of "distilling and fermenting and brewing, seething and drying, and making waters and spirits and pills and powders."[15] This made the Dudley women an excellent resource for the others because, although a few handbooks were available, most housewives relied on their neighbors to learn this lore.

For example, one recipe for "dropsie, palsie, ague, sweating, spleen, worms, and jaundice" that also strengthened "the spirits, brain, heart, liver and stomach" is typical not only for the number of steps involved but for the sheer quantity of ingredients it demanded:

> Take Balm leaves and stalks, Burnet leaves and flowers, rosemary, red sage, taragon, tormentil leaves, Rossolis, red Roses, Carnation, hyssop, Thyme, red strings that grow upon Savory, red Fennel leaves and roots, red Mints, of each one handful; bruise these herbs and put them in a great earthen pot and pour on them as much white wine as will cover them, stop them close, and let them steep for eight or nine days, then put to it cinnamon, ginger, angelica seeds, cloves and nutmegs, of each one ounce, a little saffron, sugar one pound, raisins . . . one pound, dates stoned and sliced, half a pound, the joints and legs of an old Coney, fleshy running Capon, the red flesh of the sinews of a leg of mutton, four young chickens, twelve larks, the yolks of twelve eggs, a loaf of white bread cut in sops, and two or three ounces of Mithridate or Treacle, and as much . . . Muscadine as will cover them all.[16]

Such a recipe necessitated community involvement. What if you had run out of fennel or couldn't afford to buy saffron or cinnamon off the boats from the West Indies? It was easy to lack essentials or to be unable to purchase what was needed. Wealthy, organized, and knowledgeable as they were, Anne and her family must often have played the role of town apothecary, supplying the needy with medicine and medical counsel.

But faced with the unpredictable growing conditions in America and the many unfamiliar plants, everyone had to try new concoctions and experiment with strange new roots and leaves. The risks were high. Using the wrong herb or too much of a dangerous plant could literally kill one's patient. Still, some brave souls desperately scoured the countryside for plants that might hold within the secrets of a cure.

Puritans like Anne believed that those who were truly close to God had a better chance than others at this task because they would be better able to detect God's presence in the universe. According to the seventeenth-century theory of "signatures," God had left His "handwriting," or clues to the uses of all the herbs, in telltale markings on their leaves, flowers, roots, and juice. For example, the liver-shaped leaves of liverwort meant that it would help with disorders of the liver. The bright red of poppies indicated that they were useful for diseases of the blood, or to stanch bleeding. Puritans also assumed that the cures for most afflictions lay close to home; for instance, if a man suffered from rheumatism because of "living in a damp and swampy" area, his nurse should make a tincture from the willow bark that grew nearby.[17]

Each housewife, then, had to be a detective seeking out the advice of experienced foragers and a chemist experimenting with new ingredients, at the same time that she prayed fiercely over her creations. But if preparing medical tinctures could be a confounding and even dangerous enterprise, cooking was no simple matter either.

Fireplaces were the command centers of the colonial home. They were equipped with an arsenal of cranes and hooks so that pots could be hung at varying levels. Anne first had to determine the kind of fire she needed. Low embers for custards, greater flames for roasting, a steady burn for stews. Then there were the utensils and pots to choose from. Double boilers "could be made by putting hay in the water at the bottom of a large iron kettle so a smaller kettle could rest inside." There were "spiders," or frying pans that balanced over the white ashes on their iron legs; spits for roasting foul and joints of meat; "toasting forks, long-handled dippers, earthenware dishes, glass bottles and copper kettles."[18]

One could never let down one's guard against the flames. For example, the beam that supported the entire fireplace could occasion disasters. All too often the wood closest to the fire would char and crumble, until suddenly the entire timber would shatter into pieces, falling into the flames, spilling hot kettles and spraying boiling pottages on anyone who could not jump back in time. The recipes themselves required "discretion and experience." Like anything else in Puritan culture, a woman's cooking expressed the state of her soul. Everything from her pie pastry to the ales and beers she brewed had to be touched with "grace."[19]

These exacting preparations occasioned many visits back and forth between houses. When at last it was time for Anne to set up housekeeping in her own home, Ipswich must have seemed more like a town than she had dreamed possible only a few months before. Her family had contributed four more houses to the little collection of thirty or so dwellings: Anne's home stood next to her parents', while Patience's and Samuel's houses were only a few doors farther down the lane.

Not that anyone lived far from anyone else on the frontier. Each settler was required to build his home within a half-mile radius of the meetinghouse and then as close to others as possible. Living too far out made you an automatic target for Indian attacks. Also, proximity helped keep up spirits and allowed neighbors to keep an eye on each other. In fact, too much time alone occasioned suspicions of nefarious behaviors. As Anne reflected: "The arrow of a slanderous tongue" did not simply "kill the body" but "mangles [a person] in his grave."[20] One mother instructed her newly married daughter to spend as much time as possible with her neighbors, advising her "that she might better do her work" in "another body's house" rather than spend too much time in isolation.[21] Privacy was a dangerous commodity in the wilderness: It was against the law to walk more than a mile away from the settlement by yourself.

As in New Towne, the acreage the settlers owned spread out in a radius from the huddled dwellings of the town and was used for the joint grazing of the livestock and for growing crops. Wealth was not generally measured by the size of one's house lot, since too much land could set you too far away from your neighbors for comfort. Instead it was the size and quality of one's house that denoted one's stature in the community. To create a fine home, complete with wainscoting, a snug door, and glass windows, was one way to beat back the taint of the wilderness, assert your gentle birth, and preserve your English identity. Thus it was always important to Dudley that his homes were carefully built, and Simon followed suit.

Though the little settlement felt slightly more civilized than Anne had anticipated, it was impossible to forget that they lived in a kind of war zone. Word came from the General Court that they needed to be on heightened alert; rumor had it that the nearby tribes were threatening to attack. The court declared that the settlers were required to carry a gun whenever they went outside. As the highest-ranking military man in the settlement, Patience's husband, Captain Denison, was "put in charge" of establishing a schedule of continuous watches and preparing the men in the village for battle.[22]

It was unsettling to live with this constant vigilance. Any unusual sound in the middle of the night could foreshadow a violent invasion. In this first year, Anne would find the nearness of the other houses a great comfort, but over time the cramped and huddled town began to seem somewhat stifling. Safety was sometimes a poor exchange for the narrowed eyes of her neighbors.[23]

As spring turned into summer and no attacks came, Anne and her family began to settle into the routine of life on the edge of the forest. As she and her sisters felt braver, they may have ventured beyond the common green to gather berries, herbs, and kindling. Like New Towne, Ipswich was situated on a pleasant river that curled through the settlement toward the ocean. That meant there was plentiful fresh water and fish and a convenient meeting place for the women, and their servants, especially during the long hot days of August.

If Anne or her friends felt ambitious, or if they could persuade one of their husbands to escort them with his gun, they could tramp through the grass until they reached the longest, whitest beach that anyone had ever seen. Although it was hard work to clamber over the dunes to reach the water's edge, it was worth the struggle because of the enormous clams that shot up their little spouts of water. Anne and her sisters had never seen such natural bounty, and it began to seem that God truly intended them to flourish here in this new little settlement.

CHAPTER THIRTEEN

❧❧

Such Things as Belong to Women

For if she had attended her household affairs, and such things as belong to women, and not gone out of her way and calling to meddle in such things as are proper for men . . . she had kept her wits, and might have improved them usefully and honorably in the place God had set for her.

— JOHN WINTHROP

A good name is as a precious ointment, and it is a great favour to have a good repute among good men.

— ANNE BRADSTREET, "Meditation 73"

ART IS NOT ALWAYS created under auspicious circumstances, and the years 1636–38 not only were a politically dangerous time for New England but also represented an especially demanding era in Anne's life. Yet these were the years in which Anne set her mind to starting her poetry career in a serious manner, despite the fact that her days were spent with a baby daughter and a little boy who could race into any number of threatening situations.

Her duties were seemingly endless; she had to convert her rough frontier household into a safe and civilized home, and oversee the servants, the health of the livestock, and the crops — which meant everything from monitoring the size of the pigs to making cheese and pressing cider apples — and so Anne did not have much opportunity for leisure or for time to herself. Indeed, the idea of reading, writing, or poring over literature of any kind must have seemed an unlikely dream to this young mother. But when life on the frontier felt unbearable, she would discover that it was poetry that enabled her to survive without falling into depression.

Anne's life during these years was made more difficult because Simon and Dudley were often called to Boston. By the spring of 1636 Mistress Hutchinson and her followers had become increasingly obstreperous. The woman's "apostles" were now declaring that they had no need of any minister, or any church, for that matter, except one directed by the mistress herself. One avid follower had been heard to declare that Hutchinson "preaches better Gospel than any of your black-coates that have been at the Ninneversity," and that she would "rather hear such a one that speakes from the meere motion of the spirit, without any study at all, than any of your learned Scollers, although they may be fuller of Scripture."[1]

Inflamed by Hutchinson's teachings, her followers, who now included men as well as women, had taken to the road, "gadding" to other churches in the colony to heckle the ministers during their sermons. One minister underscored how alarming their "attacks" were by writing that they "discharged" their criticisms like "pistols . . . at the face of the Preacher."[2] Simon and Dudley were simultaneously disturbed by the news and relieved that they had exiled themselves and their families from the poisonous heresies that were polluting the southern settlements, as Ipswich was too far north for any of the Hutchinsonians to attempt to visit. However, their presence at the meetings of the General Court was urgently necessary, because the new governor, Sir Henry Vane, seemed to be doing nothing to quell the disturbances Mrs. Hutchinson was creating. In fact, he was one of her biggest fans.

Not that stopping Hutchinson was an easy task. Though Winthrop, Dudley, and Simon were court officials, they were powerless to curb her actions until she committed some kind of obvious crime. She was not a minister with whom they could remonstrate, as they had Roger Williams. She was not a fellow magistrate whose disturbing ideas they could silence by stripping her of rank. As a woman, she was beyond their jurisdiction despite the fact that she was nominally lower in the hierarchy. Her footsteps were invisible, hidden as they were in the inner sanctums of females, inside birthing rooms and the chambers of her own house.[3] Thus, Dudley, Simon, and the others had no choice but to bide their time and trust in God's providence.

As fall drew into winter, Anne would have heard reports that Hutchinson and her followers were becoming increasingly odd in their behavior, asserting their own righteousness and their ability to discern who possessed God's grace and who did not. Many prominent Boston men had been drawn into her circle of admirers, and her enemies worried that her ideas had begun to contaminate the court itself and therefore the government of Massachusetts.

For Anne the immediate effect of the mounting crisis in Boston was that she was left in charge of the Ipswich household for weeks at a time. During the day this was not so terrible. There were the servants, her sisters, and her mother to help with the children and the chores. The male laborers, her brothers-in-law, and her own brother tended to the outdoor work, and she had little time to be lonely or to miss her husband.

But the nights were tedious, and these were the times she most felt the absence of the loving Simon. She had to admit to herself that she craved the "heat" of his passion, and although she knew that "my dumpish thoughts, my groans, my brakish tears / My sobs, my longing hopes, my doubting fears" could not bring him back to her, still she allowed herself to lament her loneliness. "If he love, how can he there abide?" she would cry in a future poem that was a surprising departure from the stoicism of her earlier years.[4]

And yet the nights afforded her a privacy that was otherwise impossible. At last the children and servants were asleep, and Anne found herself looking forward to the hours alone. Later she would write Simon, "The silent night's the fittest time for moan."[5] Not, of course, that the nights were ever particularly silent in Ipswich. Outside there was a veritable cacophony of knocks, rattles, and creaks that could be frightening since any sudden noise — the creak of a branch, the settling of the house, the call of an owl — could be the first sign of an Indian raid. But at least there was no chatter of human voices. No three-year-old Samuel asking the same questions over and over. No rage-filled infant demanding to be picked up and rocked and nursed. And so Anne did not give way to melancholy. Instead, during the hours that she "curtailed from her sleep," she began to spill out her ideas, arguments, and visions in ambitious and fiercely opinionated verse.[6] With only a stick of pine tar that sputtered and filled the room with its dim light, and as baby Dorothy nestled in her little cradle and Samuel lay curled on the big bolster that served as the family bed, Anne turned back to her first love, poetry.

Although she never mentioned Hutchinson's name in her work, it would have been impossible not to have the woman on her mind. Anne's family was steeped in the political disaster that was clearly building toward a crisis. Of more personal concern to Anne, the Hutchinson dilemma had directed everyone's attention more pointedly than ever to the question of the proper role for women in society and what should be done to those who had stepped out of bounds. The debate over the limits that should be placed on female behavior was alarmingly linked to the problem of being a woman and setting pen to paper. Anne had heard cautionary tales such as Winthrop's declaration that one writing woman had committed suicide by throwing herself down a well because she had addled her wits by reading and thinking too much. Women were too frail in both body and mind to engage in much intellectual activity, or so most people believed, and Mistress Hutchinson was the proof. Her brain, Hutchinson's male critics argued, was clearly too weak to discern between Satan's blandishments and the word of God.

This was a terrible thought, but it was the one Anne had to confront if she were to move forward with her own writing life. That the "Scriptured," older Hutchinson could be tricked by the devil meant that Anne herself could be deluded, since it was clearly no easy matter for a "foolish woman" to stave off Satan. Females, the Reverend Thomas Weld thundered in one of his texts criticizing Hutchinson, were generally "weaker to resist" temptation than men, as they were "more flexible, tender, and ready to yeeld."[7]

Thus if the brilliant and learned Hutchinson was an "Eve" who had poisoned the minds of the Bostonian Adams with her tempting words, if she had misled the women under her care and could not perceive the difference between good and evil, truth and falsehood, and if the leaders whom Anne admired deemed Hutchinson an "American Jezabel," how could Anne dare to write even one word?[8]

She did not want to raise the ire of the government like Hutchinson had, or fall into the snares of evil. According to the magistrates, Hutchinson had pitted wives against husbands and turned households upside down. Reverend Weld accused Hutchinson of purposely raising "disturbances, divisions, contentions . . . among us, both in Church and State, and in families, setting division betwixt husband and wife."[9] The connection Weld made between civic unrest and familial discord was typical of the Puritan point of view; to set a wife above a husband was a challenge to the hierarchy as a whole. Hutchinson's actions undermined not only individual families but the entire colony as well.

On the other hand, it was also conceivable that Anne harbored some admiration for Hutchinson and was inspired by her courage. Perhaps she secretly disagreed with Dudley and Simon's assessment of the older woman. But even if this was the case, it was still dangerous for Anne to begin writing. With all of the rumors afoot, she could easily become the next target of wrath. As one critic of Hutchinson declared, it was "phantasticall madnesse" to believe that "silly Women laden with diverse lusts" could ever be held "in

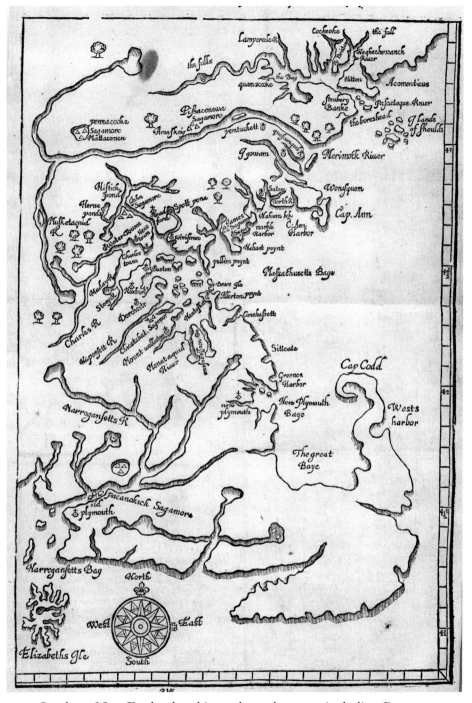

Southern New England and its early settlements, including Boston.
Frontispiece map in William Wood, *New Englands Prospect*, 2d ed.
(London, 1635). *(Massachusetts Historical Society)*

Woodcut from Foxe's Book of Martyrs, "A lamentable spectacle of three women, with a sillie infant brasting out of the mothers wombe, being first taken out of the fire, and cast in againe, and so all burned together in the Isle of Garnsey, 1556, July 18." *(Annenberg Rare Book & Manuscript Library, University of Pennsylvania)*

Replica of *The Arbella*, built in 1930 to honor the 300th anniversary of the settlers' arrival. *(Jim McAllister)*

Replica of the simple dwellings of the early settlers.
Pioneer Village, Salem, Massachusetts. *(Jim McAllister)*

An example of the kind of house the Bradstreets might have lived in.
Jackson House (1664), Portsmouth, New Hampshire. *(The Halliday Historic Photograph Co., Historic New England/SPNEA)*

A typical seventeenth-century New England hearth. Old Whipple House kitchen, Ipswich, Massachusetts. *(Photograph by Mary H. Northend, Historic New England/SPNEA)*

Replica of the interior of a colonial house. These are some of the items a Puritan woman might have had in her kitchen. Pioneer Village, Salem, Massachusetts. *(Jim McAllister)*

For my deare sonne
Simon Bradstreet

Parents perpetuate their liues in their posterity, and their maners in their imitation Children do naturally rather follow the failings then the vertues of their predecessors, but f am perswaded better things of you once desired me to leaue some thing for you in writing that you might look vpon when you should see me no more, f could think of nothing more fit for you nor of more ease to my selfe then these short meditations following, such as they are bequeath to you, small legacys are accept by true friends much more, by dutyfull children, f haue avoyded in recching vpon others conception becaufe f would leaue nothing

2.
but myne owne, though in value they fall short of all in this kinde yet f presume they will be better prisd by you, for the Authors Sake. the lord blesse you wth grace heer and crown you wth glory heerafter, that f may meet you wth reioyceing at that great day of appearing, wch is the continuall prayer, of
your affectionate
mother AB
March 20
1664

Dedication page of Anne Bradstreet's autobiography, in her own handwriting. *(Stevens Memorial Library)*

Simon Bradstreet circa 1680. *(Boston Athenaeum)*

THE
TENTH MUSE

Lately fprung up in AMERICA.

OR

Severall Poems, compiled
with great variety of VVit
and Learning, full of delight.
Wherein efpecially is contained a com-
pleat difcourfe and defcription of

The Four
- Elements,
- Conftitutions,
- Ages of Man,
- Seafons of the Year.

Together with an Exact Epitomie of
the Four Monaichies, viz.

The
- Affyrian,
- Perfian,
- Grecian,
- Roman.

Alfo a Dialogue between Old England and
New, concerning the late troubles.

With divers other pleafant and ferious Poems.

By a Gentlewoman in thofe parts.

Printed at London for Stephen Bowtell at the figne cf the
Bible in Popes Head-Alley. 1650.

Title page, *The Tenth Muse. (Stevens Memorial Library)*

Anne Bradstreet, detail from a window in St. Botolph's Church, Boston, Lincolnshire, circa 1950. *(Miriam W. Butts)*

Memorial Stone to Anne Bradstreet, erected September 12, 2000, in commemoration of the 350th anniversary of the publication of *The Tenth Muse*, North Andover, Massachusetts. *(Miriam W. Butts)*

Anne Dudley
Bradstreet

1612 — 1672

Mirror of Her Age, Glory of her Sex,
whose Heaven-born-Soul
leaving its earthly Shrine,
chose its native home, and
was taken to its Rest,
upon 16th Sept. 1672
John Norton Jr. 1672

higher esteeme" than men, especially "those honored of Christ, indued with power and authority from him to Preach."[10] At the very least, it could be seen as vanity for Anne to write her words on the precious parchment her family hoarded for use on special occasions.

God-fearing and devout, during these late nights Anne had to stare down her own belief in her weakness, as well as her fears of being attacked, to begin to commit her thoughts to parchment. Though she had never heard of any other woman attempting such a feat, perhaps the memory of her father's voice, all those years ago in the paneled rooms of Sempringham, gave her courage. As it was, she prayed that each line she formed would be in the service of the Lord. If Hutchinson's preaching was destroying New England, then Anne was determined to pen righteous words on its behalf, to help save the colony from the dissension, discord, and factional fighting that now plagued it. Perhaps she could also rescue the reputation of women, proving that they were capable of achieving work of Puritan merit.

But what did writing in the name of God mean? To begin with it meant stealth. Anne's poetry had to be a covert activity because of the criticism she would face if anyone hostile to the idea of writing women found out. Her father supported her efforts right from the beginning, as did the rest of her family, but every day her neighbors flooded her home, borrowing supplies, exchanging recipes, helping her sew hems, hull strawberries, or knead the dough for bread. This was not the time for any female to disclose her ambitions as a writer or a thinker no matter how vividly she expressed her belief in Puritan orthodoxy.

So, during the day, Anne went about her duties as a Puritan wife and mother. On Sundays and Thursdays, whether it was raining, blowing sleet, or so blazing hot that her skirts clung to her clammy legs, Anne, like all Ipswich inhabitants, attended religious services in the little meetinghouse down the dirt track from her home. Undoubtedly she rejoiced that she was able to hear the word of God preached by such a learned man as Nathaniel Ward. But there were some troubling aspects to his sermons as well.

In support of the colony's ministers and magistrates, who were faced with the "boldness" of Hutchinson and her followers, Ward railed against the effrontery of women in general and enjoined his congregation, especially the ladies, to avoid the sin of pride. Using humor and ridicule, he emphasized the terrible danger of allowing women to get out of hand. Few things were more dangerous than the "loose tongued Liberty" of females.[11]

Ward also hated the diversity of beliefs, or "poly-piety," that was springing up in New England thanks to individuals like Anne Hutchinson. He reserved a good deal of his biting sarcasm for denigrating what he called "universall Toleration," as such permissiveness would allow the ungodly the right to express their outrageous and destructive opinions.[12] Ward's sermons could only reinforce Anne's anxieties about toeing the line. People would read her words more suspiciously than those of a man, and even male Puritan writers had to stand up to the ministers' scrutiny: Were their beliefs in keeping with orthodox opinion or not?

Between Hutchinson's notoriety and Ward's misogyny, it may have seemed to this twenty-four-year-old woman that the curtains were drawing closed on her aspirations as a female intellectual. She could not fully disagree with Ward's attacks on the frivolity of women. She had once resisted her father's dream of a pilgrimage to America, for reasons Ward would have deemed shallow if he knew. On a deeper level, she would later record that her "flesh" and her "spirit" were often at war, with her "fleshy" lusts all too frequently triumphing over her soul's desire to spurn material concerns.[13] She often felt far away from God, and so probably the minister was right: There was nothing more frail than a woman. But what Anne did not realize was that Ward valued nothing more than an inquiring mind and a pious soul, even if these were located inside a female body.

Ward was a writer with a huge library of books, and there was little chance that Anne could let such a resource go untapped in her new wilderness home. Books were prized possessions, and the settlers passed them around to one another in order to defray the costs of importing new volumes to America. Given Anne's insatiable hunger for reading and for knowledge in all of its various forms, from science to history, it was likely that she had already read the books her father and husband had brought to Ipswich. She also probably had access to John Winthrop Jr.'s collection. But with her father and husband away so frequently, it was likely she longed to have someone to talk to about the heavy tomes of history and theology. Since she was used to learning from men, and was well equipped to discuss religion, politics, and literature with Ward, in hindsight it seems inevitable that this young woman parishioner and her minister would join forces.

How these two intellectuals actually began to meet and talk is unknown. Perhaps Anne summoned up her nerve and sought him out. Or possibly they fell into conversation after services when Simon was away. Whatever prompted them to find each other, it was a fruitful and inspirational relationship for both. Suffering from ill health and often lonely, having been a widower for twelve long years, at age fifty-six Ward loved nothing more than intelligent conversation. As a young man, he had immersed himself in the most glamorous circles, practicing law in Europe, where he spent most of his time in the royal court of Heidelberg, conversing with princes and princesses. He came to Puritanism relatively late in life and did not become a minister until he was in his thirties. He had always been famous for his wit, and he once said, "I have only two comforts to live upon: the one is in the perfections of Christ; the other is in the imperfections of Christians."[14]

Of course, the Ipswich minister was also a very pious man. Engraved above his mantle were the Latin words SOBRIE, JUSTE, PIE, LAETE (prudently, justly, piously, and gladly).[15] To Ward, laughter and joy were as important to his religion as these more sober qualities, and it must have been far more pleasant to talk to a pretty young woman who looked at him admiringly than to the hoary old men who came by occasionally to quarrel. Anne, too, undoubtedly felt fortunate to listen to Ward, who, when he pulled out all the stops, was irresistibly charming.

Ward's passionate engagement with the unfolding political events back in England and his vast knowledge of English law and history were particularly compelling. To his credit, as the months passed, Ward grew increasingly impressed with Anne's intelligence, despite his prejudices against women. Indeed, over the years his admiration would grow to such an extent that he would lend his support to the publication of Anne's verse, signing his name to an important introductory poem. Of course, he still managed to criticize women in general even as he praised his female disciple. "It half revives my chill frost-bitten blood, / To see a woman once do ought that's good," he grumbled.[16]

Despite the old minister's gruff exterior, to Anne it was men like him who made living in Ipswich bearable; her education could continue. In fact, over the next years she would immerse herself in her studies with an astonishing energy, given the demands of the rest of her life. What better way to contradict the pernicious events in Boston than to be reading English history, Scripture, science, and theology? Even as Hutchinson's prominence was giving powerful and intelligent women a bad name, Anne was equipping herself with more ammunition to write learned poetry, a territory that was considered exclusively male. Before long she would be fueling her work with an encyclopedic knowledge that would surpass that of most of her male contemporaries.

As for Ward, he basked in Anne's admiration, and it was during the most intense period of their intimacy that he wrote his two most important works, a body of laws for the colony and his best-seller, *The Simple Cobbler of Aggawam in America*, a compilation of aphorisms and pious sermons that Puritans everywhere devoured. Anne's intelligence astounded Ward, and he was beginning to see that the education of women was so urgent an aspect of life in the New World that he would allude to this idea in his drafts of the laws for New England and in his sermons.[17]

Anne must have been thrilled to find that he respected her ideas. The two lonely writers needed each other; they fostered each other's creativity. Indeed, it seems likely that neither Anne nor

Ward could have produced such important work during this period without the sustaining force of their relationship.

And so if Simon was kept away from Ipswich by snow, ice, and treacherous roads, Anne's loneliness seemed less oppressive now. She had found herself a companion far more literary than her husband and more attuned to her work. This was a heady new experience; though Dudley had prized her acumen, he had never rid himself of his authoritarian stance as her father.

Not that Anne ever lost sight of her other duties. That Dudley and the rest of Ipswich did not criticize Anne for spending so much time alone with the crusty old minister and lavishing her energy on scholarship was a testimony to how well she played her part. She was clearly a pious, devoted mother and showed no inclination to follow in Anne Hutchinson's footsteps by flaunting her erudition in public. And no one could suspect Ward of impropriety. He was a man who took religion too seriously to be challenged. At any rate, probably no one realized how close a friendship was developing between the young woman and older man; Ward offered Anne the brilliant conversation and political insight that her husband could not, and she undoubtedly gave him that "gladness" of heart which he believed was an intrinsic part of daily living.

FINALLY, IN THE FALL OF 1636, after the heat of the first August in Ipswich had passed, news came to Anne and her family that Boston had reached a boiling point. Hutchinson's followers had tried to push the Boston church into accepting her brother-in-law, John Wheelwright, as one of its appointed ministers. Although Winthrop, as a member of the church, had used all of his political pull to prevent the appointment and Wheelwright had retreated to Maine, the congregation muttered and complained, and the town itself was up in arms. Even Cotton seemed moved by Hutchinson, although ultimately he would join his fellow ministers and condemn her with vehemence.

Sulkily, the Bostonians declared that they had been victimized by the colonial establishment. Although there were a few dissenting voices, most people believed that they were unique among the other settlements. What they meant, of course, was that they were more holy and more "chosen" than any of the other towns. If the leaders of this movement were not squelched soon, Winthrop feared Boston would try to head out on her own and split off from the rest of Massachusetts, ruining the founders' idea of a unified Puritan New England and demoralizing the other communities.

By January 1637 the colony had deteriorated into two enemy factions: Boston versus everyone else. The General Court ordered a day of fasting and penitence to try to resolve the differences between the outraged leaders of each group. But on this day of supposed reconciliation, Wheelwright returned from Maine to preach a sermon announcing that those who opposed Hutchinson's ideas were "enemies . . . to Christ," and that those who were truly pious "must kill them with the worde of the Lorde."[18] Ominous though this declaration was, Wheelwright did not mean that the people of Boston should actually slay their opponents, but he did intend to foment protest against the magistrates' power.

That fall, the synod of Massachusetts ministers met and for twenty-four days carved out what they believed were the defining attributes of Puritan orthodoxy to help them take a united stand against Hutchinson and her followers. The only minister who disagreed with their tenets was Wheelwright, and this sealed his fate. In November the General Court banished Mistress Hutchinson's brother-in-law for refusing to surrender his "heresies." Momentous though this decree was, everyone knew that Wheelwright's exile was only a prelude to the real showdown. It was time for the magistrates to confront Mistress Hutchinson. Desperately they trumped up some claims against her.

First they charged her with threatening the social system of the colony. This made sense to Hutchinson's accusers, since the familial, legal, and theological lives of the settlers were so intertwined. In the eyes of Dudley, Simon, and their colleagues, Hutchinson had not only betrayed the magistrates of the colony by "countenancing and encouraging" those who had plotted against the New England government, but she had also broken the fifth commandment, dishonoring the settlement's officials, who were "the parents" of the colony; Hutchinson had stepped out of bounds as a "child" of New England.

The severity of this charge is perhaps not readily apparent; but in New England, children could face legal action for disobedience to their parents if anyone observed their behavior. When rebellious sons and daughters had reached the age of sixteen, they could face the death penalty simply for cursing or hitting a parent. Although no child was ever executed, plenty were prosecuted for insubordination. One young man, for example, was convicted for calling his father a "Liar & Drunkard & holding up [his] fist against him," and a girl was dragged into court for shouting at her mother, "a pockes of the devill what ayles this madd woman."[19]

The court's stance was similar on conflicts between husbands and wives. A woman's defiance of her husband was not a purely personal matter but a legal offense. At the time of the Hutchinson trial, husbands in New England still possessed the English legal right of "correction" of their wives, that is, using corporal punishment to enforce obedience. In a dramatic move, only three years later, the Massachusetts court would claim this right for itself, declaring that "if there be any just cause of correction complaint" it should "be made to Authorities assembled in some Court," so that the magistrates would become, in effect, not only parents of the settlers but the symbolic "husbands" of Massachusetts wives.[20]

The second charge against Hutchinson was even more convoluted than the first. Since the court could not claim that she had committed any criminal act, the magistrates could only fall back on the accusation that she had "entertained" seditious individuals. The third accusation was perhaps the most serious of all, as it was based on Hutchinson's claims against the ministers. In Massachusetts Bay you were not allowed to insult the colony's preachers or undermine their authority in any way. Hutchinson had accused them of preaching the erroneous "covenant of works": that you could get to heaven by virtue of your own efforts. A truly pious individual understood that only through God's grace could you be saved, and so Hutchinson's accusations were considered shockingly libelous.

As the days grew bitter and short, both sides prepared for the trial. Simon and Dudley removed to New Towne, where business ground to a halt as deputies and delegates piled into the rectangular meeting-house, the only structure big enough to hold such a gathering. For Anne, who was well advanced in her third pregnancy, it was out of the question to travel such a long distance simply to be a spectator. And she was not alone. For most women living in remote towns, it must have been frustrating to know that such momentous events were occurring out of their immediate reach. They would have to wait for the men to return home to tell them what had happened.

It would be difficult, though, for most observers, including Simon and Dudley, to describe with any real accuracy the drama to come or the woman at its center. Dudley declared, "Mistress Hutchinson, from that time she came, hath made a disturbance."[21] Winthrop, who had been reelected governor that spring, now called Mistress Hutchinson "the breeder and nourisher of all these distempers," illustrating his conviction that she was a woman gone wrong, having misused her maternal abilities so grievously.[22]

On that opening day in November, however, Mrs. Hutchinson appeared fearless and easily overturned the magistrates' reasoning with her own biblical references. When Winthrop demanded to know the reason behind the large meetings at her house, she asked with cutting politeness, "May not I entertain them that fear the Lord because my parents will not give me leave?"[23] Understanding the system in which she lived, Hutchinson did not contest the paternal authority of the court directly. Instead, her use of the double negative suggested that there was a higher law than that of the court and she was simply adhering to God's commandments.

Her flustered listeners could not come up with a scriptural refutation of her point, and so Winthrop attempted to smooth this over by exclaiming, "We do not mean to discourse [argue] with those of your sex," in the hopes that a reminder of her subordinate status as a woman would lessen the power of her logic. Still, her point hung in the air, unrefuted.[24]

Winthrop's spluttering retort notwithstanding, this was exactly what the trial was predicated on, formal and public debate with a female — a radical event, since women were by definition not meant to inhabit the realm of governmental or church authority. The very proceedings, then, threatened to upset colonial definitions of the proper code of behavior, particularly if the magistrates did not win.[25]

The pressure was on for both sides, therefore, although there was little chance that the magistrates would lose their case, since they significantly outnumbered the Boston contingent of Hutchinson supporters. Still, the Bostonians were powerful and vociferous and would certainly kick up even more chaos if they felt that injustice had been perpetrated. As for Anne Hutchinson, she knew she was fighting not only for her dignity and integrity but for her life. The prospect of exile hung in the air like a death sentence.

With such high stakes, the opponents were vigilantly attuned to any sign of weakness on the part of the other. Of course, the magistrates had the advantage because they could spell each other and lend their colleagues moral support, whereas the forty-six-year-old Hutchinson stood in isolation, facing them on her own and arguing her case out of sheer willpower, intelligence, and faith. Her strength was all the more astonishing as she was pregnant and would, in fact, collapse at the end of this first day of questioning.

As the trial ensued, it seemed she had carefully prepared her arguments before the trial, or else she was so conversant with the Bible that her answers flew off the tip of her tongue. She rarely hesitated, and spoke quickly, without the need to consult notes. For example, when the court asked her to justify the meetings at her house, she replied promptly and used the Bible to support her actions, citing Titus 2:3–5, which spoke of the godliness of elder women preaching to younger ones, and a story in Acts, where a godly woman named Priscilla, accompanied by her husband, instructed a young man in the ways of Christ.

The court could not refute these passages, and Winthrop could only bluster angrily: "You show us not a rule." Hutchinson responded with admirable calm, "I have given you two places of Scripture." To this the discomfited governor exclaimed, "But neither of them will suit your practise." With what might have been an audible snort, Hutchinson said in a mockery of their literal mindedness, "Must I show my name written therein?"[26]

But although the mistress was triumphing in this battle of wits, her successes were only further alienating her enemies. Each of her competent references to Scripture and her very confidence only made it more evident to her enemies that she was trespassing in male territory. She should not be so well versed. She should not be so adept at debate. Clearly she was attempting to usurp the role of the ministers — a direct assault on the powers of the court. Thus the magistrates ended the first day's arguments by growling, "We see no rule of God for [your behavior], we see not that any should have authority to set up any other exercises besides what authority hath already set up, and so what hurt comes of this you will be guilty of and we for suffering you."[27]

The real issue at hand (one that also applied to Anne Bradstreet and her writerly ambitions) was how much room there was in New England for two systems: a male and a female one. Convinced of her own righteousness and impelled, apparently, to teach those who came to her door, Hutchinson had had no alternative but to operate outside the existing conventions. She could not stand up and preach in church, so she preached in her own home, sitting in her own chair. Now, on the first day of the trial, the magistrates had drawn the line. Theirs was the only acceptable authority, and any "preaching," "prophesying," or teaching other than that by court-sponsored individuals — the ministers — was prohibited.

On the second day of the trial, the magistrates confronted Mistress Hutchinson with her "insults" to the preachers. Attacking the colony's officially sanctioned ministers amounted to blasphemy and even sedition. Hutchinson remained undaunted and responded by demanding that each preacher swear to the truth of his statements.

This raised the ante of the debate, and the ministers balked. If any of them swore and then could be proved wrong, they would be guilty not only of lying under oath but also of violating the law of God.[28]

Into this breach strode John Cotton, Hutchinson's original advocate. He declared that Hutchinson had never, as far as he recalled, definitively claimed that the other ministers were in error or "under a covenant of works." The Bostonians in the audience must have uttered a silent cheer at this point, because the case against Hutchinson was beginning to unravel. That she had supported those who were seditious — that is, her brother-in-law — was not a serious enough charge to condemn her, and now it seemed that her most serious offense — libel against the ministers — could not be proven by the court.

Hutchinson capitalized on this moment by asserting that the ministers had no right to testify against her anyway, as they had gained their information in a "private" session with her. She said that she had assumed that her interviews with each preacher were confidential, as was the general rule in New England.

This was a disturbing new development in the case, as no one in the colony relished the idea of ministers publicizing the information they gained under the minister-congregant pact of confidentiality. For a moment it appeared that Hutchinson would be victorious — and perhaps she would have been if she had not suddenly stepped forward: God had spoken directly to her, she cried. Her brilliance in the court was because the Lord had "put" the scriptural passages she had cited into her mind. In fact, she declared that He spoke with "the voice of his spirit to my soul" in precisely the same way that he had spoken to Abraham, by an "immediate revelation."[29]

Even Cotton could not stand by her now. Puritans believed that God no longer communicated directly to His flock. The age of revelation was over. Hutchinson had uttered shocking words that proved she was in the grip of the devil. The court hastily sentenced exile, eager to separate themselves from this sinner as quickly as possible. Winthrop rejoiced that it was from "her own mouth" that her guilt was determined.[30] Even Hutchinson's supporters were aghast at her declaration that she was a prophet and had experienced miracles on the scale of the biblical patriarchs.

At this point, most of Hutchinson's followers fell away, although some of the most loyal adherents struggled to defend her for a few more months. Her civil trial was at an end, although she still had to face a church trial the following March. When she presented herself at these proceedings, she seemed a broken woman. Pregnant, ill, and exhausted, she publicly recanted, but the ministers still voted to excommunicate her. An apologetic, weakened Hutchinson was still a dangerous woman. They did not want her near their congregants.

After this rather anticlimactic finale, all resistance to the court's edict appeared to die. The Boston church returned to the fold of the other New England congregations, and Boston residents even seemed to make peace with their neighbor and governor, Winthrop, who was glad that they no longer regarded him as "their greatest enem[y]." He wrote, "The Lord brought about the hearts of all the people to love and esteem [Him and their pastor] more than ever before, and the church was saved from ruin beyond all expectation."[31]

That spring the magistrates forced Hutchinson, her husband, and her children out of the Bay colony and into the wilds of the unknown territories. The Hutchinsons found refuge in Rhode Island and later moved on to New York. For all the settlers, including Anne and her neighbors in Ipswich, it seemed that quiet might now return to Massachusetts Bay. They had cleansed the colony. Even the formidable John Cotton was reprimanded for his role in supporting Anne Hutchinson, and he hastily distanced himself from the former superstar. The Hutchinson trial had made it clear that in order to survive in Massachusetts Bay, you had to abide by the rules. There was no room for renegades.[32]

CHAPTER FOURTEEN

Old England and New

HUTCHINSON'S METEORIC CRASH rang a warning bell to all ambitious women in New England. You had to toe the theological line if you wanted to survive, and you could not stray from your prescribed role as a female in Puritan society. If a woman dared to write verse, therefore, she would have to compose lines that would not compromise her station in life. She would have to assume the role of an obedient wife and daughter, not a preacher, and certainly not a prophet.

It was a dangerous business, then, that Anne had embarked on in the midnight hours. Although she would never condone Hutchinson's actions, she would never condemn them either. Whether for good or evil, Hutchinson was an example of the kind of power an intelligent female could wield.

During the turmoil of this period, Anne wrote her second poem, "An Elegy upon That Honorable and Renowned Knight Sir Philip Sidney," a work obsessed with the idea of women and power. There was an avalanche of ambition behind this poem. The great English poet had been dead for almost two generations and held little claim on the consciousness of those who were not literary aspirants. But to Anne, Sidney was an important avenue toward being considered a poet herself. She knew that the most famous poet of the last generation, Edmund Spenser, had elegized Sidney and thereby claimed the mantle of the greatest living English poet for himself. In the same way, Keats would immortalize Homer, Shelley would immortalize Milton, and Eliot would link himself to the Metaphysicals. One day Anne herself would be claimed by the great American poet John Berryman as his stepping-stone to greatness in his 1951 poem "Homage to Mistress Bradstreet."

If you were a male aspirant to the laurels of poetic fame, you wrote elegies to the dead poets you admired as a way of asserting your own literary identity. As far as Sidney was concerned, Anne had perhaps more right than any other living writer to invoke the legacy of her predecessor, since Dudley had always told her she was related to the celebrated Sidney by blood.

With her "Elegy," therefore, Anne claimed the right to be considered the next great English poet, although for Anne to aspire to any kind of poetic fame was a profoundly ambitious dream. The English reading public loved poetry. From Shakespeare to Herrick, from Quarles to Milton, they devoured new books of verse as though they were starving for meter and rhyme, regarding the best collections as page-turners as well as instructive examples in beauty and faith. Poets were important people and writing poetry was regarded as a supremely impressive vocation, but, of course, it was a vocation reserved entirely for men. Hutchinson had demonstrated the trouble women could get into if they trespassed into male territory, and so, whether or not Anne made a conscious decision to distance herself from Hutchinson's boldness, she took an entirely different approach from the older woman; she masked her ambition behind twenty-two lines of apparent self-denunciation.

She imagined that the nine classical Muses of art and literature who lived on Mount Parnassus, according to Greek mythology "took from me the scribbling pen I had . . . And drave me from Parnassus in a rage."[1] In Anne's version of the Muses, the famous damsels of inspiration do not have it in them to help another woman and are infuriated by the female poet's presumption.

But Anne counters this apparent blow to her skill by asking the reader to "wonder not if I no better sped."[2] On first reading, she seems to mean we should not be surprised that her efforts were not very successful. But according to Puritan theology, it was only logical that the Muses would kick a Christian poet off the Greek mountain. As a Puritan poet, Anne believed she was destined to travel another sort of path with a different source of inspiration, the Holy Ghost, or the Muse of the Christian God.

That she was anxious about the idea of venturing into the male literary world was still evident three years later when she would write a poem on another one of her literary heroes, Du Bartas, who had dazzled her back in Sempringham. Again she considered the theme of female inadequacy compared with the prowess of men, asking the same implicit question: Was it possible for a woman writer to achieve any kind of excellence?

At first it seems that she has acquiesced in this poem and is asserting that only men can be great poets. Never, Anne writes, could she aspire to such heights as Du Bartas, the pinnacle of piety, learning, and skill. She bemoans her "faltering tongue"; her muse is "a child" who "finds too soon his want of eloquence"; she is "weak brained," "sightless," and "mute." If only, she laments, she could have his "pen" (and, earthy woman that she was, she would have enjoyed the play on the word *penis*). It is not until the final line of the poem that she makes her own claim for "Fame." Flawed though she is, it is she who will resuscitate the male writer from death with her words. She ends the poem with the proud statement, "He is revived."[3] By whom? By Anne Bradstreet, of course.

For Anne the problem of poetic greatness and lineage was far more complicated than for her male counterparts: Where could a woman fit into the tidy line of male inheritance? Two years later, in

1643, Anne would at last offer her answer by turning to her father's great heroine, Elizabeth I, the warrior queen.

> *Now say, have women worth? Or have they none?*
> *Or had they some, but with our Queen, is't gone?*
> *Nay masculines, you have thus taxed us long,*
> *But she though dead, will vindicate our wrong.*
> *Let such as say our sex is void of reason,*
> *Know tis a slander now but once was treason.*[4]

Anne was becoming bolder. She had dropped the self-deprecation of the two earlier tributes and, with the Hutchinson debacle still in recent memory, declared that Elizabeth was not just equal to male rulers but was in fact the "pattern of kings." "Was ever people better ruled than hers?" she demanded. "Did ever wealth in England more abound?" Anne was proud that Elizabeth was a fighting queen, one who had "wracked," "sacked," and "sunk" the Spanish Armada. She had put on armor and commanded the troops at Tilbury like an "Amazon."[5]

To Anne, a woman, not a man, was an example of the glory of England, so it was not surprising that she painted Elizabeth as a kind of messianic symbol. If a woman could rule over men, if the weak could triumph over the strong, then anything, Anne implied, was possible. But sadly, this wondrous "Phoenix" was gone; never would the queen return until "the heaven's great revolution." Anne ended the poem with a fantastic vision of "many worlds," where the fabulous could become true: Elizabeth would be resurrected; her "living virtues [would] speak"; and, amazingly, she would shine as an example for men to follow.[6] It would be a glorious reversal of Anne's real-world hierarchy, where men were the perennial leaders and women the inevitable, eternal followers.

Given the dangers, politically speaking, of a woman's being so outspoken, these were especially inflammatory words. Not that Anne meant to retroactively support the Hutchinson "revolution" that had almost taken place. But the raft of misogynist complaints that had been unleashed in response to the Hutchinson crisis must have troubled her. She knew better, however, than to declare her ideas out loud. Only under the cover of night, while the town slept, did she venture to assert her own frank arguments.

These writing times were few and far between, as Anne was often too exhausted to stay up after the children were asleep. If it was hard for anyone to find time alone in colonial New England, it was doubly hard for a young mother; by the time she had written the poem to Elizabeth, Anne had borne five children. To embark on a journey as a writer was such an implausible undertaking that even she must have sometimes wondered why she spent her energy this way.

But each of her early poems was not only an attempt to sort through the difficulties she experienced as a woman writer but also her response to the hardship of her life. When it began to leak out that she was composing poetry in the dead of night, she reported the whispers of those who believed that she was overstepping her place, "I am obnoxious to each carping tongue / Who says my hand a needle better fits."[7]

Buoyed by the education she had received as a child as well as by her father's belief in her poetic vocation, she felt she could best serve the colony through her literary efforts. She also seemed to understand that to survive her life in the wilderness, she had to focus on her intellectual well-being as well as the exigencies of daily life. She had more success than her contemporary in walking this thin line. Anne would be praised for maintaining "her exact diligence in her place," while Hutchinson would be pilloried for generations for her various trespasses.[8]

In fact, ironically, Mistress Hutchinson's downfall ushered in the most fertile decade of Anne Bradstreet's life — fertile in every sense of the word. From 1638 to 1648, Anne wrote more than six thousand lines of poetry, more than almost any other English writer on either side of the Atlantic composed in an entire lifetime. For most of this time, she was either pregnant, recovering from childbirth, or nursing an infant, establishing herself as a woman blessed by God, the highest commendation a New England Puritan mother could receive.[9] Once Anne had settled into the rhythm of bearing children, babies seemed to stimulate her work.

Perhaps this was because Anne had found reliable servants to help her take care of the house and to tend the little ones, but it was also probably no accident that these two kinds of creative activities went hand in hand for her. Rather than viewing children as an obstacle to a productive working life, Puritan parents saw each child as an asset to the family's blessings and wealth. The more hands, the lighter the labor; the more healthy Puritan children who came of age in America, the greater the chances of longevity for the English colony, and so it was everyone's responsibility to have as many children as possible and to instruct them in the ways of Puritanism. To Anne, each new baby was also an incentive to be a good pious mother, and her poetry became part of her attempt to teach her children the tenets of her religion.

In 1638, just months after Mrs. Hutchinson's exile, Anne bore her third baby, a healthy little girl. Poor Mrs. Hutchinson, however, had suffered a catastrophe. Driven out of Boston when she was pregnant and forced to give birth in the wilderness, she had produced a horribly damaged infant, or so rumors claimed. Some people even whispered that Hutchinson's child was not human but a demon fathered by Satan.

That Hutchinson had borne such a deformity was a dreadful testimony to her sinful nature, according to the stern beliefs of New Englanders. To them a woman's womb proved her virtue and piety or demonstrated her hypocrisies. Before her trial, Hutchinson had risen to power in part because she was seen as a virtuous mother. After her guilt was proven, it fit Puritan logic that she would no longer be favored by God. If each child was a physical manifestation of the mother's spiritual condition, then, as the minister Thomas Weld argued, "See how the wisdome of God fitted this judgement to her [Hutchinson's] sinne every way, for looke as she had vented misshapen opinions, so she must bring forth deformed monsters."[10]

Anne could take heart, therefore, that just after she had written her first serious poem, the elegy to Sidney, her new baby had arrived without blemishes. This had to mean that her work was not tainted by sin; she was pure of heart. Throughout Anne's writing life this connection between childbirth and the condition of her soul would be a powerful theme. Any doubts she had about her poetry would be magnified with each pregnancy and countered by each healthy birth. Her community, too, saw each of her healthy babies as a testimony to her godliness, despite what might otherwise be seen as increasingly maverick behavior.

But although Anne had so far managed to channel her own ambitions to fit inside the Puritan system, she was beginning to fear for her brazen younger sister, Sarah, who seemed tempted to take tentative steps along Hutchinson's treacherous path. Sarah had always been more rebellious than her sisters, and she appeared to relish some of Hutchinson's strange ideas, particularly that of modern-day prophesy — that it was still possible for people to hear the voice of the Lord. Anne feared that her beloved Sarah might someday share the fate of this wretched woman. Of the sisters, Sarah was most like Anne — brilliant, emotional, restless, and an original thinker. In fact, Anne had named her new little girl after her middle sister, skipping over Patience, the next oldest, who should have followed, in the family-naming tradition.

But Sarah was intent on independence and left her parents' home to marry Major Benjamin Keanye soon after her little namesake was born. It was troubling that Sarah's new home was in Boston, the place where her fascination with Hutchinson had probably begun. Indeed, it was ironic to all of those who knew the Dudley girls that the steady, compliant Mercy, who had also recently married, would remain close to her parents and sisters in Ipswich, while the problematic Sarah was forty miles away from their supervision. All too soon she would avail herself of her freedom, presenting a kind of dark mirror to her eldest sister of what could happen to a woman who strayed too far from convention.

Meanwhile, back in Ipswich, under the watchful eye of her family and friends, Anne struggled with her own faith. As she wrote a few years later, "Many times hath Satan troubled me concerning the verity of the Scriptures, many times by atheism." Devout as she was, Anne frequently wondered, "How could I know whether there was a God?"[11] However, unlike Sarah, Anne had her poetry and her close relationships with Ward, her father, and her husband to help her sort through her complicated feelings. And with three children to raise in the rigors of her religion, she could not afford to give in to her doubts, at least not openly.

IN 1639, THE YEAR AFTER little Sarah's birth and the Hutchinson crisis, Dudley was once again elected to the post of deputy governor. He decided, grudgingly, to move closer to Boston to attend to the growing needs of colonial government. In the years since they had arrived in the New World from England, Boston had become a bustling Puritan center, and emigrants continually flowed in, undeterred by reports of the Hutchinson debacle. By the early 1640s there would be more than twenty thousand settlers who had busily "planted fifty towns and villages, built thirty or forty churches, and more ministers' houses, a castle, a college, prisons, forts, cartways ... many having comfortable houses, gardens, orchards, grounds fenced, corn fields, etc."[12]

For the first time in her life, Anne did not follow her father. Her duty lay with her husband, and Simon did not want to leave Ipswich. Dudley and Dorothy settled in Roxbury, a little village near Boston. Pregnant for the fourth time, with little Sarah only a year old, Anne was truly on her own now. Her quiet mother would be far away during Anne's next labor, and as the eldest sister, it would be her duty to help guide Mercy and Patience through their own pregnancies and births.

Whether she was being stoic or was exhilarated to have this new freedom, Anne never seems to have complained about her parents' departure. But she could not stay silent when it came to her husband's absences, and used her skills as a poet to express her frustration and her love in deeply personal verse that she never intended to publish.

Simon had been appointed by his father-in-law and Winthrop to help oversee the creation of what the Puritans called "the United Colonies of New England" — a group of settlements that would include Massachusetts Bay, New Haven, the Connecticut valley, and Plymouth. Given the firm opinions of all involved, particularly the New Havenites (led by the stern Thomas Hooker, the Bradstreets' old New Towne minister), Simon was kept very busy with negotiations. Although Anne Hutchinson and Roger Williams would have been shocked to hear it, there were those in the west who saw Winthrop and Dudley's government as being too tolerant of different points of view and so resisted connecting their fates to Massachusetts.

Simon was well suited to this mission, but this meant that he was rarely in Ipswich. Pioneer life was already difficult for Anne to bear, and Simon's absence made it more so. She expressed her longing for him in verse that revealed potent sexual imagery. Urgently, she needed him to come "burn / Within . . . my glowing breast, / The welcome house of him my dearest guest."[13] When her new baby son was born in 1640, she named him Simon, as though she wanted to keep some part of her husband nearby at all times. Because their religion supported and encouraged sexual passion between husband and wife, Anne did not have to hold back her feelings. Instead, she framed her eroticism with a directness that is still startling to read today.

Using images from the natural world, she compared herself not only to the earth itself but also to a deer, a turtledove, and even "the loving mullet, that true fish" that would rather die than live without her mate. She needed Simon physically and declared:

> *Return my dear, my joy, my only love,*
> *Unto thy hind, thy mullet, and thy dove,*
> *Who neither joys in pasture, house, nor streams,*
> *The substance gone . . .*[14]

Without Simon's body, or "substance," Anne was miserable.

Simon raced home whenever it was possible for him to escape his work, but no matter how hard he tried, he was never in Ipswich enough for his passionate wife. Suffering as she did, Anne did not at first realize that there was a positive aspect of her husband's time away. But each month he was gone, she was forced to develop her confidence and her competencies. As the single head of a frontier household, she had many duties to perform, since Simon's tasks became hers, and so Anne gradually grew extremely capable in many areas. She oversaw the family's business transactions, kept careful records of their finances, made decisions about the family's property, including the buying and selling of livestock, and disciplined the staff of sometimes unruly male laborers.

By necessity, Anne had evolved into what has been called a "deputy husband," a wife who legally, politically, and economically acted for her spouse, signing his name if she needed to, and even speaking as his representative in sessions of the local court if "he" had to testify in a local crime or debate (although this last was a rare occurrence).[15] Fortunately, Anne's "trespass" into male territory was culturally and legally sanctioned. Because husbands were often away for extended periods, everyone agreed that it was a pious wife's duty to assume her husband's chores.

The side effects of this transfer of responsibilities could be permanent. Women in Anne's position often grew markedly independent and had no compunction about joining in public debate. Those women whose husbands died and who were therefore rendered permanent "deputy husbands" sometimes chose to preserve their status as widows (if they were wealthy enough) in order to maintain their clout as representatives of the estate, a position far more powerful than that of a mere wife.[16]

Gradually Anne became one of the leading settlers in Ipswich in her own right. Accustomed as she was to debating with strong-minded men like her father, Anne filled her new "husbandly" responsibilities with skill, while her flourishing household met with the approbation of her neighbors. It helped, of course, that she had the enthusiastic blessing of the town's minister, Ward.

During these years, the late 1630s to the early 1640s, the leaders of the colony believed that it was particularly important that the devout in New England maintain their piety in the face of temptation, as ominous changes were afoot. Of course, Puritans had always regarded their king with suspicion. Charles was married, after all, to a French Catholic, and his bishops had actively persecuted their favorite ministers. To dissenters like Anne, Charles was a restless, spendthrift young man. They had little sympathy for his dreams of glory, were unimpressed with his good looks and high fashion, and saw his bloodthirstiness as self-aggrandizing and foolish. Irritatingly, he refused to listen to the wisdom of the Puritans in the House of Commons and instead attempted to get what he wanted with charming overtures and bonhomie, and then when this did not work, with bristling threats.

Finally, in a shocking breach of custom, Charles refused to allow the Puritan-controlled Parliament to convene. This was because in 1629 the House of Commons had refused to grant him the right to levy taxes to fund his passion for war. No other English monarch had dared to do such a thing. But Charles believed that he possessed the divine right to govern and that therefore no one should be allowed to disagree with him, let alone block his will.

Alarmed by Charles's dismissive attitude toward Parliament, in 1637 the Massachusetts General Court had commissioned Ward to draft a legal document that ensured that such an outrage could never be perpetrated in New England. Anne watched as Ward threw himself into this task, resigning from his post as minister to devote himself entirely to the job.

Ward wanted his code to protect the colony from potential oppression by the General Court, but he also wanted to uphold the traditions of English common law in the New World. Each event back home directly impinged on his thinking as he sat up late into the night, researching and writing the *Body of Liberties*. New England, unlike old, should be bound by God's Scripture, Ward believed. In his introduction to the *Body*, he wrote that no law should exist that could "be proved to bee morallie sinfull by the word of God."[17]

Given the intrinsic loneliness of such an endeavor, it must have been sustaining to have an intelligent young acolyte who hung on his every word and seemed as obsessed as he was with the creation of a godly New England. Notwithstanding his questionable attitudes about women, Ward even defended wives against abuse from their husbands. Perhaps his relationship with Anne was teaching him to reconsider some of his entrenched ideas as he added the crucial sentence, "Everie marryed woeman shall be free from bodilie correction or stripes by her husband, unlesse it be in his own defense upon her assault." Although it was typical of Ward to imagine women as the aggressors, still he called for a decisive split with English common law, which had allowed men to punish their wives with a "reasonable instrument" for hundreds of years.[18]

Ward penned his laws with painstaking care, and by 1641 the court had adopted a version of his work as the colony's order of governance. This document was of profound importance for the settlement; now it had its own principles that would, they hoped, prevent the mistakes of the Old World. Suddenly Massachusetts Bay seemed more separate than ever before, with its own legal system, like any distinct national entity.

Meanwhile Charles raced on, brandishing his sword at the Scots, collecting money however he could without a Parliament-sanctioned tax (for example, by slapping people like Theophilus in jail for protesting), and thereby alienating his subjects even more. At last, in 1640, a year before Ward finished his legal code, the war-hungry king ran out of money and was forced to reconvene Parliament so that they could levy taxes to fund his ambitions. As the Puritans saw it, Charles had received his comeuppance and it was time to pay him back for curtailing the rights of the legislature and for mistreatment of the people. Everyone in New England, including Anne and Ward, must have realized what Charles did not, that calling Parliament back into session after a ten-year hiatus was like lighting the tail of a bomb. Charles flatly refused to compromise and would not "offer reprisals" for his past actions. In response,

Parliamentary leaders became even more intransigent.[19] The incendiary relationship between the king and his Puritan subjects had flared to a truly dangerous point.

Anne and her neighbors immediately felt the ramifications of this stalemate between Charles and his government. As soon as the confrontation began, the steady stream of pilgrims fleeing England stopped. English Puritans felt that at last there was hope and rallied to fight the restrictions they had been laboring under since Charles had acceded to the throne. By 1642 it was clear that the Great Migration was over and New Englanders would have to learn to fend for themselves, economically speaking. Crops were soon worth "little more than half what they had been, and cattle were down from twenty or twenty-five pounds a head to eight, seven, or even six." No one was sure how the colonists would survive without the built-in market of new arrivals rushing off their ships and purchasing the settlers' old tools and furniture; their cows, pigs, and food supplies; and even their warm clothing for the winter.[20]

During this suspenseful time, some pious New Englanders reversed the migration process and caught the next vessels back home in order to join the legal battle against the king. Those like Anne who stayed behind wondered about the fate of the colony: Would the faithful in Massachusetts abandon the New World to fight for purity in the Old? Reports from England declared that Puritans and other dissenters had become increasingly defiant as they arrayed themselves against the king and his policies.

Ward joined Winthrop and Dudley in anxiously following the struggle. Having practiced law for ten years in London, the minister still had many friends who were in the thick of things. Thus, it was probably from Ward that Anne learned how talks between the king and Parliament had ground to a standstill.

In the spring of 1642, both the Commons and Lords announced for the last time that they would not renounce their list of grievances against Charles. They wanted to abolish the ancient feudal tax laws that Charles had revived to fund his army. They demanded that Parliament be summoned every three years and that it could not be disbanded without its own consent. Finally, they wanted the end of the hierarchical system of bishops and archbishops. The king responded by declaring that his very existence depended on his repudiation of their claims: "If I granted your demands, I should be no more than the mere phantom of a king," he raged.[21]

This stalemate was exactly what Ward sought to protect New Englanders from in his *Body of Liberties*. The old system seemed to be failing their beloved England. A full-fledged violent conflict loomed between Charles and his subjects; by the summer, both sides had put an end to negotiations and began to prepare for armed conflict. About halfway through her fifth pregnancy, Anne brooded over the future. No one knew what might happen to Massachusetts Bay. It seemed an inauspicious time to bring an infant into the world.

On July 21 Winthrop and Dudley responded to the crisis in England by calling for a fast day. Like Ward, most people in the colony still nurtured a traditional loyalty to the king even though they disapproved of many of his actions. He was the ruler and standard-bearer of the English people. How could there be an England without a monarch? Besides, it was unpleasant to consider how Charles might punish Puritans in general and Massachusetts in particular once he regained control of the government. For of course he would; after all, he was the king.

That fall, news came that New Englanders' forebodings were coming true. Back in August, the king had fled from the capital; Parliament howled that Charles must be returned to them immediately "by battle or other way."[22] Although at first it seemed that Charles had few supporters and could easily be cowed into submission, Royalists mustered their forces and began to march on London. The reports broke off at this point, so when Anne went into labor, she could only picture the worst: the demise of Puritanism in England and America. Happily, Anne delivered another healthy baby, little Hannah, and perhaps she derived some comfort from the new infant's plump legs and tiny face. But while Anne suckled Hannah, more bad news sailed across the Atlantic. Guns had been fired. Englishmen had killed Englishmen. The king's forces had trounced the Parliamentary army at Banbury on October 23. A civil war had begun.

Anne seems to have been frustrated at waiting helplessly to receive more news. No longer simply interested in her own ambition or, for that matter, in showing the world that pious women could read, write, and think for themselves, Anne's ideas about her identity as a poet had enlarged. This elevation of purpose seems to have occurred in part because of her relationship with the politically minded Ward, but also because of her role as a "deputy husband" in Ipswich. Over the last decade, she had been increasingly pushed into public matters as a prominent citizen of the town. She longed to rattle her spear against corruption and heresy like a man, and from watching Ward, she saw that the pen could serve as a redoubtable weapon. It was true that she couldn't write laws, but she could still write verse, and this verse could be political, angry, and "manly" in tone, even if she was only a woman.

Cooped up indoors but fully recovered from the birth of her new baby, Anne was ready to launch herself into her new work. The poem she planned was longer than any of her earlier attempts. She would have to chant the lines to herself over and over, storing her ambitious work in her mind, since parchment was so scarce. But faced with the deadening hardship of daily life, nothing was probably more helpful for warding off despair, boredom, and a sense of purposelessness than the endless mental activity of composing, revising, and memorizing. In fact, the process was akin to prayer, just as her father had once taught her.

But unlike male poets of the time, Anne came up with her lines as she rocked her baby to sleep in the middle of the night, as she stirred the soup on the fire, or as she bathed a child's cut. And so, as she turned her attention to the martial poem she wanted to write, she again decided not to underplay her identity as a woman but to put it to good use.

The idea must have flashed into her mind with the glitter of a gem. The poem would feature two characters: a mother, who represented Old England, and a daughter, who personified New England.

Through their dialogue, Anne would find an opportunity to display her impressive knowledge of English history and politics and also fight for the Puritan side of the argument. Old England would wail, and her daughter would try to ease her suffering. But they would also argue — a situation that must have been all too familiar to this headstrong daughter of the stern and traditional Dorothy. Not to mention that she now had three lively girls of her own who must have frequently challenged her rule of the house.

It is true, of course, that Anne's idea of Old England as New England's mother was common enough. Her own father had used this figure more than ten years earlier onboard the *Arbella* in "A Humble Request," when he and the other writers depicted themselves as children of their mother country. Perhaps the most famous example was the English Puritan John Milton. In an essay chastising Charles's government, Milton evokes a weeping Mother England who bears a strong resemblance to the mother Anne would create only a year or so later. Reflecting on the fact that tens of thousands of colonists had already fled the oppression of the king's bishops, he wrote,

> O if we could but see the shape of our dear mother England,
> as poets are wont to give a personal form to what they please,
> how would she appear, think ye, but in a mourning weed, with
> ashes upon her head, and tears abundantly flowing from
> her eyes.[23]

But Anne would not present Old England in a static or solitary fashion. Instead, "A Dialogue between Old England and New" would read almost like a play. She infused tension, suspense, love, and anger into the story, even as she expressed her own feelings over the looming civil war. It was no accident, for example, that New England utters the initial word of the poem, "Alas," as she describes her mother's decrepit condition. Here Anne speaks in the voice of the New World, a vantage point that was impossible for the England-bound Milton to achieve. Old England, Anne declares, is a wrecked old woman bound for damnation unless strong, healthy New England can save her.

Not that Anne wanted England to go up in flames. New England, in Anne's version, is saddened by her mother's "ailing" condition and regards it as her duty to help her. Thus the daughter demands a catalog of her mother's "woes" that she might "sympathize." Eventually, England confesses that her illness is caused by her "sins":

> *. . . the breach of sacred laws.*
> *Idolatry . . .*
> *With foolish superstitious adoration,*
> *Are liked and countenanced by men of might,*
> *The Gospel trodden down and hath no right;*
> *Church offices were sold and bought for gain,*
> *That Pope had hope to find Rome here again.*[24]

Instead of regarding the colonists as an inspiration, England acknowledges that the New Englanders "wert jeered . . . / Thy flying for the truth was made a jest." As for the venerable Puritan ministers, who had attempted to point out the corruption of their mother country, Old England admits:

> *I mocked the preachers . . .*
> *The sermons yet upon record do stand*
> *That cried destruction to my wicked land;*
> *. . . . .*
> *Some lost their livings, some in prison pent,*
> *Some find, from house and friends to exile went.*[25]

Under pressure from her daughter, the mother admits she deserves her punishment. "Their silent tongues to heaven did vengeance cry, / Who say their wrongs and hath judged righteously / And will repay it sevenfold in my lap." But New England cannot sit idly by as her mother plunges into despair; the fates of parent and child are intertwined. As Old England says, "If I decease, doth think thou shalt survive?"[26]

Anne understood all too well the resentment that often lies between mothers and daughters. At last New England dispenses with the customary reverence that children are supposed to feel toward parents and takes over the poem with a shocking ferocity. The daughter's final speech outlines what Old England would have to do (with New England's help) to save herself from destruction.

> *These are the days the Church's foes to crush,*
> *To root out Popelings head, tail, branch, and rush;*
>
> . . . .
>
> *. . . thine armies brave send out*
> *To sack proud Rome and all her vassals rout;*
>
> . . . .
>
> *Bring forth the beast that ruled the world with's beck,*
> *And tear his flesh and set your feet on's neck;*
>
> . . . .
>
> *This done, with brandished swords to Turkey go,*
> *For then what is't but English blades dare do,*
> *And lay her waste for so's the sacred doom.*[27]

Truly, this was Dudley's daughter writing. Anne poured all of her pent-up anger and fear about the current political situation into these stanzas. England could save herself only through righteous warfare against the infidel, and the enemy was everywhere — Rome, Turkey, Palestine. It was not enough for England to redeem herself and purify her own church and state. She would have to launch herself into the world to spread the true beliefs of the dissenter and vanquish the "idolatries" of all other faiths.

A manuscript version of this poem was probably passed among the friends of the Bradstreet-Dudley clan long before it was published. If so, Anne's words about the righteousness of New England would have gratified her fellow New World Puritans who had chosen not to return to England to fight the king. Such men could read her poem and feel that they had chosen the right side in the conflict. Not until England had purged herself of her sin and corruption should her colony feel impelled to help her. Those who remained in New England could see themselves as righteous instead of cowardly.

An astute reader could also have seen that Anne was firmly on the side of Parliament, a dangerous position for a colonial to assert. Although she qualified her attack on Charles by saying that anyone who was "false to king" or who "hurt . . . his crown" should be "expell[ed]," she was also blunt about which side was England's "better part"; it was Parliament who "showed their intent, / To crush the proud . . . / To help the Church." Indeed, in Anne's poem Charles seems sulky rather than wise — "The King, displeased, at York himself absents" — and he blocks Parliament's attempts at righting England's wrongs.[28]

This was an exciting poem to read, packed as it was with bloodshed, predictions of the future, and a long, exhilarating recital of the monarchy's sins. Though it seemed aimed at a larger audience than any of her previous poems, Anne did not know how it would be received by others. No other New Englander, male or female, had written such political verse about the civil war. Not only had she trespassed into male territory with this kind of political poetry, but she also condemned the king. When at last she copied it out onto paper and sent "A Dialogue between Old England and New" to her father and Ward, she waited with trepidation to hear what they thought.

Fortunately for Anne, there is no record of either man criticizing her ambition; instead both appear to have been thrilled. "A Dialogue" articulated important ideals that were close to the hearts of New England leaders. Later Ward would gloat that she had surpassed all other writers, including men, declaring, "Let men look to't, lest women wear the spurs."[29]

With the approval of these two important mentors, Anne's confidence could only soar. While she loved her husband, it was Ward's and Dudley's opinions that mattered most when it came to her work.[30] And she had an agenda now. Anne wanted to write in the pithy, "plaine" voice of her new home, and she wanted to add her opinions to the ongoing political debate. In other words, with "A Dialogue" she announced her intention to be a sort of pundit, a public commentator; she was intent on joining the larger world of debate and ideas, one traditionally closed to women.

To do this she would have to invent a simpler, pared-down aesthetic to match the purity of her religion and the newly settled land. This technique would take her many years to develop, but she had come to a turning point. No longer did she want to pull out all the stops and splash out the sort of froth that she had experimented with in her elegies to Sidney and Du Bartas. Her life in Ipswich may have been challenging, but it had offered her a path toward redemption. She was not the miserably uncertain girl she had been back in England and on the *Arbella*. Instead, she was beginning to believe that she did indeed possess the God-given "vocation" to shout out the words of the New Jerusalem.

CHAPTER FIFTEEN

Now Sister, Pray Proceed

To add to all I've said was my intent,
But dare not go beyond my element.

— ANNE BRADSTREET, "Air"

A DIALOGUE BETWEEN OLD ENGLAND AND NEW" was
the first American poem to wave the New England flag.
Anne's claim that she and her family and friends should be
admired by those they had left behind was made even more audacious by the fact that she was also writing in a new "Puritan" style of
verse, at least whenever New England spoke. This was not the
poetry of the last century, with its ponderous, old-fashioned solemnities. Nor was it like the verse of the previous generation, the
English Elizabethans, whom Anne had admired when she was
younger. She had flung past the elegant phrases and the complicated wit of her first poems, brandishing a biting poetic sword and
inventing a "New England" who spoke in a frank, "plaine" voice that
flew in the face of good manners.

At first glance, this change in style was not readily apparent. New England's lines still rhymed like those of her mother. The poem relied on wit and allusion. But New England's stanzas were briefer, more direct, and less flowery than anything Anne had written before. New England used brutal examples to make her points and often interrupted her mother, so that some of her lines were shorter metrically than others. This technique created a poem that at times seemed to mimic the breaks and rush of spoken language and thus seemed more choppy than ordinary verse of the period. Where were the carefully rounded turns of phrase that sounded "poetic"? Where were the beautiful images from Greek mythology? What kind of verse was this?

Sadly, Anne's depiction of England as an ailing, weakened mother foretold a tragedy in her own life. In December 1643 Anne's own mother was suddenly desperately ill. Although everyone assumed that Dorothy was in fine health, one morning after breakfast, just as she was compiling a list of things to do that day, she was gripped with "what felt like a gas pain in her chest . . . [and] by noon of the next day, when the doctor arrived, she was in agony."[1] A week later she died, having succumbed to death so rapidly that it was a shock to everyone.

For Anne and her sisters, it was heartbreaking to have lost their mother and to have missed the opportunity to attend her deathbed, since this was an important ritual in Puritan New England and in the Old World, too. An individual's final moment was often a public event. Some people actually rehearsed the lines they wanted to say, as they knew they would be surrounded by their family and neighbors. The last utterance of a dying person possessed an almost sacred charge (depending of course on the individual's reputation for piety during his or her lifetime). Often these sayings were passed along from neighbor to neighbor and were even transcribed in the family records as a harbinger of truth or a forecast of the years to come.

But in facing death, Dorothy appeared to have been as quiet as she was in life; at least no one left a record of her last thoughts.

And so it was Anne, ironically, who had the last word, just as New England, the daughter, had gotten the final speech in the poem Anne had composed six months earlier. Compelled to elegize her mother and to give voice to her unsung and quiet talents, she wrote "An Epitaph on My Dear and Ever-Honoured Mother, Mrs. Dorothy Dudley, Who Deceased December 27, 1643, and of Her Age, 61."

In this sad little poem, Anne carefully listed all the qualities for which her mother was respected:

> *Here lies,*
>
> . . . . .
>
> *A loving mother and obedient wife,*
> *A friendly neighbor, pitiful to poor,*
>
> . . . .
>
> *Religious in all her words and ways,*
> *Preparing still for death, till end of days:*
> *Of all her children, children lived to see,*
> *Then dying, left a blessed memory.*[2]

Anne's evocation captured precisely what a pious Puritan woman should look and act like, but there was an unspoken truth buried in this poem as well. Without Anne's words, this particular matron might have been forgotten. Anne could see that it was actually up to her, the literary daughter, to make sure her mother left behind a "blessed memory." Otherwise the grandchildren — Anne's children and the children of her sisters and brother — would forget Dorothy in a few years. Anne wrote, "As the brands of a fire, if once severed, will of themselves go out although you use no other means to extinguish them, so distance of place together with length of time (if there be no intercourse) will cool the affections."[3]

IN THE IMMEDIATE AFTERMATH of Dorothy's death, Anne might have sought comfort from her father, but despite the fact that he declared himself "melted with sorrow," Dudley was intent on finding a new wife, and with characteristic impetuosity he seized upon a nearby widow, marrying Katherine Hackburne (née Dighton) on April 14, four months after the death of Dorothy.[4] Of course, his children could not help but speculate about the duration of this courtship. Had it really only begun once their mother had died? Or had Katherine, his neighbor, been one of those helpful widow ladies who arrived with pie and other comforts to entice the soon-to-be-grieving widower into her own bed?

Whatever had really happened, Anne was aware that she would never know the whole story and it was a fait accompli. Katherine began to produce children with alacrity, and suddenly Anne's elderly father had a new family. Although this was a fairly common phenomenon in the colonies — older widowers marrying young women after spouses had died — no doubt this was a somewhat alarming and discomfiting experience for Anne.

It must have been impossible not to feel some degree of loyalty on behalf of her mother, who had been so easily supplanted by another woman, and Anne's next poem would express her anxiety over this idea. Also, Anne might well have been jealous of her father's new children, although Dudley did his best to reach out to his daughters, writing Mercy that, now that her mother was gone, he would hire her a midwife for her upcoming labor and would also send her a "souce in a bag," that is, a sausage. He added that he would try diligently to serve as a guide, urging her to let him have "thy letters as thy mother had and I will answeare them."[5]

With Anne it was easier for Dudley to maintain his ties. Although no letters exist, Anne refers to their conversations in her poetry on several occasions, suggesting that they had remained in communication about their shared literary passion even after Dudley moved away from Ipswich.[6] Still, no amount of contact with her father could make up for the loss of her mother. Racked by grief, probably disturbed by her father's remarriage, and always highly imaginative, Anne began to picture her own children bereft of a mother, and she realized that she did not want to fade away as her own mother had. She obsessed over her own demise, dwelling on the tears and sorrow of her husband, not to mention the looming threat of a "step-dame" for her "little babes."

Pregnant again in 1645, she penned a mournful dirge to Simon called "Before the Birth of One of Her Children."

> *How soon, my Dear, death may my steps attend,*
> *How soon't may be thy lot to lose thy friend,*
>
> . . . .
>
> *If any worth or virtue were in me,*
> *Let that live freshly in thy memory*
> *And when thou feel'st no grief, as I no harms,*
> *Yet love thy dead, who long lay in thine arms.*
> *And when thy loss shall be repaid with gains*
> *Look to my little babes, my dear remains.*
> *And if thou love thyself, or loved'st me,*
> *These O protect from step-dame's injury.*[7]

Although in this poem she vividly imagines the aftermath of her own death, Anne writes with the same passion that inspired her other love poems to her husband. She wants to make sure Simon will not behave like her father, hastily installing a new wife into their household. She tells Simon exactly how to remember her, begging him to go on loving her as though she were still alive. Through Simon's continued attachment to her, she will be able to live on in spirit and still be the mother and wife of the house. It was hard, after all, to contemplate surrendering control of your affairs when you had single-handedly run your complicated household and raised five children from diapers to their first lisps of the Puritan-sanctioned catechism. Anne did not want some other woman to step into her shoes and take over her family.

She also hoped that her children would honor her merits, not for her own sake, but for theirs and for the sake of the colony in general.

The upcoming generation in New England needed the example of a pious mother to follow, just as she had needed Dorothy. In a later poem, Anne would return obsessively to this same theme and instruct her sons and daughters, now grown, to tell their own children about her and to pass on the lessons she taught. Conceiving of herself as a mother bird to baby birds now grown, she wrote:

> *When each of you shall in your nest*
> *Among your young ones take your rest,*
> *In chirping language, oft them tell,*
> *You had a dam that loved you well,*
>
> . . . .
>
> *Taught what was good, and what was ill,*
> *What would save life, and what would kill.*
> *Thus gone, amongst you I may live,*
> *And dead, yet speak, and counsel give . . .*[8]

There was a lesson here. It was not enough to live a "worthy" life; it had to be remarked upon by others for its example to resonate in the future. This was not about fame or perennial recognition. Instead, it was the duty of the Puritan mother to pass on a spiritual legacy to the next generation. Of course, writing an epitaph was one way Anne could mourn her mother; but she also felt her children needed "to see" their grandmother so they could emulate her piety. And Anne could use poetry to pass on her own beliefs to her children in case she died prematurely and they started to stray. What better way could she serve New England? Anne would pursue this idea of feminine legacy and the passing of tradition between mothers and daughters in her next series of poems.

Before Dorothy died, when Anne was working on "A Dialogue," Dudley had sent her a copy of a poem he had been writing to inspire her to try her hand at yet more ambitious verse. His poem is no longer in existence, but from Anne's description of it, it featured four women who were allegorical figures of "the four parts of the world."[9]

Whenever her father laid down the gauntlet, Anne rose to the challenge, and this time was no exception. In the years preceding Dorothy's death, she had embraced this fresh project even though she was not yet finished with "A Dialogue." After her mother died, she drove herself to compose an even more compendious and far-reaching poem. In fact, before her very eyes, the poem got longer and longer and then split into four parts, and then another four parts, until she had what she called *The Quaternions*, four poems with four sections each. When she was done, she would have written sixteen poems and more than eighteen hundred lines, an enormous accomplishment for any poet. Perhaps this flurry of work helped take Anne's mind off the loss of her mother. But it is also possible that Dorothy's absence gave Anne the freedom she needed to take more literary risks. After all, it was Dudley, not Dorothy, who had always encouraged her creative drive.

Anne must have had some sense of pride in these poems, because later she would confess that her characters might "seem . . . to claim precedency" over her father's, but of course she hastened to add that this was only a trick of the eye, since it was impossible for her "humble hand" to have "rudely penned" anything superior to her father's verse.[10]

The sheer size of *The Quaternions* is particularly impressive given that Simon continued to travel much of the time and Anne still had all her duties as a mother and a deputy husband. Yet somehow she seized the opportunity and the time to pen poems that would display her encyclopedic learning and would also address the complexities of the relationships between mothers, daughters, and sisters as well as the difficulties of feminine aspiration.

Pent up, lonely, and brimful of ideas, in the initial poems of *The Quaternions* she set herself the vertiginous goal of telling the story of creation. Those who felt that women should not addle their wits with too much information and too much political involvement could not be too badly offended, as this was one of the most popular subjects from Scripture.

Of course, Anne had stolen this idea from Du Bartas, the long-winded sixteenth-century poet she admired so fervently and had elegized earlier that year. But her poem bore little resemblance to his. To begin with, she released herself from the necessity of relying exclusively on scriptural knowledge for telling her story and included the latest scientific discoveries. Even more important, while Du Bartas had bogged down in attempting to describe the first seven days of the universe, Anne came up with her own narrative structure. By refusing to tell the story chronologically and by resisting the point of view of an omniscient (and implicitly male) narrator, she created a story with suspense, tension, and character development. As in "A Dialogue," her people spoke directly to each other, as though they were in a play.

Once again, Anne drew on her experience as one of four sisters and as the mother of three girls. In "The Four Elements," the first poem of *The Quaternions*, she used female characters to stand for the cardinal elements of the universe — air, water, earth, and fire. This was not in itself an unusual decision; many other writers had used allegorical female figures in their poetry. But their characters were usually stiff emblems of some abstract quality: patience, virtue, mercy, and so on. Anne, on the other hand, breathed life into her women, making them into "sisters" who jockeyed for position.

Each element shouted that she was the most important to the universe. This was the kind of competitive anger, knowledge, and passion that good Puritan females weren't supposed to possess. In Anne's poem this feminine rage threatened to destroy the world:

> *All would be chief, and all scorned to be under,*
> *Whence issued winds and rains, lightning and thunder;*
> . . . .
> *The sea did threat the heavens, the heavens the earth,*
> *All looked like a chaos or new birth:*
> *Fire broiled Earth, and scorched Earth it choked.*
> *Both by their darings, Water so provoked*
> *That roaring in it came . . .*[11]

Although Anne allowed for the possibility of the creation of a new order from the clash between these sisters, she focused most of her energy on describing a bone-rattling apocalypse that was meant to chill her readers into repenting their battles, reestablishing the harmony that they were supposed to enjoy and thereby forestalling the wrath of God and the blight of His judgment.

Ultimately, Anne's elements attempt to resolve their quarrel through rational debate, suggesting that if even women, generally considered the weak-minded sex, could rely on reason to quiet their problems, then so could the Puritan leaders in both England and New England. Otherwise England would be destroyed.

To flesh out each character's argument, Anne had to study fiercely. She would have to master the physics, chemistry, and practical applications of each element to make the debate compelling and informative. She was fortunate to live in Ipswich, with its many good private libraries. Dedicated as she was to running her household smoothly, she still threw herself into her research, knowing that she would have to squeeze her hours of scholarship into her already full days.

Ironically, the restrictions Anne faced as a female writer seemed to work in her favor. Because she drew upon the material she knew best, the experience of women, and of women in families, her work had an earthy quality lacking in the sermons and poems of her male counterparts. In addition, the potential criticism that she faced as a female writer pressed her into creating more finely wrought and imaginative work than was required of her male contemporaries. Men were not subject to the limitations she had to circumvent and could simply write diatribes, pamphlets, and sermons, whereas the inventiveness that poetry demanded suited Anne and served her well.

Still, Anne could never escape the problems she faced as a woman writer. In the introductory poem (which she addressed to her father), she worried that no one would believe she had written these poems herself. She was especially concerned that people would think she had copied her words from Du Bartas:

[I] . . . feared you'ld judge Du Bartas was my friend,
I honour him, but dare not wear his wealth;
My goods are true (though poor), I love no stealth,

. . . .

I shall not need mine innocence to clear,
These ragged lines will do't when they appear.[12]

The fact that she worried about such accusations was an indication of the uniqueness of her achievement. This was an ambitious
project for any poet, let alone a woman. Anne knew that it would be
impossible for many of her contemporaries to explain the power
and intelligence of her work except by charging her with plagiarism.
Here was a new use of feminine self-deprecation. Her "poor" lines
would attest to the authenticity of her work.

Yet Anne's "sisters" exploded the idea that women were always
the dulcet, obedient individuals they were supposed to be. It was as
though her characters embodied her own hidden ambitions, to
which she could never confess. In the world of poetry, her "elements" could be as pushy, smart, and aggressive as they wanted;
each sister shoved the others to the side in order to demonstrate her
own importance. Nowhere did Anne paint a picture of the pious,
demure Puritan lady Dorothy had raised her to be. Her women
shouted, raged, and insulted each other as bawdily as any man.

But "The Four Elements" was not simply a free-for-all, since
Anne also made sure to apply her copious research. Earth gave a
brief overview of the geography of Greece; Fire spoke of the great
towns she had razed to the ground, from Troy to Zion; Water outlined her services to the ancient Egyptians; and Air explained that
she occupied "every vaccuum," a radical scientific concept for the
era (though ultimately it would be proven untrue). Each of these
learned ladies tried to outdo the other in the scope of her knowledge. No one had ever heard of such a thing — a tribe of debating
bluestockings — although it is tempting to wonder if this is how
Anne, Patience, Mercy, and Sarah argued among themselves.

By the time she was done composing this poem, these women were Anne's intimates. She had steeped herself in their "qualities" and imagined who they would be if they were really alive. She had read late into the night, holding lines of verse in her mind during the day and writing the new sections of the poem down only after the children slept. Samuel, Dorothy, Sarah, Simon, and Hannah must have quickly become accustomed to their mother's distracted looks, her habit of tuning out their demands while she worked, and her way of listening, it seemed, to voices no one else could hear.

So while she stood at the huge fireplace, tending each of the little fires — the embers that allowed a corn pudding to simmer slowly in its kettle, the low flame in the back that baked the bread for the week, and the roar near the front that roasted the chicken they would eat that day for dinner, Anne might have heard the orange tongues declare,

> *Ye cooks, your kitchen implements I frame*
> *Your spits, pots, jacks, what else I need not name*
> *Your daily food I wholesome make, I warm*
> *Your shrinking limbs, which winter's cold doth harm.*[13]

On the hot summer days when it seemed miraculous that the river had not completely dried up, the trickle that splashed over the pebbles on the riverbed seemed to gurgle, "If I withhold, what art thou? Dead dry lump, / Thou bear'st no grass nor plant not tree, nor stump." While Earth declared defiantly, "I come not short of you, / In wealth and use I do surpass you all." Even the gentle Air itself seemed to sigh, "I am the breath of every living soul. / Mortals, what one of you that loves not me / Abundantly more than my sisters three?"[14] How could Anne ignore the quarrel that was going on all around her, even if it was, so to speak, a civil war of her own invention? After all, the scholars said that whenever the powers of darkness disrupted the harmony of the elements, the result was invariably natural disasters of all kinds, as well as a mirroring chaos in the microcosm of the human world.

She could not stop, then, with Air, Earth, Fire, and Water. According to Aristotle, whom Anne read in translation, the human being was a miniature version of the universe itself. Man, too, was a mixture of four elements, known as "humors" — blood, choler, melancholy, and phlegm.

Although all four humors were present in each individual, one humor was believed to dominate according to a person's overall health and personality type. Blood, which was in charge of distributing the humors throughout the body, was supposed to bestow a generous temperament on those who were "sanguine" in nature. Choler, which governed the heart and gave the body the necessary "heat" to function, was responsible for a martial spirit. Melancholy, which was in charge of the bones, liver, stomach, and spleen, tended to make one sad but also wise. And Phlegm, which was responsible for the governance of the brain, gave one an intellectual bent, since it was in charge of reason, imagination, and memory.

According to contemporary science, if the four elements battled with each other, the four humors would reflect this dissension and human beings would have to contend with illness, disaster, and plague. To Anne there was clear evidence of the universe's lack of harmony, from the civil war in England to the death of the best and the holiest, such as the Lady Arbella all those years ago. Even the Hutchinson debacle was an example of how the finest individual could be toppled by the brutal forces of the devil.[15]

Again, Anne translated this academic idea — that dissension among the elements would produce chaos in each human being — into what she knew best. Air, Fire, Water, and Earth would become pregnant and produce daughters, the four humors, who would vie for primacy in a companion piece to "The Four Elements." Each humor shared many of the qualities of her "mother element." Happily, this new poem, appropriately titled "Of the Four Humors," also required more research, an activity Anne seemed to thrive on. Now she would have to read all she could find on human anatomy, medicine, and the actual workings of the humors — which organs they were associated with and what powers they governed in the body.

Once she mastered the science she needed, she poured her knowledge into shaping the quarreling cousins in their own battle for pre-eminence. When Phlegm asserts her primacy as the seat of the senses, her description of the miracle of human eyesight reveals that Anne had read the foremost expert on anatomy, Dr. Helkiah Crooke, and was as up-to-date on the science of sight as was possible:[16]

> *The optic nerve, coats, humours all are mine,*
> *The wat'ry, glassy, and the crystaline;*
> *O mixture strange! O colour colourless,*
> *Thy perfect temperament who can express?*
> *He was no fool who thought the soul lay there,*
> *Whence her affections, passions speak so clear.*[17]

When Phlegm goes on to describe the mechanics of the spine and ligaments, she gloats over her attributes, giving her recital far more verve than the textbook versions of anatomy that Anne had studied so copiously. Like a playwright, Anne transformed the inert knowledge of the specialists into lively monologues her readers could follow.

Anne's politics were not far beneath the surface of "Of the Four Humors." The most warlike of all the sisters, Choler appears rash, foolish, and overly aggressive. She also declares that her martial humor is dominant in males: "Yet man for Choler is the proper seat: / I in his heart erect my regal throne, / where monarch like I play and sway alone."[18] Choler's pride and machismo do not speak well of the swaggering men she governs. Anne could not resist this dig against the pointless bellicosity of males, and of Charles in particular.

Anne drove this point home by making the last, most "yielding," and feminine of the cousins, Phlegm, the one who is able to stop the violence in her family. Anne was well versed in the scriptural tenet that the last shall be first and the weak shall be made strong. She based much of her life as an intellectual woman on this premise. Thus it is Phlegm who unites her cousins and then the four mother elements too.

Let's now be friends; it's time our spite were spent,
Lest we too late this rashness do repent,

. . . .

Let Sanguine with her hot hand Choler hold,
To take her moist my moisture will be bold:
My cold, cold Melancholy's hand shall clasp;
Her dry, dry Choler's other hand shall grasp.
Two hot, two moist, two cold, two dry here be,
A golden ring, the posy UNITY.
Nor jars nor scoffs, let none hereafter see,
But all admire our perfect amity;
Nor be discerned, here's water, earth, air, fire,
But here's a compact body, whole entire.[19]

Phlegm's vision of harmony was Anne's own. Each humor accepted the fact that she needed the others to make a whole that was greater than the warring parts. In this time of civil war, when Parliamentary forces were battling the king's army and when no one knew which side would win, there was nothing Anne yearned for more than this kind of "UNITY."

Although her vision was essentially a cooperative one, Anne acknowledged that it could come about only after fierce competition, revealing her hope that the bloodshed and warfare in England would cease. Of course, Anne also had a subsidiary hope: that men might learn to bend an ear to women and that what they heard might change the course of history.

As the civil war showed no sign of letting up, many of Anne's friends and neighbors continued to be torn about where their duties lay. Leaders of New England, such as Winthrop, began to receive letters begging them to come back and lend support to the Puritan cause against Charles. One old friend of Winthrop's who sat in Parliament lamented, "Now we see and feele how much we are weakened by the loss of those that are gone from us, who should have stood in the gap, and have wrought and wrasled mightily in this great business."[20]

It was hard to resist such pleas for help, but most prominent New England Puritans were not particularly eager to jump into the fray, as they were worried about the direction of their coreligionists back in England. Old World Puritans agreed that royalist principles must be dismantled but were less clear about what to put in their place. Increasingly, they seemed to be leaning toward the Bay colony's biggest bugaboos. Either they wanted to cling to Presbyterianism, where a synod of elders had control over the administration of all the churches — a hateful idea to New England Puritans, who felt that each church should be self-governing — or they sought complete freedom to form the kinds of churches they wanted regardless of whether they adhered to the laws of the "true religion." To the colonists, this libertarian approach would result in a ghastly proliferation of dissenters, from Anabaptists to Familists to Quakers, all of whom were anathema to the stern folk in Massachusetts.

Winthrop and Dudley therefore deemed it important to remain in New England and safeguard their system of church governance. But a divide was emerging between Old and New World Puritans. Without continuity, could American Puritans still think of themselves as English? Were they the true English Puritans, while the Old World folk had simply lost their way?

This last was the conclusion of most of Anne's family and friends. Any other idea was too threatening to consider. Suddenly Anne's poems from this period, "A Dialogue," "The Four Elements," and "Of the Four Humors" seemed to speak to the moment. Anne was now writing as a serious-minded, learned poet and a social critic. Already her poetic accomplishments were impressive, although no one seems to have realized that one day her work would garner the attention of the English-speaking world.

CHAPTER SIXTEEN

Foolish, Broken, Blemished Muse

The subject large, my mind and body weak
With many more discouragements did speak.
— ANNE BRADSTREET, "The Four Monarchies"

ANNE KNEW THAT HER DAYS IN IPSWICH were numbered when Simon announced his dream of moving his family from the relative ease of the settled town and plunging them deeper into the wilderness. Like his father-in-law, Simon felt impelled to conquer the wilderness in the name of Puritanism. It was against the creed of his religion to sit back and rest on his laurels; a pious man or woman must continually strive to please God, no matter the challenge. Anne agreed with her husband, but it was still awful to consider yet another wrenching move.

She had little choice in the matter, however. Over time, Simon must have reminded Anne more and more of her father, with that same relentless drive to succeed, selfless dedication to the colony's success, devotion to Puritanism, and slightly quixotic idealism. Of course, Simon was far more genial and relaxed than Dudley had ever been. But as he grew into a civic leader in his own right, he modeled himself after the father-in-law he revered.

By the end of 1643, Simon had completed most of his work for the colony and could devote himself to building his estate. His work as a mediator among the strong-minded New Havenites, the rigid Plymouth Pilgrims, and his own colony's leaders had helped him grow in confidence.

Now, just like his father-in-law, Simon was dissatisfied with his current situation and believed he could establish a true utopia, this time in Cochichawicke, a fertile territory fifteen miles west of Ipswich, bounded to the north by the Merrimack River and "two miles eastward to Rowley."[1] In 1634 John Winthrop Jr. had bought this land from an Indian sachem for six pounds and a coat, and Simon had been hoping to make this move ever since he had heard of the virgin territory.

The dream of yet another new settlement was a family affair. John Woodbridge, the husband of Anne's sister Mercy, was among those who had originally raised the idea in 1638, when he and others sought from the General Court the right to "begin a plantation."[2] For years Woodbridge had cherished the dream of being the minister of a new Puritan settlement. This seemed the perfect opportunity, but there was one stumbling block. When he was a young man, Woodbridge had fled England before he could be ordained. Dudley, who was eager to have a clergyman in the family, urged the young man to "perfec[t] your former studies" so that he could assume the pulpit in the new territory.[3] Woodbridge went to Harvard to complete his preparation, and when at last the happy day came — in 1645 he was anointed as a Puritan minister — Dudley immediately saw to it that he was appointed to head the church of the new settlement. That same year Chochichawicke was renamed Andover, a comforting improvement from the English point of view, and a meetinghouse was constructed for Woodbridge to preach in.

Now that Mercy's husband had attained his dream position, he was eager to move at once. Simon, who seemed to have been waiting for his brother-in-law's ordination before he made his move, agreed.

And so Anne and Mercy knew that it would soon be time to say good-bye to their homes in the thriving town of Ipswich and to their sister Patience. Although none of the women left any record of complaint about being separated, it must have been difficult to face their leave-taking.

Fortunately for Anne, Simon had the good sense to build his new home before transplanting his large family. He had erected a sawmill on the Cochichawicke Brook the year before, and since it was the only one within miles, money and goods began to pour into the Bradstreets' already overflowing coffers. Simon and Anne had arrived in the New World as one of the colony's wealthiest families, and by the 1640s Simon's real estate investments, as well as his sale of livestock and agricultural produce, had made them even richer.

With Anne and the children safely installed in their old home in Ipswich, Simon did not have to rush the building of this new house, nor did he have to cut costs, since he could get his logs sliced into boards at his own mill. It was a luxurious opportunity, and Simon made the most of it, hiring carpenters and lavishing money on paneling, doors, imported windows, and perhaps even a gable or two. Within a year or so, his workmen had created a splendid homestead situated on twenty acres of land, the finest location and the most beautiful English structure in Andover.

Sometime early in 1646, when Anne was pregnant with their sixth child, Simon announced that they were ready to move. If the prospect of yet another long journey through the forest, this time with five children in tow, was alarming, Anne left no evidence that she dreaded it. Instead, she might well have been excited at the prospect of her new home.

When she first walked inside, she would have been able to smell the freshly cut wood that was bright and pure, as yet undarkened by smoke. The wide floorboards would have been yellow pine, with the curving white ripples typical of that grain. The fireplace was so enormous that more than one person could stand inside it. The tiny paned windows let in light but not cold, and the door fit snugly to keep out drafts.

In addition to the Bradstreets, twenty-two other homesteaders had settled on the edge of the virgin forest. Firewood was stacked for the winter, and the land surrounding the house plots was cleared of stones and trees and leveled as much as possible to make room for planting.

Still, despite the solace of her beautiful house, it must have been wrenching for Anne to leave behind Ward, her mentor and confidant. With whom would she talk about poetry, history, and politics? Who would guide her thinking and answer her questions? How could she continue to grow as a poet and a Puritan without his care and focused attention? Her father, too, would be even farther away; visits would be more difficult and mail more unreliable.

These sorrows were partially eclipsed by the situation in England. A fierce Puritan general, Oliver Cromwell, had risen to power and had shocked the world by announcing, "If I met the King in battle I would fire my pistol at the King as at another."[4] Much as the New England Puritans hated Charles, this was still an alarming flouting of tradition. To residents on both sides of the Atlantic, it seemed that the world was being turned upside down. On June 14, 1645, Cromwell and his New Model Army won the decisive battle of the war at Naseby, and Charles and his men fled. It seemed only a matter of time before the king would be captured.

In the midst of this unsettling crisis, Ward had hastily finished *The Simple Cobbler of Aggawam*, the manuscript Anne had watched evolve. Ward's middle-of-the-road position about the war seemed to appeal to people; he believed in the sanctity of the king even as he asserted the glories of true Puritanism. Published in London, the book went through four editions in the first year.[5] Overnight, Ward was a celebrity, and moderate English Puritans begged him to come back to the Old World to speak on their behalf. Like other New Englanders, Anne was proud of his success, but for her it was a bittersweet sort of joy, since she knew his fame would take him away from her for good. At seventy years old, once Ward left America, it was unlikely he would ever return.

But for Ward there was no real incentive to stay in Ipswich. With Anne in Andover, he had lost what was probably his greatest pleasure in life — their long hours talking about each other's writing and the excitement with which they read each other's work. At any rate, he felt he had a mission to accomplish back in England. In 1647, a year or so after Anne's trek to the wilderness, he left for England.

Heartbroken though she must have been, Anne did not utter any "moans." Perhaps she did not have time to give way to despair now that she was plunged back into life on the frontier. She had delivered a sixth child, Mercy, and had a new homestead to get in order. But in Andover, whether she complained or not, Anne was in something of an intellectual desert. There were few people in this remote outpost with whom she could share books and ideas, no one who would read her poetry or discuss international politics. She had been separated from all the libraries of the Ipswich intellectuals, and though she knew that she was not completely alone in her new home, it must have seemed that way at times.

It was no coincidence, then, that Anne named her new daughter after her reliable sister. Although she and Mercy were separated by nine years and might sometimes seem as different as the quarreling siblings Choler and Melancholy, or Earth and Air, they needed each other just as much, especially on the frontier. Anne's world would have been incomplete without her sister's steady loyalty and quiet appreciation.

But the waters did not run so smoothly with their sister Sarah. It had been almost ten years since Sarah had left home to live in Boston with her husband. With the difficult weather, depending on the season, it was overwhelming to consider traveling, especially as Anne, Mercy, and Patience were either pregnant or nursing babies during most of these years. Sarah, on the other hand, had produced only one child, a daughter named after her sister Anne, and could perhaps have braved the journey, but it seems something stopped her. Perhaps it was the dangers of travel and the distance between settlements, but it seems there was something more to her hesitation than a geographical divide.

Although Andover was so remote that it was hard to receive news from Boston, most important information did eventually find its way there. Almost immediately after little Mercy's birth, Anne and Mercy learned that their sister was acting strangely. Although the exact details of her behavior were unclear, she appeared to be questioning the authority of the ministers just as Hutchinson and her followers used to do. This is surely what Anne and her family had always feared, that the impressionable young girl had gotten poisoned by her exposure to the older woman. Sin was contagious, after all.

In spite of Sarah's odd behavior, or perhaps because of it, her husband took her back to England when he traveled there for business. But England in 1646 was not the place to bring an unstable young woman with a passionate temperament. On every street corner, men and women prophesied that the end of the world was coming: Charles was Satan in disguise; Jesus walked the earth. At twenty-six Sarah became swept up in the excitement. John Winthrop Jr. received a report that alarmed all of Sarah's family with its brief description of her as "a great preacher."[6] It appeared that Sarah had taken to speaking publicly of her beliefs, another ominous echo of Hutchinson's behavior.

Clearly Sarah had put aside the Puritan lessons of modesty and humility and was now following the commands of her own heart. Anne and her sisters could not help but brood over their sister's actions. It began to seem that she was bound to face the same fate as New England's false prophetess. Then even more disturbing information arrived. Sarah had suddenly turned up back in Boston without her husband and was promptly officially "admonished" for "prophesying" in "mixt assemblies."[7] What was Sarah doing in public, exposing herself to the curious eyes of both men and women, disgracing herself and her family?

As the months passed, it became evident that Sarah's disgusted husband had no intention of coming back to Massachusetts. He was fed up and wrote angry letters to his father-in-law, accusing Sarah of adultery, heresy, and lust. To his old ministers in Boston, John Cotton and John Wilson, he declared that he had

> hazarded my health and life, to satisfy the unsatiable desire & lust of a wife that in requittal impoysoned my body with such a running of a reines that would, if not (through mercie) cured, have turned unto the french Pox. It is cleare . . . that no poyson can be received from the bodie of a woman, but what shee first has received from the infected body of some other.

That he had never strayed from his marital bed went without saying, Keanye asserted, vowing that he had never bestowed "the due benevolence of a wife" to any woman besides Sarah.[8]

Condemned by her own husband, Sarah was in a desperate situation. Soon she could face penalties of exile, imprisonment, even death. Dudley wrote to Keanye, imploring his son-in-law to grant Sarah a divorce and desist from pushing her into a court trial for indecent behavior. Keanye pounced on the opportunity, eagerly scribbling his official repudiation: "[Sarah] has not lefte mee any roome or way of reconciliation: And theirefoare as you [Dudley] desier, I do plainely declare my resolution, never again to live with her as a Husband."[9]

Getting divorced was no easy matter in Puritan New England. But Dudley was currently serving the colony as deputy governor yet again, and he applied pressure to the General Court until his colleagues relented in 1647, granting his daughter this unusual reprieve. Such an act immediately raised eyebrows on both sides of the Atlantic, and the Dudley family's reputation began to suffer. One settler wrote to the governor that much "offense [had been] taken, at the late Divorce granted by the Court." He continued: "How weighty a business it is, as I neede not tell you, so I would humbly desire that some course may be taken so to cleer the Courts proceeding, as that rumors might be stopped."[10]

But Winthrop stuck by his old friend, and Sarah's divorce remained on the books — not that this helped her pull herself together. At twenty-seven she had made the decision to go her own way. Reports came to Anne that Sarah had begun having illicit love affairs, waltzing around Boston on the arms of men her family did not even know. She swore at the authorities and resumed preaching on street corners. Soon she was excommunicated from the church for "odious, lewd, and scandalous unclean behavior."[11] Dudley's daughter, Anne's sister, excommunicated! Dudley swung into action, arranging for Sarah to be married to a man of lower social station. He paid the man a generous allowance for the simple task of controlling his headstrong daughter. But despite her father's efforts, Sarah would die in poverty at the age of thirty-nine, unhappy and alone.

The effects of Sarah's behavior on her siblings are impossible to measure, although Anne's image of the sisterly circle of unity points to the extent of the disaster for the Dudley women. To lose one sister to such hellish pursuits could only devastate the other three. At the same time, it tainted their own reputations. Perhaps all the Dudley sisters were suspect. Although Patience and Mercy seemed acceptable, Anne's intentions could be seen as odd. Was poetry writing really so different from prophesying?

Dudley undoubtedly suffered over these blows to his family's pride, but Anne lived far enough away from Boston to be protected from most of the gossip. Despite her constant introspection and recurring self-doubt, Anne's confidence in herself and her poetry had grown. She knew she was doing God's work; she had earned Ward's blessing and had recently gained the respect and friendship of her brother-in-law, the newly minted minister of the Andover church.

Anne had not stopped writing before or after her move. Poetry was solace during the icy winters and the long nights. Back in Ipswich, she had completed two more poems, "Of the Four Ages of Man" and "The Four Seasons," as companion pieces to "The Four Elements" and "Of the Four Humors." This completed the "four times four" of *The Quaternions*.

But Anne was only thirty-four years old. She had not finished writing, and besides, she had ended her last poem on a bitter note. Sharply disappointed in "The Four Seasons" — the final of the four poems of *The Quaternions* — she concluded that work by castigating herself for her own limitations, plaintively begging her readers' forgiveness:

> *My subject's bare, my brain is bad,*
> *Or better lines you should have had:*
> *The first poem fell in so naturally,*
> *I knew not how to pass it by;*
> *The last, though bad I could not mend,*
> *Accept therefore of what is penned,*
> *And all the faults that you shall spy*
> *Shall at your feet for pardon cry.*[12]

Although no one else seemed to share her negative assessment of the work, this was an unsatisfactory stopping place, and Anne resolved to try again and tackle a fresh project. This time she allowed herself to dream of pushing past the topics of her last work — the natural sciences and the cycles of the material world — to enter a new arena of knowledge: the history of the ancient world. What better way to connect with the two older men in her life whom she loved and yet who were now far away — Ward and Dudley. She had already displayed an impressive grasp of recent English history and politics as well as a vast store of scriptural information in *The Quaternions* and the elegies, but to tell the story of "the four monarchies" of the pre-Christian era would require mastering a fresh course of reading and would allow her to grapple with the principle of monarchy in general, a topic that was on every English person's mind in 1646.

Characteristically, Anne must have relished the prospect of so much research; there was no more fruitful way for her to escape her fear, isolation, and loneliness than through this kind of immersion in study. Although it is unclear where she found the books she needed, whether she sent servants to Ipswich to borrow volumes or whether she and Simon had purchased new editions from England, it is evident from her verse that she raced through as many works about ancient civilizations as she could find. She also steeped herself in one of her childhood favorites, Sir Walter Raleigh's *History of the World*, drawing inspiration from his opening salute to the reader:

> For who hath not observed, what labour . . . bloodshed,
> and cruelty, the Kings and Princes of the World have
> undergone . . . to make themselves and their Issues Masters
> of the World? And yet hath Babylon, Persia, Egypt, Syria,
> Macedon, Carthage, Rome, and the rest, no fruit, no flower,
> grass, nor leaf, springing upon the face of the earth, of those
> seeds: No, their very roots and ruines do hardly remain.[13]

Even as Sarah shrieked heresies on the streets of Boston, Anne's imagination was caught by worlds long gone. It was impossible not to glean lessons for herself and her family from the nation builders of the past. Her brand-new home, her chests and tables, her children, the flickering light of the candles they could now afford — she knew all this could vanish overnight if God willed it. Just as the Assyrians had turned to dust, so might the New Englanders, unless they kept the memory of Christ fresh in their hearts.

During her second winter in Andover, pregnant for the seventh time, Anne launched herself into this enormous story, seizing upon the bloodiest moments in the fifteen centuries before Christ had saved the world. Truly, this was history from a Puritan perspective. Though she was venturing out of female territory, she was not straying from the orthodoxy of her faith. And she was convinced that if she could tell the story the way it should be told, she could prove that New England was poised at the apex of human history.

Another poet might have been tempted to choose the easiest poetic method in order to sprint straight through to the end. But Anne had never had any traffic with anything facile, and she determined to use one of the most difficult poetic forms of all — the heroic couplet — stretching herself to write iambic, or five-beat lines that rhymed, one after another. This challenge was especially daunting given the gigantic dimensions of the unwritten poem that lay before her like a dark, unplanted field. Ultimately, she would have to remain metrically accurate while wresting more than twenty-five hundred rhymes out of a language that, unlike Italian and French, resisted easy assonance of any kind. In fact, only a few years later, Milton would declare that it was the chain of "rime" that had held English poets back from creating truly lofty poetry out of the English language.[14]

But Anne would likely have vehemently disagreed with such a statement. Rhyme was a discipline that helped elevate the writing of poetry to a religious meditation. And it was also how she helped herself remember her lines until she could find the time to write them down. Such weighty subject matter merited a muscular approach, although she wilted now and then as her task came to seem insurmountable. Sometimes she would pause in the middle of her story to call attention to her weakness as a writer; for example, warning the reader that she would "rudely mar" any description of the glories of Babylon if she attempted to pen them with any accuracy.

> *This task befits not women like to men*
> *For what is past, I blush, excuse to make*
> *But humbly stand, some grave reproof to take;*
> *Pardon to crave for errours, is but vain,*
> *The Subject was too high, beyond my strain. . . .*[15]

Of course, there was a strategy at work here as well. Anne's apology may well have been sincere, but it would also help deflect the charges of plagiarism and trespass that she so dreaded.

If Ward were near he might have assuaged her occasional doubts about her abilities. In a kind of tribute to their friendship and his patient support of her work, she carefully copied the Latin phrase *Ne sutor ultra crepidam* (that the shoemaker should stick to making shoes) from the title page of her dear friend's *The Simple Cobbler of Aggawam* into her apology.[16] In doing so, Anne hinted that despite the criticism she might face as a female writer, she, like her old friend, would never abandon her true "cobbler's trade" of mending "feet" — a double entendre that Ward would appreciate, since "a foot" was the unit of measurement for metrical poetry.

In this determined spirit, she penned graphic accounts of the ruthless women of antiquity that more than counterbalanced her own protestations of weakness, particularly her descriptions of the careers of famous evil-doers. About Semiramis, the Assyrian soldier-empress, she wrote that she was "a brave virago" and was remarkable for her "valor." She relished the tale of the warring Greek queens, Euridice and Olympias, noting that Euridice's soldiers refused to "shoot" their "darts" at their old queen, Olympias, and concluding their tale with a boisterous description of Olympias's vengefulness after she defeated the younger queen. Anne made sure that her readers appreciated the multitude of Olympias's sins. The viperous old woman dug up the bones of her enemy's brother "and threw his bones about to show her spite." After she murdered her husband, she "slew," "stopped the breath," or "fried" the children of his other wives.[17]

Despite the horror Anne evinced at such wrongdoing, the number of lines she lavished on these cruel women suggested that there was something about them — their arrogant sense of freedom to create whatever havoc they desired — that fascinated her. Perhaps it was this last idea that had the most pull, the idea of liberty from the restraints of proper female decorum under which she and her sisters labored. Or maybe it was simply that female courage in all its manifestations was on Anne's mind during those first difficult winters in Andover.

BEFORE LONG Mercy must have told her husband about her elder sister's obsession with ancient history, although it seems unlikely that John could have missed Anne's immersion in her research, since there were probably books and papers stacked all over her kitchen table. But however he discovered his sister-in-law's under-taking, John was soon intrigued. He himself aspired to writing poetry, "though," he admitted, "my verse be not so finely spun" as Anne's. Later he would write that he wanted "to show my love" for his sister-in-law in whatever way he could. He admired everything about her, from her "sweet hand" to her "blush" when he praised the beauty of her lines.[18]

Surprisingly, Mercy raised no protest (that we know of) when John expressed his excitement about Anne and her work. Mercy must have known that John would not abandon her for her sister; he was too righteous and upstanding a Puritan. And clearly Anne was securely in love with Simon. Still, the intensity of her brother-in-law's admiration must have provided Anne with some comfort during these years. With Simon rarely home, she was often alone with her children and the servants in the big home her husband had built for her, and it seems likely that she wanted to talk about the books she was reading and the poetry she was writing. Like Ward and her father, John was devoted to poetry, as well as being remarkably well informed about the events in the Old World. And so Anne embarked on another passionate friendship with yet another intelligent, sensitive man. Again her work benefited. Buoyed by his belief in her, Anne labored at her chosen task, writing history in a land that appeared to her to have no history.

Meanwhile the drumroll of extraordinary events in England continued. Reports from England flooded the colony. The king had been captured. He escaped. He was captured again and escaped again. It was a game of cat and mouse, but what unearthly stakes! Most New Englanders were stunned: a king, captured? Surely this proved the "vanity" of all earthly pride, Anne decided, and immediately penned a short poem culled mainly from the Bible's bleakest book, Ecclesiastes, reflecting, "He's now a slave, that was a Prince of late."[19]

But there was a flip side to these chaotic happenings. If monarchs could be captives, then women could be political commentators, and though Anne's writing time had always been stolen from the rest of her duties, she managed to write more than five thousand lines of

"The Four Monarchies." Just as *The Quaternions* had allowed her to grapple with the conflicts that tormented England and her colony, her new poem allowed her to contemplate these terrible events from the wide lens of Christianized history.

Still, early in the spring of 1647, she felt an ebb in her spirits. As she wrote the lines that described the last king of the final, "fourth monarchy" (the Romans) — "The government they change, a new one bring, / And people swear ne'er to accept of king" — Anne stopped abruptly.[20] Even while she was contemplating the exile of the Tarquins from Rome, Cromwell and his men were resolving

> that it was our duty . . . to call Charles Stuart, that man of
> blood, to account for the blood he has shed and mischief he
> has done to his utmost against the Lord's cause and people in
> this poor nation.[21]

Present reality was suddenly more powerful than historical tales. The parallels between the past and present must have been overwhelming. Anne knew, with a sudden shock, that her grand idea was not bearing fruit and that her poem was not living up to her expectations. She complained, "Essays I many made but still gave out, / The more I mused, the more I was in doubt."[22] It was hard to admit that her "endeavours" had failed, but Anne acknowledged to herself that her poem was only barely limping along. It was time to halt, regroup, and change course, and only a woman so dedicated to her craft would have had the courage to admit this.

If there was no point in trying to flog dead words into life, Anne may also have been downcast that she was due to lose her new friend, John. In 1647, only a year after their move to Andover, Woodbridge had received a summons to return to England to fulfill a momentous duty. The leaders of the Puritan army wanted a New England minister to guide their negotiations with the king, who had been captured for the final time. Apparently an American Puritan seemed more neutral than his English counterparts and was therefore more acceptable to the suspicious Charles. Woodbridge came from a substantial family; he had a reputation for piety, but he had not actually raised arms against the king like so many of his English counterparts. Mercy and Anne trembled at the thought of losing him, even if only for a few months. Without Simon or John, they would have to struggle together in the frontier.

As for Woodbridge, bidding farewell to his wife, children, and his friend and sister-in-law was painful. Perhaps as a kind of consolation for his grief at departure, John sailed for England with a collection of Anne's poems by his side. This emissary act would turn out to be a momentous event for both Anne and America, but how it came about, no one knows. Did Anne hastily put the finishing touches on her manuscript and place it in John's hands? Perhaps this accounts for the abrupt stop to "The Four Monarchies." Did he urge her to let him have a copy to remember her by?

There were others who might have been involved, too. Perhaps Ward had urged Anne or someone in her family — John or her father — to send her new poems to him. John could not have proceeded very far in bringing Anne's work to England without her father's blessing also, and undoubtedly Simon's as well. The Dudley and Bradstreet names were at stake.

Certainly, Dudley had a vested interest in getting Anne's poems to England. He was hopeful that English Puritans would read his eldest daughter's manuscript with admiration so that he and his family could recoup their pride in their family name. Sarah's disgrace had brought shame upon their lineage. For Dudley, Anne's verse was a sign of God's grace, and her skill reflected positively on him as a Puritan father. Perhaps one daughter's heresies could be redeemed by another's piety.

Whether he, Simon, or even Woodbridge expected the poems to be published is unclear. What is evident is that they wanted the manuscript to circulate in the right circles. What better way to advertise the New England way than with Anne's prodigious learning and skill? It was time for English Puritans to read her words and be amazed at the spokeswoman America had produced.

CHAPTER SEVENTEEN

❧❧

The Tenth Muse

Is it possible? . . . It is the work of a Woman, honored, and
esteemed where she lives.
— JOHN WOODBRIDGE, "Epistle to the Reader"

T O SURRENDER HER MANUSCRIPT was brave on Anne's
part, as she must have known her poems would not stay in
John's luggage for long. He believed the public should read
her poetry, and although he would later claim that she knew nothing of his plans, Anne could hardly have been ignorant of the fact
that her team of supporters would try to circulate her manuscript
around important circles in England. If her fans succeeded with
their ploy, her work might well be condemned. As she had once
remarked to her father, any poetic prowess on the part of a woman
might lead critics to say she had stolen her lines from another poet.[1]
It was impossible, after all, for many people to believe that a female
could write skillful poetry.

With potential hecklers in mind, she had written a last-minute prologue to her largest, most ambitious poem, "The Four Monarchies." Immediately she sounded her note of humility, declaring:

> *To sing of wars, of captains, and of kings,*
> *Of cities founded, commonwealths begun,*
> *For my mean pen are too superior things:*
> *Or how they all, or each their dates have run*
> *Let poets and historians set these forth,*
> *My obscure lines shall not so dim their worth.*[2]

But of course this was what "The Four Monarchies" set out to do — to chronicle wars, generals, kings — exactly what Anne said was too challenging for her to tackle. A less "feminine" subject was hardly imaginable, and so Anne tried to save herself from attack by complaining that unlike the male poets she admired — Du Bartas, Sidney, and the Greeks — her muse was "foolish, broken," and "blemished." Acknowledging her vulnerability, she wrote, "A poet's pen all scorn I should thus wrong, / For such despite they cast on female wits."[3]

But Dudley's pride ran in her veins, and unable to remain entirely humble, she took issue with this last point, just as she had in her elegy to Queen Elizabeth.

> *Let Greeks be Greeks, and women what they are*
> *Men have precedency and still excel,*
> *It is but vain unjustly to wage war;*
> *Preeminence in all and each is yours;*
> *Yet grant some small acknowledgement of ours.*[4]

She did not mean to threaten men's primary position in the universe, she argued, but male "precedency" should not blot out the achievements and gifts of women. All male critics had to do was to bestow upon female writers even a "small" appreciation for their abilities. Canny politician that she was, Anne never claimed women's talents were "small," only that male "acknowledgement" was.

When Woodbridge finally arrived in London, he could not at first concentrate on promoting Anne's work, as he was thrust immediately into mediating between the king and the emissaries from Parliament. Helplessly, he watched Charles rebuff the attempts of the leaders to make peace. As the truculent Commons became increasingly impatient with the king, John understood that the crisis was escalating and that the worst was bound to happen. Inevitably, he would be stuck overseas for an indefinite amount of time, and so he sent for Mercy and his children, perhaps wishing he could bring Anne over as well.

But Mercy traveled without her sister, and by the time she landed on her native shore, it was evident that the talks between the king and his people had come to a standstill. This was a terrible blow to men like Ward and Woodbridge. On the bright side, however, John was released from his duties as a mediator and could now devote his time to the poems of the sister-in-law he so admired.

The first thing he seems to have done was to collect testimonials from men with worthy reputations, attesting to Anne's merits as a writer and as a pious Puritan. Ward soon joined him in this endeavor, contributing his own celebratory verse as well. After a few months, Anne's advocates had gathered twelve pages of prefatory poems by well-respected pious men to supplement the manuscript. These poems praised Anne's faithfulness and modesty, assuring the reading public that this verse was the product of a virtuous woman and not some fame-seeking troublemaker. It was common to have a few pages of such support, not unlike modern-day blurbs on the back of a book, but this was far more than was usual and illustrated her supporters' zeal on her behalf as well as their awareness of the criticism she faced as a woman writer. All in all, eleven individuals (including Ward, Woodbridge, and his brother, Benjamin) wrote commendations of her work.[5]

Meanwhile, Charles had been caught trying to persuade the Irish and the Scots to invade the country. He now appeared to his enemies to be the most pernicious traitor in the history of the land. Reconciliation appeared impossible. Woodbridge, Ward, and other moderate Puritans were heartbroken at the shipwreck that loomed. The angriest citizens, many of them Puritans, shouted that it was time for a trial to put the villainous monarch to the test.

To Ward and Woodbridge it must have seemed the perfect time to celebrate Anne and the mission she stood for. Both men believed she was an example of all that was exceptional about Massachusetts, and her poems were an excellent advertisement for the Christian venture in America.

But just as she had predicted, even though she was not yet published, suspicions had begun to circulate about the truth of her performance. Had this New England woman really written these poems without male assistance? How had she managed to acquire so much learning? And where did her metrical talents come from? Was she actually only a "Du Bartas girl," a female who had purloined her lines from the poetry of the French Protestant heavyweight?[6]

It was time to squelch these vicious doubts. Ward showed the manuscript to his own publisher, Stephen Bowtell, and somewhat surprisingly, Bowtell decided to publish this unknown colonial woman without delay. Nothing, he suspected, would sell better during these turbulent times, with the Puritans controlling the country, than the verse of a pious Puritan woman from New England, if only because of the curiosity factor. Besides, any author recommended by Ward would have been in favor with Bowtell, as *The Simple Cobbler of Aggawam* had been an extraordinary success for the time.

Back in Massachusetts, possibly unaware of their efforts on her behalf, Anne felt abandoned. For the first time in her life, she had no family around her — all of her sisters and her father were far away. The year after John's departure, she gave birth to another son, whom she named Dudley in an attempt to cheer up her father, whose spirits were probably still sagging from Sarah's blows to his family's reputation. But even the healthy delivery of a new baby could not make up for her loneliness. Of course, she was actually hardly ever really by herself, but her crowded household of children and servants, all dependent on her, may have made Anne feel even more alone. Apart from Simon, home only rarely, nowhere could she find an intellectual or spiritual equal. Resourceful as ever, Anne decided that, bereft of friends, sisters, mentors, and her husband, she would have to view this loneliness as an opportunity to cleave more closely to the Lord.[7]

Always serious about her religion, she became even more committed to an interior discipline of prayer and meditation, and her poetry began to reflect this change. With the last words of "The Four Monarchies," she had decided to give up writing such showy, learned, political poetry. Now, instead of reading tomes of history, she went for long walks by herself in the woods near her house.[8] The settlement had grown large enough to make it safe to wander down by the gentle curving river, although it was unwise to stray any farther.

The news from England was more and more terrible. By 1649 the king, far from being above the law, had been declared by Parliament guilty of treason. On January 30, after donning two shirts so that he would not shiver in the cold and be thought fearful, he gazed up at heaven one final time, quietly laid his head down on the block, and was beheaded before a huge mob that miraculously remained silent until after the royal blood spilled onto the ground. Immediately, English Puritans sent gleeful accounts of the gruesome event to their contacts in the New World. But Anne's friends and family were not so quick to jump on the bandwagon.

Even though she disparaged his behavior, his papist tendencies, and especially his traitorous dealings with the Irish, Anne was shocked. After all, Charles had been the king. Graphic reports made their way to Massachusetts. One eyewitness said the Puritans had lowered the height of the chopping block so that if Charles struggled, they could hold him down. Of course, as it turned out there was no need, since Charles had too acute a sense of history and theater to resort to such a last-minute wrestling match. Reportedly, though, the king's last words concerned such details:

King. "It [the block] might have been a little higher."
Executioner. "It can be no higher, sir."

King. "When I put out my hands this way, then —"

Then having said a few words to himself, as he stood, with hands and eyes lifted up, immediately stooping down he laid his neck upon the block; and . . . his Majesty, thinking [the executioner] had been going to strike, bade him, "Stay for the sign."

Executioner. "Yes, I will, and it please your Majesty."

After a short pause, his Majesty stretching forth his hands, the executioner at one blow severed his head from his body; which, being held up and showed to the people, was with his body put into a coffin covered with black velvet and carried into his lodging.[9]

Another witness recorded that "such a groan as I never heard before and hope never to hear again" emerged from the mob.[10] Of course this famous sigh was as symbolic as it was bloodcurdling. Charles had met his execution with such dignity that even some Puritans could not avoid regarding him as a martyr. To a people raised on *The Book of Martyrs*, nothing guaranteed a following more quickly than submitting to a seemingly unfair public execution.

Charles's death annihilated centuries of English tradition. Certainly royal pretenders to the throne had been executed before, but no sitting monarch had ever been sentenced to die by his own people. Whether or not one supported his cause, his execution asked the English people to question what they believed and to whom they were loyal. As a result, people began to see that even kings were fallible, vulnerable to the will of the land, and not God's chosen hand servants. There was a touch of empowered liberation to this sort of realization, as well as a growing cynicism. The future was frighteningly uncertain, and so it was only fitting that Cromwell, the military commander who rushed in to fill the vacuum, was compared to a rush of "three-forked lightning" by the poet Andrew Marvell.[11]

With the sacred links to the past severed, England seemed a volatile place to be. Anne could not help worrying about John,

Mercy, and Ward. Winthrop's son Stephen, who was stationed in London, wrote home in consternation, declaring, "New England seems to be the only safe place where I believe we must come . . . at length if we can."[12]

Comparatively speaking, the colony did seem a far more peaceful and certain place than the Old World in the immediate aftermath of the execution. But then New England lost its own famous leader, John Winthrop. At the age of sixty-one, after a final illness, he died on March 26, 1649, in his home in Boston. For all but seven years of the colony's existence, Winthrop had stood as its leader. To the colonists, the loss of both the king and their old governor in the space of two months seemed a double calamity. With Winthrop's chair empty, the time seemed ripe for disaster to strike.

Anne coped with these events the best way she knew how, through the writing of poetry. She set herself the task of penning an elegy to the dead king, whom she had hated but who she did not think deserved to die. Cromwell and his band of followers had decreed it traitorous to lament Charles's death, but Andover was a long way from London and Anne was used to employing literary disguises. It was not difficult for her to come up with a device that allowed her to mourn the king and protect herself and her friends at the same time, although it must have seemed strange to think that they faced danger from other Puritans.

She wrote with conviction and speed, perhaps because she suspected her manuscript was soon to be published and wanted this poem included, but she may also have hoped to comfort Ward in what she knew would be his profound grief. He had written *The Simple Cobbler of Aggawam* to forestall this violent event but had failed. Her brother-in-law, too, would likely feel he had not carried out his mission of mediation. But she could not be outright in her condolences. If anyone suspected the men of sympathizing with the dead king, they might be killed.

In her elegy "David's Lamentation for Saul and Jonathan II Sam. 1:19," Anne assumed the voice of David, the Israelite poet and ancient king of Israel who had ascended to the throne after the death of King Saul and his son, Jonathan. This was the only time she adopted a male identity in her poetry, and this was in keeping with her sense that she had to conceal her political views behind a blameless facade.

The verse begins innocently enough: "Alas, slain is the head of Israel." But of course any mention of a "head" and a "slain" king in one line could only bring to mind Charles. In case anyone was inclined to miss her point, she emphasizes the actual royal scalp, writing, "The shield of Saul was vilely cast away, / . . . / As if his head ne'er felt the sacred oil."[13] After all, even if they hadn't been there, her readers, too, were likely haunted by the images: the king's head tumbling into the chute, the damp spray of blood shooting forth from his arteries, the awful gape of his ghastly neck.

It was a bleak poem that Anne rushed to finish. When at last they read her verse, Woodbridge and Ward knew immediately that this elegy belonged in her book. They placed it last, as her triumphal effort, the one that spoke most directly to her time and people.

Adopting David's point of view had allowed Anne to make another point that New England Puritans found especially appealing. David had mourned the old king, but the fact remained that Saul had disobeyed the Lord and had even sought to murder David; that is why both he and his son had to die. Everyone understood that David was the rightful leader, and Anne's assumption of his voice equated New England with the new, holier Israel, one that might mourn the passing of the old but represented the hope of the future. This final elegy reinforced Anne's "Dialogue"; England, like Saul, was condemned to die. New England, like David, was bound for glory.

Anne might well have rejoiced to be living in the promised land, but though she might prophesy that Israel (in the guise of New England) would flourish and conquer the Philistines, it was sad to see the new sweep away the old, even if ordained by God. "How are the mighty fall'n into decay?" she lamented, bearing witness to New England's glorious ascent, while old England's bloodied corpse lay in the sand.[14] There was another significance in her speaking with David's voice — a rush of exhilaration came from identifying herself with the man who was not only Israel's greatest king but also the author of the most beautiful poems in history, the Psalms. If only in the lines of this poem, she could at last speak with the authority of the greatest male poet of all time.

ON JULY 1, 1650, a little book, measuring only five and a half by three and three-quarter inches, was offered for sale. It was called *The Tenth Muse Lately Sprung Up in America*, a title John had chosen himself. It was easier for men to envision a woman as an inspiration, or a muse of poetry, rather than an author, and so Woodbridge's title was well conceived. Anne's work, he implied, was worth reading not because she claimed to be a poet in her own right but because it would encourage other, male, writers to produce new poems. In his prefatory letter he suggested that Anne had had no intention of allowing anyone to read her work. Indeed, the only person's "displeasure" he "fear[ed]" in publishing the book was hers (a disingenuous remark, since the reading public, too, was liable to attack him for publishing a woman). John wrote that "contrary to her expectation, I have presumed to bring to public view, what she resolved should . . . never see the sun."[15]

John's presentation worked, and Ward's seal of approval finished the job. *The Tenth Muse* thrilled the public, taking it by storm. Given the tense mood of the country, Anne's poetry struck the perfect note. She spoke on behalf of harmony and peace, even as she advocated violence against infidels. Her New England seemed the repository of hope for the Old World and held forth the promise of healing.

This was balm for her readers, when optimism was rare and doom seemed inevitable (except for the eager Puritan extremists, whose spirits had never been more buoyant). Far from being threatened, English readers saw the volume as a curiosity — few women had ventured into the literary marketplace, let alone one who had ventured to "the Occidentall parts of the World" — and sales steadily mounted as everyone eagerly read this pioneer woman's words.[16] There are no records of any of the criticism Woodbridge, Ward, and Anne herself had feared. Instead, Anne Bradstreet became a kind of heroine. She embodied the spirit and the voice of these Puritan times. And, indeed, seven years after publication, *The Tenth Muse* was still selling briskly on both sides of the Atlantic.

For some the event was as strange as if a monkey or a parakeet had published a volume of verse. Women were not supposed to have brains capacious enough to hold the enormous amount of information Anne wielded. Perhaps they could write a letter or a prayer or two, but they could never master the noblest form of all — verse. Even Woodbridge had declared,

> *Some books of women I have heard of late,*
> *Perused some, so witless, intricate,*
> *So void of sense, and truth . . .*
>
> . . . .
> *. . . I might with pity,*
> *Have wished them all to women's works to look,*
> *And never more to meddle with their book.*[17]

Despite the clamor that erupted when *The Tenth Muse* arrived in the marketplace, Anne did not at first know her poems were in print. It took several months for the news to sail across the ocean. In some ways it was fortunate for her that there was this delay, because once the letters began to arrive telling her of her little book's good fortune, and once the volume itself landed on the shores of America, there was nothing she could do to stop the printing press.

At last, at thirty-eight years old, Anne held her book in her hands. It must have been with a mixture of joy and trepidation that she grasped the leather binding and sliced the pages apart. She knew that at this point there was nothing she could do to fix her poems; the many mistakes she found scrambled across every page were there to stay. Whether they were the result of publisher's errors or her own lack of skill, she "blush[ed]" at the many "irksome" imperfections.[18]

In her poem "The Author to Her Book," she called *The Tenth Muse* the "ill-formed offspring of my feeble brain" and then extended this metaphor, saying that since she had "affection" for her child, she had attempted to "amend" the book's "blemishes," but had failed.[19]

> *I washed thy face, but more defects I saw,*
> *And rubbing off a spot still made a flaw.*
> *I stretched thy joints to make thee even feet,*
> *Yet still thou run'st more hobbling than is meet;*
> *In better dress to trim thee was my mind,*
> *But nought save homespun cloth i' th' house I find.*[20]

Cleverly, Anne adjusted her meter to reflect her poetic apologies, adding an extra syllable to the "hobbling" line so that the verse itself appeared to limp. The "homespun" material she used to dress her "brat" was an assertion of her new style.[21] No more aping the learned English male poets. She was a Puritan mother living in America, and as such her poetry could only be roughly hewn. Of course, as in "The Prologue," the announcement of her humility would serve her well, according to the Puritan ethic.

Although there are no records of how many colonists bought *The Tenth Muse*, one indicator of the book's popularity in New England is that it was the only book of poetry in the library of Edward Taylor (the next generation's distinguished poet) fifty or so years later.[22] This meant the volume's popularity was widespread as well as long lasting, since Taylor lived in the western part of the state. Some historians have felt it fair to surmise that nearly every Puritan home in New England contained a copy of *The Tenth Muse*.[23] And Anne herself became one of the few women to gain an entry in Cotton Mather's history of the period, written forty years after her book's publication. Looking back on Anne's achievement with nostalgia, Mather called her poems "a monument for her Memory beyond the Statliest Marbles."[24]

In the opening lines of "The Author to Her Book," Anne reiterated John's prefatory letter and declared that she had never thought to publish her poems herself. Instead, she claimed, the manuscript was "snatched" by "friends" who were eager to publish her work, and she was shocked to be catapulted into the public eye. Although she admitted she had sent the book "out of door," she insisted she was free of ambitious aspirations.

The Tenth Muse was 220 pages long and printed in a tiny typeface. There were thirteen poems in all, including her elegies to Du Bartas, Elizabeth I, and Sidney, *The Quaternions*, "The Prologue," "The Four Monarchies," and "David's Lamentation for Saul and Jonathan." It was impossible for her readers to miss her piety and skill. Clearly Anne Bradstreet was a learned, faithful woman whose work demonstrated the redemptive effects of emigrating to America. No Old World woman had ever achieved such a feat; perhaps New England had enhanced her abilities in some mysterious way, as though God looked with favor on both her project and the colony.

When he overheard remarks like these, Dudley could breathe a deep sigh of exultation. Anne's book went a long way toward helping her family recover from Sarah's disgrace. She had restored the reputation of the Dudley name and had become an unwitting celebrity. John had made sure to tell the reader in his prefatory letter that Anne was above all a woman who was "honoured, and esteemed where she lives for her gracious demeanour, her eminent parts, her pious conversation, and discreet managing of her family occasions." Her poems had not impaired her commitment to her family as a good mother and wife. Her neighbors saw that she had not shirked her duties and instead had "curtailed . . . her sleep, and other refreshments" in order to devote her time to her writing. Indeed, John declared, she had spent only "some few hours" on her work.[25]

This was clearly not true, but what else could Woodbridge say? The appearance of any woman in print was suspicious enough — as John wrote, "The worst effect of [a man's] reading will be unbelief, which will make him question whether it be a woman's work, and ask, is it possible?" — and so a volume of this weight and magnitude needed copious explanation. No other woman in the history of the English language had managed such an accomplishment. It would be more than a century before another female would publish work with this kind of ambition and on this large a scale. Understandably, then, Woodbridge tried to reassure readers that Anne was not trespassing in male territory. *The Tenth Muse* was a "Womans Book" and needed to be read with sympathy by male readers, not with "envie of the inferiour Sex."[26]

And yet no one balked at her achievement. Her book galloped through printings. In 1658 it was listed as one of "the most vendible books in England" in the bookseller William London's catalog, next to "Herbert's The Temple, Mr Milton's Poems . . . and Mr Shaksper's Poems." Fifteen years later, "a very learned English woman who had tutored the daughters of Charles I" exclaimed, "How excellent a Poet Mrs. Bradstreet is (now in America) her works do testify."[27] One young man wrote a fan letter:

> *Your only hand those Poesies did compose,*
> *Your head the source, whence all those springs did flow,*
> *Your voice, whence changes sweetest notes arose,*
> *Your feet that kept the dance alone, I trow:*
> *Then, vail your bonnets, Poetasters all,*
> *Strike, lower amain, and at these humbly fall,*
> *And deem your selves advance'd to be her Pedestal.*[28]

It seems likely that Anne wrote back to this particular devotee, whose name was John Rogers, because she had heard of him from her sister Patience. He was courting Patience's daughter Elizabeth, and when at last he married her, John was thrilled that Anne became his aunt by marriage.

Although it was slightly overwhelming to receive such impassioned testimonials from young men, Anne also relished the attention. She cultivated her relationship with young Rogers, who was a man "of so sweet a temper" that he had few enemies and would, in fact, one day become president of Harvard College. This would turn out well for Anne, as it would probably be Rogers who would oversee the printing of her *Selected Works* years after she had died.[29]

Anne had achieved even more than her bold father had dreamed of when he had devoted himself to her early education. Dudley could only rejoice. New England and Anne were his two largest sources of pride, and now they had merged in a breathtaking climax. His intelligent eldest daughter had become the spokesperson for the American Puritan way.

Sadly for Anne, she was able to bask in her father's pride for only a few years. Dudley died in 1653, when Anne was forty-one. Characteristically, she turned her attention to writing an elegy for him, fulfilling what she termed was her "duty" even as she sought comfort in verse. Though it must have been a struggle to express her admiration and love when laboring under such grief, she turned out eighty-five lines, lavishing far more attention on this tribute than she had on her brief twenty-line poem for her mother.

> *My mournful mind, sore pressed, in trembling verse*
> *Presents my lamentations at his hearse,*
> *Who was my father, guide, instructor too,*
>
> . . . .
>
> *For who more cause to boast his worth than I?*
> *Who heard or saw, observed or knew him better?*
> *Or who alive than I a greater debtor?*[30]

In this poem Anne expresses the special bond she and her father had. No one was closer to him than she, she claimed, and therefore she must endure the largest share of grief at his death. Even his new wife does not have the right to interject herself between the two.

"He was my father" she declares, making no mention of her siblings. She was "his own."[31] Then, in true Dudley fashion, she shifts the poem's theme to America and her father's other daughter, New England. Just as Dudley delighted in Anne as the poetic spokesperson for New England, so Anne is proud of his role in the creation of the colony. He must be acknowledged for all he did so that the voices of "malice" and "envy" will not drown out his achievements:

> *One of thy Founders, him New England know,*
> *Who stayed thy feeble sides when thou wast low,*
> *Who spent his state, his strength and years with care*
> *That after-comers in them might have share.*
> *True patriot of this little commonweal,*
> *Who is't can tax thee ought, but for thy zeal?*[32]

The elegy's last word, "lament," summed up Anne's feelings during this difficult time. Word had come from over the ocean that her beloved friend Ward had died the previous fall, and his loss coupled with Dudley's was surely hard to bear. Then John Cotton, too, expired at his home in Boston after a short illness. She seemed to have lost all of her male teachers and guides in one blow; significantly, *lament* was the last word she would write for almost ten years. With the exception of a few devotional verses, she would not pen another serious poem until the early 1660s.

No one knows why this is, or even if it is strictly true. Some of her papers could have gotten lost, especially since in the years to come she would face a tragedy that would destroy many of her belongings. But it does seem likely that she was too alone in Andover to compose poetry. Without Woodbridge and Ward, and now without her father's support, perhaps she could no longer struggle against all the barriers that lay between a woman and a serious writing life. Or perhaps she was simply too preoccupied with running her household, as Simon continued to be busy with colonial matters of governance.

Although she could take some comfort from her eighth and last baby, who was born in 1652, she revealed the extent of her yearnings when she named the infant John, after the "brother" she missed and loved so well. Her children brought a certain kind of joy, and originally they had given her the confidence that God had blessed her and her attempts at poetry, but as time wore on, they could hardly be said to make writing easier. When little John "with wayward cries . . . did disturb her rest," she felt herself "waste" as the child "did thrive." Seven times before, she had done this, and she was "spent"; her strength was ebbing. How could it be otherwise? For almost twenty years, Anne had been bearing children; she was exhausted. By the time she was forty-four, "the wretched days" yawned in front of her, each one laden with responsibilities and hard physical labor that taxed her beyond her abilities. In one journal entry in 1656, she wrote, "My spirits were worn out and many times my faith weak."[33]

Her tasks were made all the more difficult by the fact that mysterious illnesses began to strike with alarming frequency. Sometimes Anne wondered if it were time to follow her father on the last pious journey, the one she hoped would take her to heaven and the embrace of the eternal "Bridegroom," Jesus, the one "man" who would never leave her and on whom she could count without any hesitation.[34]

Her passion for God grew, as though she were in the midst of an all-consuming love affair and had to endure time apart from her beloved as she once had mourned her time away from Simon. Employing a rather jumbled collision of divine identities, she wrote:

> Lord, why should I doubt any more when Thou hast given me such assured pledges of Thy love? First, Thou art my Creator, I Thy creature, Thou my master, I Thy servant. But hence arises not my comfort, Thou art my Father, I Thy child; "Ye shall be My sons and daughters," saith the Lord Almighty. Christ is my brother, I ascend unto my Father, and your

Father, unto my God and your God; but lest this should not
be enough, thy maker is thy husband. Nay more, I am a
member of His body, He my head.[35]

She reflected, "[God] is not man that He should lie." Instead,
like a perfect suitor, "His word He plighted hath on high." And it
was this idea that comforted her most as she yearned to "cleave
close to him alway[s]."[36] Perhaps her loneliness and pain during
these years was beneficial, since, according to her faith, it was an
opportunity to deepen her relationship with God.

Still, sometimes her suffering grew so intense that life felt almost
impossible to endure. For the first time since she was an adolescent,
she was tortured with thoughts of her own death. "In my distress,"
she cried, "I sought the Lord / When naught on earth could comfort give, / And when my soul these things abhorred." But God gave
her comfort in her despair. "Then Lord," she wrote, "Thou said'st
unto me, 'Live.'"[37]

During this bleak period, it must have felt to her that her sons
and daughters were all she had left. Although her eldest, twenty-
year-old Samuel, had just graduated from Harvard and her second
son, thirteen-year-old Simon, was at school in Ipswich, all the others were still home with her. Her two older daughters, Dorothy and
Sarah, aged eighteen and fifteen, were helpful, but they were rest-
lessly awaiting bridegrooms (Dorothy would soon marry Seaborn
Cotton, John Cotton's eldest son). The two younger girls, Hannah
and Mercy, were also useful helpmates, but in 1653, when baby
John was a year old, they were still only eleven and seven, while
Dudley was a busy and mischievous five-year-old.

And so, even as she combated the rolling tide of fevers that
struck her down, she continued the spiritual education of her
strong-willed children, who "began to sin as soon as act." She tried
to guard herself against their "pleasing face[s]" because, behind
their smiles, there often lurked "a serpent's sting." Sadly, sometimes
they seemed to delight in breaking the fifth commandment to

honor their parents; they were "oft stubborn, peevish, sullen," and were inclined to "pout and cry" for no apparent reason. All this while encountering the childhood illnesses and daily "breaches, knocks and falls" that were part of life on the frontier.[38]

To Anne it must have seemed that the household would fall apart without her efforts. Her sons and daughters desperately needed her, and yet her strength seemed to be failing her. If she were to die, she wanted to ensure that her children grew to become devout Puritans and would continue to build New England in accordance with her father's vision. Rather than trusting her children entirely to the care of servants or giving in to the temptation to succumb to her illnesses, she fought to stay alive and keep them out of the clutches of some "step-dame." And it was in this protective vein that she decided to write a spiritual autobiography for the benefit of her children. She explained why in the prefatory lines:

> *This book by any yet unread,*
> *I leave for you when I am dead,*
> *That being gone, here you may find*
> *What was your living mother's mind.*
> *Make use of what I leave in love,*
> *And God shall bless you from above.*[39]

This five-page document is remarkable as a celebration of her faith as well as an admission of her doubts. Anne urged her children to know that questioning was an essential component of Puritan belief; she wrote, "I have not studied in this you read to show my skill, but to declare the truth, not to set forth myself, but the glory of God." She had always assumed that "there is a God," but she wondered, "How should I know He is such a God as I worship in Trinity, and such a Saviour as I rely upon?" By voicing her own uncertainties, she gave her children permission to make their own journeys of faith. Not that they should stray from Puritanism but that they should not allow their delusions and questions to take them away from God. Everyone, Anne implied, could face such "block[s]," and she outlined hers in surprising detail, from her flirtation with "the Popish religion" to a profound despair, where she asked, "Is there faith upon the earth?" She had to put aside the virtuous reputation she had worked so diligently to create in order to confess such things, but nothing was more important than helping her children persevere in their "pilgrimage."[40]

Characteristically, she ended what she called her "short matters" with an apology: "This was written in much sickness and weakness, and is very weakly and imperfectly done, but if you can pick any benefit out of it, it is the mark which I aimed at."[41] In fact this would be the principle that would govern Anne for the rest of her writing life. Even in the formal poetry she would embark on once again, she would endeavor to reveal "the glory of God" rather than the splendor of her "skill." The most important thing now, she believed, was to write for the benefit of her readers. Like her father, she would dedicate herself to the "after-comers": those inhabitants of New England who would read her words after she died. Perhaps she could provide them with the inspiration to devote themselves to the true God as well as to Massachusetts Bay, God's chosen land.

CHAPTER EIGHTEEN

Farewell Dear Child

To HER SURPRISE, Anne did eventually regain her health, and her spirits. In the spring of 1657, she exclaimed, "My sun's returned with healing wings, / My soul and body doth rejoice."[1] She could not believe her good luck. By 1660 her life had become somewhat easier. She had survived her battles with illness. Her troubled and unhappy sister Sarah had died the year before at age thirty-nine, bringing sorrow but also relieving Anne and all her siblings of their worries about her behavior.

The long decade of prayer, physical suffering, desolation, and self-reliance had stood Anne in good stead as a religious pilgrim. She had discovered that she could search out the divine and receive consolation from her prayers. Truly, she had matured into a devout woman her father and mother would have been proud of. At last she felt she had gained "access unto His throne, / Who is a God so wondrous great" and she yearned "to show my duty with delight."[2]

Her children were thriving. Her daughter Sarah had married a pious and wealthy man named Richard Hubbard and lived in nearby

Ipswich. Simon graduated from Harvard that spring and began his studies as a minister. Hannah had married a man named Andrew Wiggin in 1659 and had moved to Exeter, New Hampshire.[3] Mercy, Dudley, and John were the only children left in the Bradstreet home. At fourteen, Mercy was indispensable to her mother, aiding in the cheese making, mending, cooking, and gardening.

Servants were now more plentiful and far more reliable because Andover was gradually becoming a more established community, and so Anne was likely not as overwhelmed by her household duties. The town itself had also become a more pleasant place to live. There were close to five hundred inhabitants, and more were coming. An entire generation had grown up there, married, and produced children. A few small shops had set up business, and trade had become brisk and profitable, although, of course, the settlement was still a far cry from being a center of colonial life. The road to Boston was poorly marked, and the trip could take as long as three days. There were still no bridges, and when the rivers were swollen with rain, crossings could be dangerous.

In some ways, then, Anne was more alone and isolated than ever, with most of her children out of the house and civilization a long way away, but something she had never anticipated had come to pass. The children's absence meant that a good deal of the hard labor of the last ten years was over. She had more time on her hands and more strength than she had had in years. She was "blessed" in "elder age," she declared joyfully.[4]

Gradually she turned her attention to correcting the poems in *The Tenth Muse*, revising and in some cases deleting entire passages. Without the company of her male advisers, this task had lost some of its luster, but it was also a way of remembering her old friends, and her father, too. In 1661, however, a blockbuster poem flashed onto the Massachusetts scene. Suddenly everyone was talking about Michael Wigglesworth's *Day of Doom*, and Anne's little book was rendered second best, seemingly less notable and less substantial than this gripping melodrama that graphically described each sorrowful detail of Judgment Day.

An unhappy minister, Wigglesworth was a tortured individual, prone to psychosomatic diseases, and subject to terrible waves of anxiety and self-recrimination.[5] His poem reflected his own imaginative re-creation of the punishments of the Lord. Wives shrieked as they were ripped from their husband's side and cast into hell. Piteous little babies called for their mothers as they too were plunged into "fire and brimstone [where] they wail and cry and howl / For tort'ring pain." No one was spared except for the chosen "sheep."[6]

New Englanders could not lap this up quickly enough. By the end of the first year, the book had sold eighteen hundred copies in America alone, and one out of twenty colonists had purchased it. In fact there are no complete first editions of the poem because it was "literally read to pieces."[7] It was impossible for Anne not to notice this kind of splashy success. Whether she was jealous or inspired or even unmoved, Anne made a decision that her own career was not over and began to think about writing new verse again. But while Anne had been drawing closer to God, it seemed the rest of the world was growing further away from Him.

In 1660, after more than a decade of Puritan rule, most English people yearned for a relaxation of the strict moral code of the dissenters and a return to the old ways, such as the right to drink, smoke, play games, and go to the theater. After the iron-willed Cromwell died, and Royalists and moderates were returned to power, Parliament actually entreated Charles's son, Charles II, to come back to England. The new Charles agreed, and the Puritan era was over.

This event, known as the Restoration, left Massachusetts Bay feeling isolated and alone. Now they were the only Puritan enclave and as such were vulnerable to the whims of the new king. Charles II was, quite naturally, suspicious of any individual with Puritan leanings, let alone an entire colony.

When rumors floated from overseas that the king and his advisers were grumbling at New England's very existence, the General Court knew that the situation was urgent; it was time to send their best negotiators to England. Even before he told her, Anne must have suspected her husband would be in charge of this expedition. Who else in the colonies had his credentials? Simon believed that their ties to the Old World were crucial to their survival and that their best chance was to pursue a compromise with England, one that would appease the king and yet leave them "the liberty to walk in the faith of the gospel."[8]

In January 1661 Simon boarded a ship that was coated with ice. The ocean was black with cold, but Anne knew that it was her husband's duty to brave the wintry Atlantic for the sake of the colony. The only way to preserve their existence, it seemed, was for Simon to persuade Charles that Massachusetts was no threat to the Old World.

While Simon was gone, discussions hummed in every household. What did the future hold? The first generation of immigrants and their leading magistrates and ministers were almost all dead; people feared that the founders' dream of a "godly" Massachusetts Bay might soon follow them to their graves. It seemed "the saving remnant" had become just that — leftovers of the fierce movement of the first half of the century. Now that England had chosen a different path, many New Englanders felt abandoned, and this caused the most pious among them to look inward.[9] To the devout it had begun to seem that Massachusetts was sliding away from the ideals of the original settlers. There was no one among their friends and family who seemed as religious or as visionary as Cotton, Ward, Winthrop, or Dudley.

For many, though Anne was luckily not one of them, their children were a large part of the struggle. Some younger Puritans simply refused to examine their consciences or attend services in the meetinghouses. Each congregation faced the possibility of extinction as the old members died off and new ones failed to join. Some thought the churches should adopt something the ministers called the Half Way Covenant, which permitted children of church members to be baptized but did not allow them to become full-fledged participants in church rites such as the Lord's Supper without proving their faith. But men and women like Anne resisted this idea because they feared it would lessen the purity of the original churches. They felt that congregations of "true believers" were all they had left now that the Anglicans were back in charge in England.

Yet there were some children who struggled to become more observant. In fact these individuals devoted themselves to their religion with a kind of fierce insecurity based on their sense of being less faithful than their parents. They had not made the same sacrifices for their religion as those who had crossed the ocean and homesteaded in the wilderness; consequently their admiration for the men and women who had come before them bordered on hero worship. Inevitably, Anne and Simon, as surviving members of the first-generation immigrants, had grown into icons for these young people.

What most Bay colonists agreed on was that they did not need a diversity of faith. Almost ten years earlier, Dudley had warned of what was to come, in a preface to his will:

> I . . . leav[e] this testimony behinde mee for the use and
> example of my posteritie . . . that I have hated & doe hate
> every false way in religion, not onely the Old Idolitry and
> superstition of Popery which is weareing away, but much more
> (as being much worse), the newe heresies, blasphamies, &
> errors of late sprange up in our native country of England, and
> secretly received & fostered here more then I wish they were.[10]

But in the first years of his rule, King Charles II broke with his New England subjects on this topic, issuing — to their horror — proclamations of tolerance in the mother country. His advisers were pushing him to extend this sort of open-minded policy to the colony's Bible-based government. After all, the English were still reeling from thirteen years of Puritan tyranny, where it was illegal to "keep Christmas, or to deck the house with holly and ivy." Statues had been "chipped ruthlessly into decency." Pictures that were deemed irreligious were burned. One could only serve in

Parliament by showing evidence of "real godliness." Every theater in the land had been closed. "Bull-baiting, bear-baiting, horse-racing, cock-fighting, the village revel, the dance on the village green were put down." No one could even "eat a mince pie."[11] To the majority of English people, Massachusetts Bay was no longer the shining example of virtue it had been in the turbulent 1640s; rather, it was a vestige of the terrible rigidity that had killed a king and almost destroyed their country.

In the face of this opposition from their homeland, Puritan New England snapped to attention. Suddenly it seemed their dedication to Puritan orthodoxy was in profound danger. For example, from their point of view, the Quakers, who had recently invaded Boston, "strolling naked down the aisles" of the Puritans' churches, shouting disagreement in the middle of the ministers' sermons, and in general flouting all attempts to restrain their behavior, were a shocking new challenge from Satan.[12]

The court had tried its ordinary shaming tactics, at first whipping and banishing the Friends and then resorting to chopping the ears off two individuals who were repeat offenders. But these punishments proved ineffective against the determined Quakers, and Governor Endecott grumbled that they had an "incorrigible contempt of authority." The next band of marauding Friends who shouted on the street corners in Boston were banished, but when they returned despite repeated warnings, the court decided that the time had come to up the ante. In 1659 two Quakers were hung on the Boston Common, and the following year Anne Hutchinson's old friend Mary Dyer, who had converted to Quakerism, was also executed. "She hangs there like a flag" one witness exclaimed.[13]

Most English people were scandalized when they got wind of what they could only regard as the latest evidence of New England fanaticism. Even English Puritans were worried by such fierce intolerance; they had seen the bloodshed it could cause, and they wrote letters urging their New England counterparts to relent and accept non-Puritans into their towns.

Instead of being moved by these entreaties, the Bay magistrates were alarmed. Nothing could be worse, they believed, than the kind of open society the English government now advocated. The outrage the English expressed at the execution of the Quakers exacerbated the New Englanders' sense of being the only light left in the world. In response they assumed an even more aggressive stance against outsiders and those who challenged the authority of Massachusetts churches and government. To people like Anne and Simon, who were actually moderates in this debate, New England deserved to be admired. Of course the colony should adhere to its principles of religion and governance, as these were far superior to English ones.

But if the colonists were anxious to hear the results of Simon's conference with the king, Anne was worried that she had bid farewell to her husband for the last time. In a heartfelt prayer revealing how much she still loved him, she begged God to keep Simon safe for her. "O hearken, Lord, unto my suit / And my petition sign. / . . . Keep and preserve / My husband, my dear friend."[14]

Anne devoted the months Simon was away to searching for "secret places" to "kneel or walk," to commune with God and consider the poems that lay ahead.[15] But besides her entreaty for Simon's safety, she had not yet put her pen to paper when at last he returned to Massachusetts with mixed tidings.

The king had renewed their charter, but only in exchange for certain concessions: that the court allow the free worship of Anglicans, and that anyone, not just church members, could vote. Both of these tenets were anathema to the New England Puritans, and although Anne was relieved that her husband was safely home, it seemed to her and her friends that their colony was in profound danger of becoming like the corrupt and licentious Old World.

That fall she inscribed the first words of a poem that she decided to call "Contemplations." In this work she sought to capture the depth of her reflections during her solitary walks. Gone were her Elizabethan flourishes, her claims to encyclopedic knowledge. Her style had changed as her commitment to her religion had deepened. Her old hunger for fame had gradually given way to a concern for the spiritual well-being of future generations. It was her job, she believed, to help save the Puritan faith of the colony. Unfortunately, when she scoured her books and her memory, she could find no poetic structure that seemed right, and so she invented her own stanza, laboring to make this the most finely crafted of all her verse.

She lit upon an eight-line device, piling seven lines of iambic pentameter on top of one longer line, an alexandrine, and tying the whole thing together with a more intricate rhyme scheme than in any of her other poems (*ababccc*). But she did not want her verse to sound fancy or overwrought, nor the other extreme, like a tedious sermon. Instead, she hoped to recount the twists and turns of a real spiritual pilgrimage, and so she cast pitfalls along the way, temptations that could lure the pious reader from the final righteous destination, just as she herself had been "many times . . . troubled" by Satan.[16]

Using herself as an example, Anne sought to examine the unique place of human beings in the world. Only mankind, she says, can feel God's presence and experience both sorrow and joy, yet often we seem inferior to the rest of nature. The glorious sun, trees, birds, even crickets "in their little art" all pay tribute to God's greatness. Yet the poet is "mute" and unable to do the same. The seasons are cyclical, and each winter is replaced with a new spring, but man ages and dies. The fish and birds know "not what is past, nor what to come dost fear," but go about their business, "feel[ing] no sad thoughts or cruciating cares" and "know[ing] not their felicity." Man, on the other hand, is "at best a creature frail and vain . . . subject to sorrows, losses, sickness, pain." He is vulnerable to "troubles from foes, from friends, from dearest, near'st relation" — this last was perhaps a veiled reference to the poet's own trials with Sarah.[17]

To Anne the truth of mankind's "natural" existence is that it is fleeting. She writes, "But man grows old, lies down, remains where once he's laid," lamenting that human beings "see[m] by nature and by custom cursed." In part this is because we are forever separated from the rest of nature by the fall of Adam. Cain's murder of Abel, Anne reflects, is only further evidence of our flawed nature, "branded with guilt and crushed with treble woes." With both compassion and a sense of sadness, she pities the plight of the human being:

> *And yet this sinful creature, frail and vain,*
> *This lump of wretchedness, of sin and sorrow,*
> *This weatherbeaten vessel wracked with pain,*
> *Joys not in hope of an eternal morrow;*
> *Nor all his losses, crosses, and vexation,*
> *In weight, in frequency and long duration*
> *Can make him deeply groan for that divine translation.*[18]

Despite this, rather than extolling "the heavens, the trees, the earth" over man, Anne reminds us that nature will eventually "darken, perish, fade and die," while only "man was made for endless immortality." In other words, birds play an essential role in the universe, but it is a particularly human gift to yearn for God. In fact, she suggests, it is our capacity for both reflection and anticipation that will (with God's grace) allow humankind to triumph over death. We are blessed with the ability to glimpse redemption; the problem is that we rarely exercise this capacity. Instead, "he that saileth in the world of pleasure" doesn't realize until "sad affliction comes and makes him see" that only heaven can offer "security."[19]

Finally, Anne reflects that "time ... draws oblivion's curtains" even over kings and monuments. "Their names ... are forgot. ... Nor wit nor gold ... scape times rust." The futility of seeking fame — her own personal weakness — is clear. Only with God is there any kind of permanence for the pilgrim.[20]

Despite the beauty and completeness of "Contemplations," which is now regarded as "a work of arresting integrity" and her most significant poem, Anne was not through promoting these ideas.[21] As soon as she finished this poem, she sat right down and penned another, "The Flesh and the Spirit," a work that was more directly sermonizing than "Contemplations." Of course, religion and politics continued to be intertwined in Anne's world, and so "The Flesh and the Spirit" was as much about Massachusetts Bay as it was about the Puritan faith.

To humanize the theology she meant to preach, Anne returned to her old style of twenty years earlier, creating a dialogue between yet another pair of quarreling women, Flesh and Spirit. Anne conceived of the sisters as fighting over each other's claims to precedence, just as the women did in *The Quaternions*. But in this poem, instead of the unity forged at the end of the earlier poems, there is a clear winner. Spirit conquers Flesh with a decisive flourish. Experienced poet that she was, Anne allowed Flesh to put up a good fight.

To begin with, Flesh taunts Spirit, just as Anne and her friends had been mocked by non-Puritans all those years ago in England. Indeed, even in Massachusetts, although the Puritans controlled the government and the majority of the residents were believers, still there were undoubtedly those who found their rules and their many deprivations ludicrous.

> *Sister, quoth Flesh, what liv'st thou on,*
> *Nothing but meditation?*
> *Doth contemplation feed thee so*
> *Regardlessly to let earth go?*
> . . . .
> *Dost dream of things beyond the moon,*
> *And dost thou hope to dwell there soon?*[22]

It was a rare Puritan who could adopt the voice of the enemy and even poke fun at the pious behavior of the devout. But Anne was proud of her differences from nonbelievers and loved the "dream[y]" nature of Puritanism, the capacity of the pious to envision the invisible and yearn for a world no one knew for certain even existed. To demonstrate the power of Spirit, she had Flesh dangle temptations in front of her sister so that Spirit could display her muscular faith.

Interestingly, Spirit counters each of Flesh's temptations with sensual imagery. In fact, Spirit ends the poem by declaring that her spiritual kingdom is far superior to that of Flesh because one day she would have all the luxuries of her earthbound sister and more.

> *My garments are not silk nor gold,*
> *Nor such like trash which earth doth hold,*
> *But royal robes I shall have on,*
> *More glorious than the glist'ring sun;*
> *My crown not diamonds, pearls, and gold,*
> *But such as angels' heads enfold.*[23]

Faith was based on the intangible prospect of a glorious future, and Anne sought to make this heaven a place her reader could imagine. She sensed that the tension between spirit and flesh — the difficulty of delaying gratification — would be the central problem of the next generation, given the waning numbers in the congregation. With prosperity came too much attachment to the world and too much laxness with regard to religion. The plenty that now graced families in America could prevent them from ever reaching the kingdom to come. Anne reflected that

> the gifts that God bestows on the sons of men are not only
> abused but most commonly employed for a clean contrary end
> than that which they were given for, as health, wealth, and
> honour, which might be so many steps to draw men to God in
> consideration of His bounty toward them, but have driven
> them the further from Him that they are ready to say: we are
> lords, we will come no more at Thee. If outward blessings be
> not as wings to help us mount upwards, they will certainly
> prove clogs and weights that will pull us lower downward.[24]

But even as she was warning against the temptations of the world, Anne had to stare down her own earthly attachments. In the early 1660s it began to seem that the world was too kind to her. Almost immediately after Simon returned to Massachusetts from

England, her oldest son, Samuel, who had completed his training as a doctor, married a beautiful if frail-seeming girl. His young bride, also named Mercy, seemed to "love [her husband] more than her own life," and this gave Anne great delight, for her firstborn had a special place in her heart. She had never forgotten how she had yearned for his arrival; to her he would always be "the son of prayers, of vows, of tears."[25] With joy she watched Samuel build a thriving medical practice in Boston.

Her next son, Simon, was well on his way to becoming a minister, dedicating himself to his studies with devotion. Dudley, her third son, had elected not to go to Harvard and was instead being trained by his father in the skills of a real estate owner and farmer, and her youngest, John, was being tutored by the Andover schoolmaster. Although the younger boys could be wild at times, they were, in general, well-behaved, respectful lads, and Anne was relieved that her children showed every sign of being the pious young Puritans she had trained them to be.

In 1663 wonderful news came from England. John and Mercy Woodbridge were returning home. The Restoration had made England an inhospitable place for Puritan preachers, and John felt that it was time to come back to be near their loved ones and to help preserve the "true religion" in the one place it could still thrive.

It had been sixteen years since Anne had seen her sister and brother-in-law, and the 1650s had been a tumultuous decade for all of them. When John had left, Anne had still been a young woman whom he was worried he might "too much love."[26] Now she was fifty-one years old and a grandmother, as her daughters had proved more fortunate than she had been and had produced children almost immediately upon their marriages.

For both John and Anne, age and appearance were supposed to be immaterial. John had always celebrated his sister-in-law's wisdom and the "solidness" of her work. What had always mattered to them most was conversation and poetry. Thus, when he arrived back in America, John was undoubtedly eager to see his sister-in-law's new poems, although, unfortunately, there are no records of what he thought of Anne's plainer style. Still, it seems likely that as a Puritan minister, he would have been thrilled with the religious themes "Contemplations" and "Flesh and Spirit" treated. For Anne the next two years flew by in a blaze of happiness that she had never thought she would have again. Her writing soared; she felt productive and fruitful. Her children were well and happy. And when Samuel sent word that Mercy was pregnant, it seemed to Anne that her life was too perfect to be true.

Samuel, however, was concerned about his young bride. She had never seemed strong to him, and so he wanted her to stay in Andover to be under his mother's experienced care during her pregnancy. The veteran of eight labors, Anne was also a skilled and knowledgeable nurse; she had attended countless births, and so throughout her daughter-in-law's "breeding pains," she nurtured her as tenderly as she could.

Mercy gave birth to a baby girl, Elizabeth, in February of 1664, and Anne was exhilarated. Perhaps because of concerns about her health, the new mother stayed in Andover with her mother-in-law, and Samuel visited frequently. For Anne, the baby's cries and murmurs must have made the house feel alive again. Before long Elizabeth was smiling, sitting up, and taking her first steps, although Anne undoubtedly warned her daughter-in-law that this was the stage when she had to be particularly vigilant, since toddlers were notoriously liable to harm themselves. In fact, Anne found that she had a lot of advice to give.

While Elizabeth crawled throughout the house, forcing the family to put the fireguard hastily into place and to store the sharp knife blades on high shelves, Anne decided to devote herself to writing a series of "meditations" that she dedicated to her son Simon, who had asked her to "leave something for [him] in writing that [he] might look upon, when [he] should see me no more."[27] Anne had leaped at this idea because it fit well with her sense of wanting to leave behind a legacy for her children and the generations to come.

"Diverse children have their different natures," she wrote, sounding as though she were speaking directly to Mercy. "Some are like flesh which nothing but salt will keep from putrefaction, some again like tender fruits that are best preserved with sugar. Those parents are wise that can fit their nurture according to their nature." Or, she advised, "A prudent mother will not clothe her little childe with a long and cumbersome garment, she easily foresees what events it is like to produce, at the best but falls and bruises, or perhaps somewhat worse." And, "Some children are hardly weaned; although the teat be rubbed with wormwood or mustard, they will either wipe it off, or else suck down sweet and bitter together."[28]

Anne never failed to draw God into her homespun counsel. In her eyes God became like the "prudent mother" who "proportion[s] his dispensations according to the stature and strength of the person he bestows them on," and Christians were like the infants who clung to the mother's breasts even when God carefully "embitter[ed] all of the sweets of this life, that . . . they might feed upon more substantial food, yet they are so childishly sottish that they are still hugging and sucking these empty breasts [of the world]."[29]

During the first year of Elizabeth's life, Anne wrote seventy-seven of these aphorisms, and she included many more topics besides motherhood. Some were directly political: "Dim eyes are the concomitants of old age, and shortsightedness in those that are eyes of a republic foretells a declining state." Others were moral observations: "Wickedness comes to its height by degrees. He that dares say of a less sin 'Is it not a little one?' will ere long say of a greater, 'Tush, God regards it not.'"[30]

Though she was living through one of the happiest stages in her life, Anne reflected that sadness might befall her at any moment.

All have their bounds set . . . and till the expiration of that
time, no dangers no sickness no paines nor troubles, shall put
a period to our dayes, the certainty that that time will come,
together with the uncertainty, how, where, and when, should

make us so to number our dayes as to apply our hearts to wisedome.[31]

Sadly, her words proved prophetic. There was something terribly wrong with Mercy's child. Whether it was fever or smallpox or some congenital ailment is unclear, but in the middle of a hot August night, when she was only a year and a half old, Elizabeth died.

Anne was brokenhearted. She had never lost a child, and in her sorrow, she turned to her old method of managing pain, writing an elegy to baby Elizabeth that combined theology with the intimate, loving language of a grandmother. The result was a poignant poem of great beauty. She used the stanza she had invented in "Contemplations" to lament her little granddaughter:

> Farewell dear babe, my heart's too much content,
> Farewell sweet babe, the pleasure of mine eye,
> Farewell fair flower that for a space was lent,
> Then ta'en away unto eternity.
> Blest babe, why should I once bewail thy fate,
> Or sigh thy days so soon were terminate,
> Sith thou art settled in an everlasting state.[32]

Anne had been practicing this sort of personal renunciation in her verse for years. No longer did she blame herself when bad things happened. Over time she had learned that she had no ability to influence the course of events in her life, and so she turned her heart toward God, resolving to stay true to her faith not only for her own sake but also as an example for the grief-stricken Mercy and Samuel.

But Mercy, who was pregnant again, was too shaken by this event to have a clear sense of what to do. She seems to have refused to move back to Boston and clung to her mother-in-law in her sorrow. Anne counseled her as best she could, reminding her, "If we did not sometimes taste of adversity, prosperity would not be so welcome." And "Yet . . . must we trust in the Lord and stay upon our God" even "when He seems to be . . . quite gone out of sight."[33] Whether or not she was able to take comfort from these sentiments, Mercy continued to stay in Andover, and that November, to everyone's delight, she gave birth to a healthy baby girl whom she called Anne, in clear testimony to her love for her mother-in-law.

It would have been impossible for Anne not to love her namesake, and she cherished the times that little Anne did "come to me," writing that the little sprite was like a "bubble" or a "flower."[34] But that summer, when the new baby was only nine months old and nearly a year after Elizabeth's death, another tragedy struck the Bradstreet household. A servant dropped a lit candle. Almost immediately the entire house was engulfed in heat and smoke. Anne woke to a "thund'ring noise" and someone with "a dreadful voice" shouting, "Fire!" and again, "Fire!" Three generations of Bradstreets filled the night with "piteous shrieks," and Anne "did cry" to "my God . . . / To strengthen me in my distress / And not to leave me succorless."[35]

Anne and Simon managed to get everyone out safely, and once outside, stricken and heartsick, Anne "beheld a space / the flame consume my dwelling place." The air was thick and gray, and at last she "could no longer look."[36] The line of neighbors who had rushed to help at last gave up on saving the house, working only to contain the disaster and protect their own dwellings. And so the home that she had lived in for nearly twenty years crashed in bits and pieces to the ground.

As usual, she comforted herself by scribbling down a poem, this time on a sheet of "loose paper" that was all she had left, since her writing books had all been destroyed. She had lost her family's clothes and possessions, a library of eight hundred books, and many of her personal papers, including some of her poems. She mourned

> *the places . . .*
> *Where oft I sat and long did lie:*
> *here stood that trunk,*

> *and there that chest,*
> *There lay that store I counted best.*
> *My pleasant things in ashes lie,*
> *And them behold no more shall I.*

But characteristically, Anne did not allow herself to despair. She reminded herself that God "gave and took . . . yea, so it was, and so 'twas just. / It was His own, it was not mine."[37] After all, she had already had ample practice "contemplating" the fleeting nature of earthly things.

With Simon's resources, however, it didn't take long to have a new house built. Anne turned back to her poetry, continuing to revise and edit for a second edition of her work. Now she was ruthless in her cuts, dismantling some of her early poems in accordance with her deepened faith in New England and Puritanism. Despite the fire, the inconvenience and hardship of having to start over again in a new house, Anne found the next few years to be far more rewarding than she could have imagined. She had her hands full yet again. Her new home rang with the voice of her granddaughter; her own younger children were thriving. Simon's businesses were doing well. All in all, she had little to complain about.

Still, Anne remained on her guard against disaster, and this was fortunate, because in 1669 her life took a sudden downward turn. By then little Anne was three years old, and her grandmother spent a good deal of time watching over her while her frail mother, Mercy, who was pregnant again, rested. But late that spring, Anne's heart contracted in misery and fear. Helplessly, she watched as little Anne "withered," having contracted a fever. She tried all the healing remedies she had learned over the years, but the little child's fate seemed "sealed," and she died, leaving her grandmother to lament her passing "with troubled heart and trembling hand."[38] Though it seemed impossible to console herself and the baby's parents, she penned yet another elegy, "In Memory of My Dear Grandchild Anne Bradstreet Who Deceased June 20, 1669, Being Three Years and Seven Months Old."

The result was a poem that sounded like a confession of anger at God, as though Anne were whispering her rage at the injustice of human affairs:

> *How oft with disappointment have I met,*
> *When I on fading things my hopes have set.*
> *Experience might 'fore this have made me wise,*
> *To value things according to their price.*
> *Was ever stable joy yet found below?*
> *Or perfect bliss without mixture of woe?*
> *I knew she was but as a withering flower,*
> *That's here today, perhaps gone in an hour;*
> *Like as a bubble, or the brittle glass,*
> *Or like a shadow turning as it was.*[39]

Anne made it clear that it was no easy matter for her to surrender this child to the Lord, but she chided herself for forgetting the lessons of her earlier tragedies as well as for trusting God to keep the child alive. She should have known better, she reflected, than to regard the child as "mine own, when thus impermanent." God takes all things away and she blamed him for her misery: "The heavens have changed to sorrow my delight." Finally, rather than being resigned to losing the child, she dreamed of soon rejoining her: "thou ne'er shall come to me, / But yet a while, and I shall go to thee."[40]

Little Anne might at last be in a joyful condition, but her grandmother was not. In the privacy of her writing book, she decided that she had had enough. She was ready, once again, to leave this cruel world behind, and so she wrote her own farewell in a poem without a title. In the first lines of this poem, which she penned in such haste that she actually left out all punctuation, she relished the thought of all the suffering she would leave behind in death, comparing herself to an exhausted traveler, at last able to halt his journey:

> *As weary pilgrim now at rest,*
> *Hugs with delight his silent nest,*

His wasted limbs now lie full soft
That mirey steps have trodden oft,
Bless himself to think upon
His dangers past, and travails done.
The burning sun no more shall heat,
Nor stormy rains on him shall beat.
The briars and thorns no more shall scratch,
Nor hungry wolves at him shall catch.
He erring paths no more shall tread,
Nor wild fruits eat instead of bread.[41]

Anne was tired of weeping and depleted by the "cares and sorrows" of the last three years. Her body ached. She felt weakened by the hard work of a lifetime, and she no longer felt able to cope with the hardships of her existence. It seemed to her that she was "moldering away." "Oh," she exclaimed, "how I long to be at rest / And soar on high among the blest." She ended this poem by begging God to take her into His arms and allow her to "behold" the "lasting joys" of His love, crying, "Lord make me ready for that day, / Then come, dear Bridegroom, come away."[42] Perhaps writing the elegy for the little girl who bore her name had allowed Anne to envision her own leave-taking. Now, once again, death seemed a comforting idea. Although Anne must have thought this was her final piece, two more tragic events were to occur, both of which necessitated the writing of elegiac poems.

That October, when Mercy gave birth to another baby, her first son, it was difficult for Anne, or anyone, for that matter, to be too hopeful for this new life. After all, how long would this baby last? And indeed, by November Anne sorrowed because little Simon was "no sooner came, but gone, and fall'n asleep, / Acquaintance short, yet parting caused us weep."[43] She allowed herself to consider the painful blows of Mercy's three dead babies in the next sad elegy she forced herself to write, inserting six very angry lines right in the middle of the poem:

Three flowers, two scarcely blown, the last i'the bud,
Cropt by th'Almighty's hand; yet is He good.
With dreadful awe before Him let's be mute,
Such was His will, but why, let's not dispute,
With humble hearts and mouths put in the dust,
Let's say He's merciful as well as just.[44]

Anne could not help revealing her ambivalence about God after these many losses. Although she appears to proclaim His benevolence, her inversion "yet is He good" sounds far less declarative than interrogative. In the face of God's indomitable will, she depicts herself as speechless. There is no defense for His behavior, she seems to splutter, no way to explain His cruelty. Although she quickly tries to dampen her rage, clearly she does have a matter to "dispute" with Him. Of course, Anne knew that she must not rebel against the Lord. But the phrasing "Let's say He's merciful as well as just" sounds like a qualified statement that she couldn't really credit.

Anne's poetic efforts did not help her son make peace with these terrible deaths, and whether it was in anger or despair, the following year he decided that he and Mercy needed a new chance at life and shocked his parents by announcing that he was going to leave New England for good and emigrate to Jamaica. Anne was horrified that Samuel would risk his life, abandon the Puritan colony, and leave her so far behind. But there was nothing she could say to stop him from setting sail. Instead she had to console herself with the company of her daughter-in-law. Because Mercy was pregnant yet again, Samuel had decided to leave her behind and send for her when she had recovered from her travail. Sadly, Anne must have suspected what would happen next.

Mercy was even more worn-out than her mother-in-law and in even more pain. On the third of September 1670, she bore a little girl, whom she again named Anne, surrendering to her tragic wish to restore life to her other lost child. But a few days later both she and the infant died, leaving behind an inconsolable grandmother.[45]

If she had thought that the first little Anne's death was the final straw, Anne knew this horror was all that she could bear. In the space of five years she had weathered the loss of her daughter-in-law and four grandchildren as well as the conflagration of her beloved house. Her eldest son had fled from New England, and Anne wanted only one thing, to join her father and mother in God's eternal kingdom.

ANNE NEVER DID FULLY RECOVER from the tragedy of Mercy's death. God's "corrective hand" had finally convinced her of the Puritan truth, that this world was nothing but a "vale of sorrow" and her thoughts should rest entirely in heaven. By 1671, at age fifty-nine, Anne had begun to suffer from a "consumption" that, her son Simon recorded, "wasted" her to "skin and bone." Her arm was swollen with such a terrible ulcerous sore that one servant whispered that "[I] never saw such an arm in [my] Life." Characteristically, Anne took pride in this new badge of suffering, her claim to being a good warrior for the sake of her and her father's religion.[46] No one could ease her pain, and Anne prayed incessantly for release, while her children, friends, family, and indeed most of the colony, awaited news with anxious hearts. Finally on September 16, 1672, Anne Bradstreet died quietly, her husband by her side. Her son Simon lamented that he was not there to hear her "pious and memorable expressions uttered in her sickness." But he had something even more precious; after all, she had left him and his brothers and sisters more than most parents ever do, a little book of her "living . . . mind."[47]

EPILOGUE

❧✽❧

A Voice in the Wilderness

Mountainous, woman not breaks and will bend: sways God
nearby: anguish comes to an end.
— JOHN BERRYMAN, "Homage to Mistress Bradstreet"

ANNE WAS BURIED the Wednesday after she died in the cemetery not far from her house. Over the centuries this graveyard has gradually been obliterated, and now no one knows for sure where she lies. There is no surviving gravestone and no records of a funeral service or of any elegies written for her upon her death. Simon, as always, was silent — at least in writing — about his feelings, leaving no record of his grief for his wife. Even John Woodbridge was quiet. Anne's daughters and sisters were far more traditionally inclined than she had been and had never shown any interest in writing or public speaking; Samuel was gone to a far-off land, gripped by his own grief. Her two youngest sons were ill equipped for uttering expressions of their sadness.

Only her son Simon, Anne's most literary child, commemorated his mother's demise in his journal with an entry that was oddly reminiscent of Anne's own words upon her father's death. He longed "to walk in her steps . . . so wee might one day have a happy & glorious greeting," just as Anne had hoped to "follo[w]" her father's "pious footsteps" to heaven.[1] And yet, despite Simon's diary entry, Anne's death was greeted with an echoing silence, at least from the perspective of the historian. The great elegist had no one to memorialize her.

It was not that her family did not grieve. Indeed, Anne's death left Simon and her children bereft. In the months before she died, her two younger sons had gotten into trouble with the law, as though they wanted their mother to know they still needed her supervision and were not yet ready for her to go. None of the other Bradstreet children had ever strayed like this, and perhaps Simon shielded Anne from their misdemeanors. John was caught "smoking late at night" with his buddies, and Dudley had been seen "shooting pistols and drinking in the Quartermaster's house." Both young men were dragged before the county court on May 1, and Anne would have to have been very ill not to be aware of their "crimes."[2]

Their mother's teachings were not so easily forgotten, and Dudley and John pulled themselves together after the chastening experience of an official remonstrance from the court's officials. John went on to become a successful gentleman farmer in Topsfield, the next town over, and Dudley grew into a "leading citizen" of Andover, "serving as town clerk, selectman, magistrate, and deputy of the General Court."[3] Mercy, Anne would have been glad to know, got married only a month after her mother's death and went on to bear eight children, just as her mother had. With one exception — her daughter Dorothy died in childbirth — all of Anne's children lived to a ripe old age and contributed to New England with the pious zeal and talent bequeathed to them by their parents. Even while Puritanism as a religious movement began to decline, they and their progeny kept Anne's ideals alive, becoming ministers, lawyers, doctors, and leaders of American society. For example, Oliver Wendell Holmes was one of her descendants.[4]

Simon himself went on to live another thirty years. But he mourned Anne's death for four years — an extremely long period for an eligible New England Puritan widower to remain unwed — appearing inconsolable to the many eager widows who regarded him as an excellent catch. Finally he married another Anne, the widow of a Captain Gardner, who had been killed in King Philip's War against the Indians.

Simon also remained true to the Dudley tradition of public service. He was governor from 1679 to 1686 and then again at the end of his life, when he was called in 1689 to rescue the colony, in crisis over the loss of its charter. In his final years, Simon proved that as well as being an idealistic, orthodox Puritan, he was also a compassionate and reasonable man. He was one of the few heroes of the witchcraft crisis in Salem, serving as a moderating force during the hysteria in 1692, as he was profoundly disturbed by the excesses of the trials and the many executions. When he died, all of New England grieved the loss of such a noble public servant.

ANNE MUST HAVE SUSPECTED that her family would be heartbroken but mute after her demise. She knew her loved ones well. Besides, she knew what happened after women died. How could she forget the silence that had greeted her own mother's death? Even though she was a celebrity of sorts — the only real poet of her generation, a spokesperson for New England as well as a public figure in her own right — she had long been aware that if she wanted to be remembered, she would have to create her own legacy; and of course, this is what she had done, leaving behind a spiritual guidebook for her children and for future New Englanders.

For two hundred years, her strategy worked. Only after the Civil War did her name disappear from the lists of notable American poets, not to be restored until the modernist poet Conrad Aiken in 1912 placed her poems at the beginning of his famous American anthology of poetry. Since then, her reputation has been revived in fits and starts. In 1953 the great poet John Berryman turned to her for inspiration, advancing his own career with his poem "Homage to Mistress Bradstreet."[5] In the 1970s her reputation enjoyed another upsurge during the feminist commitment to uncovering "lost" women in history. Now, as a matter of course, her poems can be found in most American literature anthologies.

Anne had labored to ensure her written legacy, working to create a fair copy of her emendations to *The Tenth Muse* before she died. Six years after her death, the second edition of her work was published in Boston, probably by Anne's old admirer John Rogers, the husband of her niece.[6] This volume was very different from *The Tenth Muse* because Anne had had the opportunity to revise her early poems and include new ones. She inserted "The Flesh and the Spirit" and "Contemplations," and so the book as a whole reflected her mature commitment to New England and her use of the Puritan "plaine style."

In an interesting gesture of self-awareness, Anne had decided against John Woodbridge's title (*The Tenth Muse*) for this edition, and the book went to press as *Several Poems*. At this point in her life it must have seemed safe enough to acknowledge the truth: She had never thought of herself as a "muse" and in fact had always had a rocky relationship with those Greek goddesses. She was not a woman who inspired poetry but one who wrote it. Her readers, especially her male sponsors, had insisted on thinking of her this way, and she had at first complied, knowing that self-effacement was the only way her work would be accepted in her society.

Nonetheless, even fear of recriminations could not stop her from protesting against such strictures and proclaiming her worth, as one female character she had created many years before had declared:

> *Who is't that dare, or can, compare with me?*
> *My excellencies are so great, so many,*
> *I am confounded, fore I speak of any.*[7]

In the end Anne had won. She would no longer be the nameless tenth muse but would be remembered as a flesh-and-blood woman, the author of a book of poetry that changed the way people would think about America, about women, and about American literature. Despite her modesty in life, she would be the star of a story that would be told for centuries, the tale of what one individual, even a person of exceedingly "small frame," could accomplish if she were brave enough, smart enough, and like the country she had helped create, boldly independent.

Acknowledgments

THIS BOOK WOULD NOT have come into existence without my agent, Brettne Bloom. I have relied on her faith in the importance of Anne's story and on her wisdom throughout the process of writing *Mistress Bradstreet*. I am especially grateful to Michael Janeway for introducing me to Brettne, Ike Williams, and Jill Kneerim, and their literary agency, Kneerim and Williams at Fish and Richardson.

I am also indebted to my dear editor, Asya Muchnick, who "curtailed" hours from her sleep to give this book the benefit of her skill and intelligence, and to her wonderful assistant, Zainab Zakari, for her good cheer and practical assistance. Thank you also to Deborah Baker for believing in *Mistress Bradstreet* from the very beginning and to Peggy Freudenthal and DeAnna Satre for all of their hard work copyediting this manuscript.

Many people at various institutions have helped support this book, especially Sally Hinkle at the Society for the Preservation of New England Antiquities, Pat Boulos at the Boston Athenaeum, Anne Bentley and Megan Milford at the Massachusetts Historical Society, and Sue Ellen Holmes and Jill Baker at the Stevens

Memorial Library in North Andover, Massachusetts. I am also grateful to The Waring School in Beverly, Massachusetts, for providing me with office space for so many years, and to Deborah Coull, the creator-owner of the most important beauty salon in Gloucester, Massachusetts.

David Hall, Laura Korobkin, Jill Lepore, and Rosanna Warren gave me superlative and generous guidance when I was writing my dissertation on Anne. A generous postdoctoral fellowship from Boston University allowed me to begin writing this book. Thank you to Laurel Thatcher Ulrich, Mary Beth Norton, David Hall, and Francis Bremer for reading selected chapters of the early manuscript and catching many of my mistakes. Those that are left are due to my errors in judgment, not theirs.

My family and friends have provided me with tireless support. I am especially grateful to Geoffrey and Brooks Richon for their loving patience. Thank you also to Carolyn Cooke, Paul Fisher, Laila Goodman, Carol Hong Richon, Johanna Rittenburg, and all of my running buddies for listening to me over so many miles.

Finally, this book could not have been written without the babysitters: Talia Allenburg, Charlee Bianchini, Ben Dulong, Olivia Gale, Ben Glickstein, Max, Becky, and Julia Lang, Casey and Reeve Moir, Margot Morse, Clea Paine, Luke Schoel, Nicole Simpson, Chet Sharp, Danielle Smick, Chris Stodolski, Becky White, and Lyda Winfield.

Notes

CHAPTER ONE: *Arrival*

1. Bradstreet, "Autobiography," in *Works*, 241.
2. Francis Higginson had written, "All Europe is not able to afford so great Fires as New-England. A poor servant here that is to possesse but 50 acres of land, may afford to give more wood for Timber and Fire . . . than many Noble men in England can afford to do." Quoted in Cronon, *Changes in the Land*, 25.
3. See Thomas Jefferson Wertenbaker's description of the Puritans' identification with the Jews in *The Puritan Oligarchy: The Founding of American Civilization* (New York: Charles Scribner's Sons, 1947).
4. It was only many years later that Anne would describe how she resisted the New World. See "Autobiography," in *Works*, 241.
5. Morgan, *Puritan Dilemma*, 57.
6. Higginson, *New England's Plantation* (1630), quoted in White, *Anne Bradstreet*, iii.
7. Winthrop, "Saturday, 12 [June]," *Journal of John Winthrop*, ed. Dunn and Yeandle, 27.
8. Francis Bremer writes, "Endecott in the summer of 1629 had supervised the erection of a large home, designed as a place for the new governor to live . . . on a neck of land protruding into Massachusetts Bay between the Mystic and Charles rivers." In Bremer, *Winthrop*, 192.
9. Cronon gives a complete description of Indian agricultural technique in *Changes in the Land*, chaps. 1 and 2.

10. Winthrop, "Saturday, 12 [June]," *Journal of John Winthrop*, ed. Dunn and Yeandle, 27.

11. Bremer, *Winthrop*, 193; ed. J. Franklin Jameson, *Johnson's Wonder-Working Providence, 1628–1651* (New York: Scribner's, 1910), 66.

CHAPTER TWO: *Lilies and Thorns*

1. John Cotton, "Limitation of Government," in *American Puritans*, ed. Miller, 85.

2. Quoted in Ziff, *Career of John Cotton*, 62.

3. Bradstreet, "Autobiography," in *Works*, 240–41.

4. "Beclouded . . ." is from a later poem, "For Deliverance from a Fever," in *Works*, 257, line 11. All other phrases are from "Autobiography," in Bradstreet, *Works*, 240.

5. Bradstreet, "Autobiography," in *Works*, 240–41.

6. Shepard, "The Journal," in McGiffert, *God's Plot*, 93.

7. Ibid., 98.

8. Edmund Morgan characterizes Dudley as "immature," "lack[ing] in discretion," "col[d]" and "belligeren[t]," in *Puritan Dilemma*, 103–4. Bradstreet, "To the Memory of My Dear and Ever Honoured Father Thomas Dudley Esq. Who Deceased, July 31, 1653, and of His Age 77," in *Works*, 202, line 43.

9. Bradstreet, "To the Memory . . . ," in *Works*, 202, lines 42, 80.

10. Ibid., lines 10, 46.

11. Bradstreet, "Autobiography," 243; "The Vanity of All Worldly Things," in *Works*, 219, lines 1–2; "The Flesh and the Spirit," in ibid., 215–16, lines 7, 27.

12. White, *Anne Bradstreet*, 37.

13. Bradstreet, "An Epitaph on My Dear and Ever-Honoured Mother, Mrs. Dorothy Dudley, Who Deceased December 27, 1643, and of Her Age, 61," in *Works*, 204, lines 17, 16, 2, 11, 13.

14. In the two centuries since the Black Death, England's population was exploding once again, and there was not enough land or food to sustain its growth. In response to years of poor harvests, the gentry had invested in an extensive project of draining the fens to create more arable fields and grazing land, and they relied on the expert knowledge of their Dutch neighbors, whose sophisticated network of canals was now legendary.

15. *Second Part of a Register, II*, quoted in Edmund Morgan, *Visible Saints*, 7.

16. Ziff, *Career of John Cotton*, 58.

17. Roger Virgoe, ed., *Private Life*, 87.

18. Ziff, *Career of John Cotton*, 49.

19. *Memorials of Affairs of State in the Reigns of Queen Elizabeth and King James I*, ed. E. Sawyer, vol. 2 (London: 1725), quoted in White, *Anne Bradstreet*, 39.

20. Bradstreet, "Autobiography," in *Works*, 240–41, 243. "The New England Primer," in *Concise Anthology of American Literature*, ed. George McMichael, 2nd ed. (New York: Macmillan, 1985), 54–55.

21. Bradstreet, "Autobiography," in *Works*, 244.

22. William Hubbard, quoted in Mary Beth Norton, *Founding Mothers and Fathers*, 362.
23. John Winthrop, ibid.
24. It was not until "God . . . shut a door against . . . us from ministering to him and his people in our wonted congregations, and calling us by a remnant of our people, and by others of this country to minister to them [in America], and opening a door to us this way," that Cotton believed it was time to emigrate. He still debated this issue, wondering if God did not want him to stay in prison in England, but finally he decided, after consultation with other Puritan leaders, that he could serve God more fully in the New World. "Mr. Cotton's Letter Giving the Reasons of His and Mr. Hooker's Removal to New England," in Heimert and Delbanco, *Puritans in America*, 95.

CHAPTER THREE: *Sempringham*

1. Cotton Mather, *Magnalia Christi Americana*, quoted in White, *Anne Bradstreet*, 54.
2. Ibid.
3. Bradstreet, "To the Memory of My Dear and Ever Honoured Father Thomas Dudley Esq. Who Deceased, July 31, 1653, and of His Age 77," in *Works*, 202, lines 33–35.
4. The title of Elizabeth's book was, appropriately enough, *The Countesse of Lincolnes Nurserie*. It was printed at Oxford and was twenty-one pages long. White, *Anne Bradstreet*, 54.
5. Richard Mulcaster, quoted in White, *Anne Bradstreet*, 58. This is the advice Sir Ralph Verney wrote to his ambitious and literary goddaughter Nancy Denton in *Memoirs of the Verney Family*, ed. Frances Parthenope, Lady Verney, and Margaret Verney, vol. 3 (1894), 73–74, quoted in White, *Anne Bradstreet*, 59.
6. *The Divine Weekes and Workes* was translated into English by Joshua Sylvester in 1605 and went through many editions by the Restoration.
7. Bradstreet, "In Honour of Du Bartas, 1641," in *Works*, 192–93, lines 28, 33.
8. Bradstreet, "Autobiography," in *Works*, 241.
9. Although it is unclear when Anne actually read these books, her comfort with their ideas suggests that she encountered them at an early age. Also, these were books that would have been readily available in Sempringham and in her father's library.
10. Philip Sidney, "Sonnet 1," from *Astrophel and Stella* in *The Norton Anthology of English Literature*, vol. 1, eds. M. H. Abrams et al. (New York: Norton, 1979), 486.
11. For this argument about literacy — the difference between being able to read as opposed to being able to write, see Hall's *Worlds of Wonder*, especially 32–33.
12. Richard Mather, *Two Mathers*, 60–61, quoted in Charlotte Gordon, "Incarnate Geography: Anne Bradstreet's Discovery of a New World of Words in 17th Century New England," PhD diss., Boston University, 2000.

CHAPTER FOUR: *A Man of Exemplary Discretion and Fidelity*

1. Cotton Mather, quoted in White, *Anne Bradstreet*, 74.
2. Anne does not describe this time in her life with any detail except to lament her "carnal heart." Instead, it is through her later poems to Simon that we learn how she viewed him as a lover, counselor, soul mate, and good friend.
3. Bradstreet, "Autobiography," in *Works*, 242.
4. Bradstreet, "Another," in *Works*, 228, lines 32, 38; "A Letter to Her Husband," in ibid., 226, line 8.
5. Bradstreet, "Autobiography," in *Works*, 241.
6. Ibid.
7. Bradstreet, "Youth," in *Works*, 56, lines 199, 202, 183–84.
8. Joshua Moody, quoted in Daniels, *Puritans at Play*, 7.
9. The most influential work that supports this idea of the Puritan ability to enjoy sex is by Edmund S. Morgan, particularly his early essay "The Puritans and Sex," *New England Quarterly* 15 (1942): 591–607. I find his arguments somewhat persuasive, but it is important to note that many of his ideas have been successfully challenged by more recent scholars, among them Michael Zuckerman, "Pilgrims in the Wilderness: Community, Modernity, and the Maypole at Merry Mount," *New England Quarterly* 50 (1977): 266–70, and Kathleen Verduin, "Our Cursed Natures: Sexuality and the Puritan Conscience," *New England Quarterly* 56 (1983): 222–24, 229–30.
10. The minister Thomas Hooker wrote, "There is wild love and joy enough in the world, as there is wild thyme and other herbs, but we would have garden love and garden joy." Quoted in Daniels, *Puritans at Play*, 12. The Puritans became famous for the bizarre cases they prosecuted in order to maintain their standards of behavior concerning sexuality. A man named Thomas Grainger who would plead guilty to "buggery with a mare, a cow, two goats, five sheep, two calves, and a turkey," would be summarily executed. William Bradford, quoted in ibid., 126.
11. Bruce Daniels writes, "Excessive passion, deviant sex, fornication, and even masturbation constituted acts of such profound rebellion against deeply held beliefs of the church and community that pious persons could not embrace any of these sins without deeply troubling their souls." Ibid., 127.
12. Bradstreet, "Youth," in *Works*, 56, lines 177, 180.
13. Cotton Mather, "The Life of Simon Bradstreet, Esq.," in *Magnalia Christi Americana*, bk. 2, 19.
14. In some communities, the couple was considered legally bound after the banns had been announced three times; in others, the initial proclamation of the banns was all it took. Once the Puritans had emigrated to New England, such premarital "confusions" were punished severely by the courts with public whippings that were made all the more humiliating because the law stipulated that the perpetrators had to be stripped to the waist. Norton, *Founding Mothers and Fathers*, 67–69.

15. Michael Wigglesworth, for example, a somewhat dour Puritan minister who had lost his wife when he was middle-aged, confessed to a woman whom he wished to marry that he was deeply attracted to her and that after they had met, "my thoughts and heart have been toward you ever since." But this assay was actually not meant to win her affections. Instead, Wigglesworth went on to assure her that he had of course questioned his desires, and only after "serious, earnest, and frequent seeking of God for guidance . . . [have] my thoughts . . . still been determined and fixed upon yourself as the most suitable person." Daniels, *Puritans at Play*, 128.

16. Bradstreet, "Autobiography," in *Works*, 241.

17. Bradstreet, "Youth," in *Works*, 57, line 224.

18. Isle of Man, "Diseases," in "Manx Note Book," ed. Frances Coakley, at www/isle-of-man.com/manxnotebook/famhist/genealogy/diseases.htm.

19. Bradstreet, "Autobiography," 241.

20. Bradstreet, "Youth," in *Works*, 57, line 221.

21. Lucy Hutchinson, *Memoirs of Colonel Hutchinson* (Everyman's Library, 1936), 51, quoted in White, *Anne Bradstreet*, 90.

CHAPTER FIVE: *God Is Leaving England*

1. Terrorized by the most visible "purifying" techniques of Puritan radicals — smashing, burning, stealing, shouting, breaking, and even murdering — frightened devotees of Rome invented the term itself as an angry epithet in a tract published in 1565 by Thomas Stapleton, an English Catholic who had fled the country in the wake of antipapist violence.

2. For an example of Anne's bloodthirsty predilections, see Bradstreet, "A Dialogue between Old England and New," in *Works*, 187, line 279.

3. Reputedly, Anne's father's ancestor had actively supported and participated in the killing of Protestants. Dudley's grandfather, George Sutton Dudley, in verifiably Dudley fashion, had been neither a quiet nor a moderate Catholic. He had stormed readily into battles, a violent warrior on behalf of his convictions, as well as an undercover assassin. Impelled by a vision of a purely Catholic England, George had plotted to overthrow Henry VIII and then to murder his son, King Edward, and he greeted the accession of Mary with relief and joy. No ancestor could have been more shameful for the Dudleys to claim as their own. George had clearly aided and abetted the queen, whom they regarded as a monster.

4. Most Puritans referred to *The Book of Martyrs* as an essential text, and many had memorized long passages from the book. It quickly became one of the cornerstones of most Puritans' education because it was placed in English churches of all stripes to allow the reading public to encounter this hair-raising work whenever they so desired.

5. John Foxe, "A lamentable spectacle of three women, with a sillie infant," vol. 2, 1764, in "Selected Woodcuts and Passages," from *Actes and Monuments* or *The Book of Martyrs* (Center for Electronic Text and Image, University of Pennsylvania Library, Annenberg Rare Book & Manuscript Library, at http://oldsite.library.upenn.edu/etext/furness/foxe/infant.)

6. "Persecutions in England during the Reign of Queen Mary," chap. 16 in Foxe, *The Book of Martyrs*, ed. William Flatbush (Center for Reformed Theology and Apologetics, www.reformed.org/books).

7. Even though it was God who determined one's eternal destination, certain actions made hell seem more likely than others, and most people believed that heresy was the kind of sin that led to damnation. Accordingly, it was better to withstand the temporary torture of earthly flames and adhere to one's Puritan beliefs than to recant and risk being plunged into their infernal counterpart.

8. Bishop Latimer, quoted in Green, *A Short History of the English People*, 359.

9. Mark Kishlansky, *Civilization in the West*, vol. 2 (New York: HarperCollins, 1995), 422.

10. Ibid.

11. Bradstreet, "A Dialogue between Old England and New," in *Works*, 187, lines 271, 279.

12. Cotton Mather, *Magnalia Christi Americana*, 16.

13. Bradstreet, "Autobiography," in *Works*, 241.

14. As the situation worsened, many of the ministers who would one day lead New England congregations fled the country: Thomas Shepard, Hugh Peter, and John Davenport, to name just a few. However, although David Cressy agrees that these "radical ministers" were indeed hounded from the country, he seriously questions the extent of persecution that most Puritans endured. He writes, "The old notion . . . that Puritan migrants to America had to escape from Charles I's England through an underground network is seriously wrong. Hardly any of the families involved in the great migration were actually fleeing from persecution." Cressy, *Coming Over*, 140. Cressy's argument is persuasive, but he also concedes that many of the Puritans *believed* that they were being persecuted and spread rumors to this effect in both the Old and New Worlds. Anne and her family are among this latter category. There is no evidence of any actual persecution, but the Dudleys were among the most important proponents of the *idea* of Puritan suffering and the need for escape. See especially Anne's rendition of Puritan victimization at the hands of Laud in "A Dialogue between Old and New England," *Works*, 184, lines 177–190. Shepard, "The Autobiography," in McGiffert, *God's Plot*, 53.

15. Shepard, "The Autobiography," in McGiffert, *God's Plot*, 53.

16. John Smith, quoted in Norton, *Founding Mothers and Fathers*, 115–16.

17. John Brereton, *A Brief and True Report of the New Found Land of Virginia* (London, 1588), quoted in Cressy, *Coming Over*, 2. For Smith's renaming strategy, see Cressy, *Coming Over*, 6.

18. Bradstreet, "Autobiography," in *Works*, 241.

19. *State Papers Domestic, Charles I*, vol. 72, no. 36, *Calendar of State Papers, Venetian — Charles I*, 1626–28, 119, quoted in White, *Anne Bradstreet*, 87–88, 81.

20. R. C. Winthrop, *Life and Letters of John Winthrop*, vol. 1 (Boston, 1869), 304, quoted in ibid., 94.

21. Francis Higginson, 'New Englands plantation' (London, 1630), quoted in Cressy, *Coming Over*, 12.

22. Johnson, *Wonder-Working Providence of Sion's Savior in New England* (London, 1654), in Miller, *American Puritans*, 29–30.

23. John Pory, Emmanuel Altham, and Isaak de Rasieres, *Three Visitors to Early Plymouth: Letters about the Pilgrim Settlement in New England During Its First Seven Years*, ed. Sydney V. James Jr. (Plymouth, Mass.: 1963), 6–17; William S. Powell, *John Pory, 1572–1636: The Life and Letters of a Man of Many Parts* (Chapel Hill: University of North Carolina Press, 1977), 83, 93, 96, quoted in Cressy, *Coming Over*, 7–8.

24. For the Sagadahoc, Maine, experiment, see Charles Andrews, *The Colonial Period in American History*, 4 vols. (New Haven, Conn.: Yale University Press, 1934–38), vol. 1, 78–97, quoted in Cressy, *Coming Over*, 3–4.

25. William Alexander, *The Mapp and Description of New England* (London, 1630), 30, quoted in Cressy, *Coming Over*, 9.

CHAPTER SIX: *Preparedness*

1. William Bradford, *History of Plymouth Plantation 1620–1647*, vol. 1 (Boston, 1912), 56, quoted in Cressy, *Coming Over*, 147.

2. Ibid.

3. Bradstreet, "The Flesh and the Spirit," in *Works*, 215, lines 14, 16–17, 20–21.

4. Bradstreet, "A Dialogue between Old England and New," in *Works*, 179–81, lines 31–32.

5. Quoted in Cressy, *Coming Over*, 92.

6. Ibid., 147.

7. Ibid., 121.

8. White, *Anne Bradstreet*, 98. For more information on the costs of passage, see Cressy, *Coming Over*, 119.

9. Cressy, *Coming Over*, 112–13, 115–16. The list of supplies is taken from the contemporary lists Cressy provides.

10. Bradford, *History of Plymouth Plantation*, quoted in ibid., 107.

11. Hutchinson, *Hutchinson Papers*, vol. 1, 54.

12. Cressy, *Coming Over*, 43–44.

13. Higgenson, *Hutchinson Papers*, vol. 1, 53.

14. Dudley, "Deputy Governor Dudley's Letter to the Countess of Lincoln," in Young, *Chronicles*, 324–25, quoted in Cressy, *Coming Over*, 45.

15. Cressy, *Coming Over*, 85.

16. For a fuller exposition of Dudley's views on emigration, see Dudley, "Deputy Governor Dudley's Letter to the Countess of Lincoln," in Young, *Chronicles*, 324–25. Aware of the stringent requirements that Dudley, and even the more gentle Winthrop, placed on all applicants, those who wrote recommendations for prospective emigrants sounded the interrelated themes of prudence, work, piety, and plenty, with the implication that those who labored diligently and well were probably among the righteous or could be converted into faithful Puritans. The minister Nathaniel Ward, a future close friend of Anne and Simon's in the New World, begged Winthrop "to reserve room and passage in your ships for two families, a carpenter and a bricklayer, the most faithful and diligent workmen in all our parts. One of them hath put off a good farm this week and sold

all, and should be much damaged and discouraged if he finds no place amongst you; he transports himself at his own charge." *Winthrop Papers,* vol. 2 (Boston, 1931–47), 192, quoted in Cressy, *Coming Over,* 47.

17. One such letter was Robert Parke's to Winthrop: "I would desire you to give me directions what household I shall take with me, and for how long we shall victual us." Cressy, *Coming Over,* 111–12.

18. Quoted in Morgan, *Puritan Dilemma,* 41.

19. *Winthrop Papers,* vol. 4, 218, quoted in Cressy, *Coming Over,* 93.

20. The unpredictable tidal water of the Witham was the main reason for the flood steps that most of the town dwellers had built to protect their homes; during storms it periodically washed through the town, although it could sometimes dry to a trickle during the summer.

21. Mercy would also repeat the crossing, but not through her own choosing. Her husband, John, felt he had to fulfill his mission to serve God in England during the civil war, and so, at last she joined him and stayed in England with him for sixteen years. See chapters 17, 18.

CHAPTER SEVEN: *Our Appointed Time*

1. This conception was popularized by the playwright Ben Jonson, who had created a ridiculous caricature of Puritans with a character named "Zeal-of-the-land-Busy" in his play *Bartholomew Fair.* In this wildly popular drama, "Busy" distinguished himself by traveling from stall to stall of the fair, destroying toys, trinkets, and gingerbread men (all of which he called "a flasket of idols") because he was "moved in spirit" against the "peeping of popery." In *Ben Jonson's Plays and Masques,* ed. Robert M. Adams (New York: Norton, 1979).

2. "Groups of traveling puritans often walked together for several hours on their way to and from worship, discussing sermons, singing psalms, and cementing the ties that linked them together as 'friends in the Lord.' As a result, gadding played an important part in fostering the social cohesion of local puritan networks and providing them with opportunities for the defiant flaunting of their lifestyles before their ungodly neighbors." Durston and Eales, eds., *Culture of English Puritanism,* 20.

3. Quoted in O'Toole, *Money and Morals,* at www.c-span.org/guide/books/booknotes/chapter/fc081698.htm.

4. Ibid.

5. Quoted in Morgan, *Puritan Dilemma,* 30.

6. Winthrop, "Anno Domini 1630, March 29, Monday," in *Journal of John Winthrop,* ed. Dunn and Yeandle, 13–14.

7. Cressy, *Coming Over,* 127–28; White, *Anne Bradstreet,* 105. Although many scholars suggest that it was not until the eighteenth century that people understood that citrus was a vital preventative agent against scurvy, there is actually ample evidence that the Puritans were well aware of the curative power of lemons in particular. Winthrop, for example, wrote home urging his wife to remember to bring this fruit with her on her voyage to America. See Cressy, *Crossing Over,* 171.

8. Richard Mather and Edward Taylor, quoted in Cressy, *Coming Over,* 152. Cressy reports one traveler, Robert Cushman, as saying, "Our victuals will be half eaten up, I think, before we go from the coast of England." Ibid., 155.

9. Ibid., 157. Cressy writes, "Errors of navigation, achievements of seamanship and the fickleness of the weather could all be seen as manifestations of divine will."

10. Quoted in ibid.

11. "The fact is that there was no uniform puritan identity or plan. Men and women from different parts of England had varied experiences of what constituted godly communities and how they were to be governed." Bremer, *Winthrop,* 182.

12. Cressy, *Coming Over,* 155. Cressy writes, "Some [passengers] diverted themselves in taverns, and felt the censure of their more sanctimonious fellow travelers."

13. Cotton Mather, *Sailours Companion and Counsellor* (Boston, 1709), vi, quoted in ibid., 165.

14. Cressy states, "A few consulted dockside astrologers who sold them prognostications for the voyage." *Coming Over,* 155. For a more complete discussion of the retention of medieval beliefs and folk customs in the Puritan mind, see David Hall, *Worlds of Wonder,* chaps. 1 and 2.

15. Historians are not sure of the date of Cotton's sermon. Francis Bremer writes: "There was a Thursday lecture at [the Church of the] Holy Rood, and Cotton and Winthrop might have been guests on such an occasion, or the church might have been made available on a different day." Bremer, *Winthrop,* 431n1.

16. 2 Sam. 7:10 (Geneva version), quoted in Morison, *Builders,* 71.

17. Cotton said, "Even ducklings hatched under an henne, though they take the water, yet will still have recourse to the wing that hatched them: how much more should chickens of the same feather, and yolke." Ibid., 72.

18. Cotton promised the settlers "firm and durable possession" by suggesting that God had "drive[n] out the heathen before them." John Cotton, "God's Promise to His Plantations," in Heimert and Delbanco, *Puritans in America,* 76, 79. Andrew Delbanco, however, argues that this identification of New England with Canaan, or the promised land, happened later and originated in old England. He writes, "It was to be a very long time before New England came to think of itself as more than 'ordinary' in this sense." Delbanco, *Puritan Ordeal,* 93. Although Delbanco's point may well be true for the vast majority of emigrants, Anne's poetry, particularly, "A Dialogue between Old England and New" suggests that she had made this symbolic leap at least by the mid-1640s.

19. Cotton, "God's Promise," 80.

20. Bremer writes that this sermon "was not delivered on board the *Arbella*" as historians had once thought. He believes that Winthrop preached to a larger audience than was available once they were onboard. He writes, "If delivered on shipboard it would only have been heard by that portion of

the emigrants who were on the *Arbella* and thus had a smaller impact." Bremer, *Winthrop*, 431n9.

21. Peter Gomes, the current resident minister at Harvard College, has reflected that Winthrop's sermon was the most important address of the millennium. Andrew Delbanco writes that the speech has become a "kind of Ur-text of American literature." Quoted in Bremer, *Winthrop*, 174; Peter Gomes, "Best Sermon: A Pilgrim's Progress," *New York Times*, April 18, 1999, late edition, sec. 5, 102; Delbanco, *Puritan Ordeal*, 72.

22. Winthrop, "A Model of Christian Charity," in Baym et al., *Norton Anthology of American Literature*, 3rd ed., 40–41.

23. Ibid., 41.

24. Winthrop, "Thursday, 8 [April]," *Journal of John Winthrop*, ed. Dunn and Yeandle, 15.

25. Quoted in Cressy, *Coming Over*, 264.

26. McGiffert, *God's Plot*, 63.

27. This was actually a repeat performance on Winthrop's part; one contemporary reported that Winthrop "at a solemn feast among many friends a little before their last farewell, finding his bowels yearn within him, instead of drinking to them, by breaking into a flood of tears himself, set them all aweeping . . . while they thought of seeing the faces of each other no more in the land of the living." William Hubbard, *A General History of New England*, Collections of the Massachusetts Historical Society, 2nd ser. 5 (1815), 125, quoted in Bremer, *Winthrop*, 170.

CHAPTER EIGHT: *The Crossing*

1. Winthrop, "Easter Monday, 29 March, 1630," in *Journal of John Winthrop* (The Winthrop Society) at www.winthropsociety.org/journal.php.

2. Winthrop left out any account of his own fear when he recorded the Dutch vessel's story in his shipboard journal ("in passing through the Needles, [the ship] struck upon a rock, and being forced to run ashore to save her men, could never be weighed since, although she lies a great height above the water"), but still it was an ominous bedfellow to share a berth with. "Tuesday, 30 March, 1630," in ibid.

3. Cressy, *Crossing Over*, 148.

4. Richard Mather, "Richard Mather's Journal," in Young, *Chronicles*, 449.

5. Winthrop, "Thursday, April 1, and 2," in *Journal of John Winthrop*, at www.winthropsociety.org/journal.php.

6. *A Humble Request* (The Winthrop Society) at www.winthropsociety.org/doc_humble.php.

7. This is based on Winthrop's report that the ladies went ashore. Clearly, Winthrop meant the highly ranked women, and Anne was one of them. But he does not supply us with all of their names. Winthrop, "Tuesday, 6 [April]," in *Journal of John Winthrop*, ed. Dunn and Yeandle, 15.

8. Winthrop, "Thursday, 8 [April]," in ibid.

9. Ibid., 16.

10. Ibid.

11. Ibid.

12. Ibid., 17.
13. Ibid. Of the English ships, three were "bound for the Straits" and three others were headed for Canada and Newfoundland.
14. Cressy, *Crossing Over,* 161.
15. Winthrop, Saturday, 10 [April]," in *Journal of John Winthrop,* at www. winthropsociety.org/journal.php.
16. Winthrop, "Monday, 12 [April]," ibid.
17. Cressy, *Crossing Over,* 170.
18. Winthrop, "Saturday, 17 [April]," in *Journal of John Winthrop,* ed. Dunn and Yeandle, 19.
19. Cressy, *Crossing Over,* 171.
20. Ibid., 171–72.
21. Ibid., 149. Cressy writes, "It is not far-fetched to imagine a bonding among Atlantic travelers of the kind that is found among veterans of other intensive group experiences. Confined for eight to twelve weeks or more to a tiny wooden world, the travelers were thrust into intimacies that might never have developed on land." Ibid., 151.
22. Bradstreet, "Another," in *Works,* 227, line 12.
23. Cotton Mather, *The Sailours Companion,* 39, quoted in Cressy, *Crossing Over,* 164.
24. Quoted in ibid., 172.
25. Richard Mather, "Richard Mather's Journal," in Young, *Chronicles,* 460–67.
26. John Josselyn, *Account of Two Voyages* (London, 1672), 9, 8, quoted in Cressy, *Crossing Over,* 174. Richard Mather, "Richard Mather's Journal," in Young, *Chronicles,* 460–67, quoted in Cressy, *Crossing Over.*
27. Winthrop, "Saturday, 8 May," in *Journal of John Winthrop,* at www. winthropsociety.org/journal.php.
28. Psalms 107 and 136. John Cope, *A Religious Inquisition* (London, 1629), 59, quoted in Cressy, *Crossing Over,* 172.
29. Winthrop, "Thursday, 6 May," in *Journal of John Winthrop,* at www. winthropsociety.org/journal.php.
30. Winthrop, "Tuesday, 11 May," ibid.
31. In his diary Winthrop did not reflect on the possible loss of the *Talbot* but softened the accounts of the deaths on the other two ships by reporting that the man's demise on the *Jewel* was not much of a loss because he was "a most profane fellow, and one who was very injurious to the passengers." He comforted himself that the two deaths on the *Ambrose* did not need to alarm anyone, because it turned out that the casualties were "sick when they came to sea; and one of them should have been left at Cowes [in England]." Winthrop, "Thursday, 27 May," ibid.
32. Winthrop, "Wednesday, 26 May," ibid.
33. Winthrop, "Thursday, 3 June," "Friday, 4 June," ibid.
34. Winthrop, "Lord's Day, 6 June," ibid.
35. Winthrop, "Monday, 7 June," ibid.
36. Winthrop, "Tuesday, 8 June," ibid.
37. Winthrop, "Saturday, 12 June," ibid.
38. Bradstreet, "Autobiography," 241.

CHAPTER NINE: *New World, New Manners*

1. Thomas Dudley, "Letter to the Lady Bridget, Countess of Lincoln, 12 and 18 March 1631," (The Winthrop Society) at www.winthropsociety.org/doc_bridget.php.
2. Bradstreet, "Autobiography," in *Works*, 241.
3. Dudley, "Letter to the Lady Bridget."
4. Morison, *Builders*, 80.
5. MS transcript of the original records of the First Church in Boston, 1630–87, collection of the Massachusetts Historical Society, Boston, quoted in White, *Anne Bradstreet*, 114.
6. Bradstreet, "Autobiography," in *Works*, 241.
7. Nathaniel Brewster Blackstone, "The Biography of the Reverend William Blackstone and his Ancestors and Descendants," at www.Dangel.net/AMERICA/Blackstone/REV.WM.BLACKSTONE.html.
8. It is not clear where Johnson died. Edmund Morgan suggests Boston. See *Puritan Dilemma*, 61.
9. Dudley, "Letter to the Lady Bridget."
10. Ibid.
11. Ibid.
12. Ibid.; Cressy, *Crossing Over*, 195.
13. John Pond's letter to his father, March 1631, quoted in Cressy, *Crossing Over*, 195.
14. John Winthrop, quoted in ibid., 195–96.
15. Quoted in Morison, *Builders*, 81.
16. Later in life she would describe her first son as "the son of prayers, of vows, of tears." Bradstreet, "Upon My Son Samuel, His Going to England," in *Works*, 258, line 3.
17. Edward Everett Hale et al., eds., *Note-Book Kept by Thomas Lechford, ESQ, 1638 to 1641* (1884; reprint Camden, Me.: Picton Press, 1988), 177, quoted in Norton, *Founding Mothers and Fathers*, 76.
18. Dudley, "Letter to the Lady Bridget."
19. Ibid.
20. Ibid.
21. Baym et al., *Norton Anthology of American Literature*, 3rd ed., 22–23.
22. Thomas Morton, *New English Canaan*, The Third Book, chap. 14, in ibid., 25.
23. Quoted in Morison, *Builders*, 16–17.
24. Dudley, "Letter to the Lady Bridget."
25. Ibid.
26. Thomas Morton, quoted in Morison. *Builders*, 18.
27. Dudley, "Letter to the Lady Bridget."
28. Quoted in Morison, *The Founding of Harvard*, 184, 186.
29. The founders of Watertown, two Puritan brethren, George Phillips and Sir Richard Saltonstall, had laid the foundations for their ambitious village on a site later known as Gerry's Landing, and they had also claimed the acreage for half a mile downstream. Ibid.

30. Dudley, "Letter to the Lady Bridget."
31. Ibid.
32. Ibid.
33. Johnson, *Wonder-Working Providence of Sion's Saviour in New England* (London, 1654), quoted in Morison, *The Founding of Harvard*, 189.

CHAPTER TEN: *Upon My Son*

1. Bradstreet, "Autobiography," in *Works*, 241.
2. Ibid.
3. Bradstreet, "Upon a Fit of Sickness," in *Works*, 222.
4. Bradstreet, "Autobiography," in *Works*, 241.
5. Bradstreet, "The Prologue." See especially the famous line "Who says my hand a needle better fits." In *Works*, 16.
6. Psalm 23 from *The Bay Psalm Book* in McMichael et al., *Concise Anthology of American Literature*, 50.
7. See especially "An Elegy upon That Honourable and Renowned Knight Sir Philip Sidney" for her preoccupation with fame. Bradstreet, *Works*, 189–91.
8. Bradstreet, "Upon a Fit of Sickness," in *Works*, 222, lines 1–2, 13.
9. Bradstreet, "Autobiography," 240–45, as well as the poems and meditations on illness and death such as "May 11, 1661," "September 30, 1657," "August 28, 1656," "For Deliverance from a Fever," in Bradstreet, *Works*, 259, 257, 254, 247.
10. Bradstreet, "Upon My Son Samuel," in *Works*, 258, line 7.
11. Ulrich, *Good Wives*, 19–21. Ulrich provides a careful examination of a woman's seasonal chores in her description of the lifestyle of an early immigrant woman, Beatrice Plummer.
12. Ulrich, *A Midwife's Tale*, 50.
13. Ulrich, *Good Wives*, 22.
14. Ibid., 23. This account of killing a pig is based entirely on Ulrich's description of this process.
15. Ibid., 22.
16. Ibid., 152. Ulrich writes, "The custom of naming a child for a dead sibling was part of a larger pattern of remembrance. Almost all New England children, whether named for grandparents, parents, aunts, uncles, or lost brothers or sisters, became carriers of the past."
17. Earle, *Child Life in Colonial Days*, 18.
18. Ibid., 23.
19. Ulrich, *Good Wives*, 129; Goodhue, "Valedictory and Monitory Writing," in Waters, *Ipswich*, 519–24.
20. Ulrich, *Good Wives*, 126–27.
21. For a more complete description of bread making in general, see ibid., 21. For the tradition of starting the bread with the first labor pangs, I am indebted to Carol Hong Richon, a practicing midwife. For food eaten by women in labor, see ibid., 127.

22. Ibid., 131. Ulrich writes, "Momentarily at least, childbirth reversed the positions of the sexes, thrusting women into center stage, casting men in supporting roles."
23. Quoted in ibid.
24. Ibid.
25. Quoted in ibid.
26. Ibid., 129.
27. Earle, *Child Life*, 15.
28. Bradstreet, "Childhood," in *Works*, 53.
29. Earle, *Child Life*, 11.
30. Ulrich, *Good Wives*, 157.
31. Ibid. These three stories are all told by Ulrich in *Good Wives*. She also provides specific examples of childhood disasters as well as a broad overview of the dangers children faced in colonial life. See especially 146–63.
32. Quoted in ibid., 146. This interpretation is also indebted to Ulrich's analysis.
33. Bradstreet, "In Reference to Her Children," in *Works*, 232–33.

CHAPTER ELEVEN: *Enemies Within*

1. Francis Bremer writes, "Some . . . were talking about the latest rumor, that a governor-general might be appointed by the king and lead a military force to suppress the colony." Bremer, *Winthrop*, 229.
2. Morison, *Builders*, 97.
3. Morgan, *Puritan Dilemma*, 116.
4. Bremer, *Winthrop*, 234.
5. Anne was not alone. Most Puritans cherished their relationship to England; letters between the Old and New Worlds were their lifeline to civilization and to all that they had lost, including, of course, their childhood homes, their families, and all the comforts they had once known. Even the formidably idealistic minister Thomas Shepard could not stop "lamenting the loss" of England. McGiffert, *God's Plot*, 63.
6. *Records of the Governor and Company of the Massachusetts Bay*, ed. Nathaniel B. Shurtleff, 5 vols. (1853). Quoted in Bremer, *Winthrop*, 246. Bremer writes that "the General Court under the leadership of Dudley and Ludlow passed a series of sumptuary regulations. No tobacco was to be smoked in inns or public places, nor in an individual's own home. No person in the future was to buy or make any apparel with lace or silver or gold embroidery. Clothes with excessive fashionable slashes (more than one slash in a sleeve, for instance) were prohibited." Bremer, *Winthrop*, 246.
7. For a more complete description of this episode in Williams's life, see Morgan, *Puritan Dilemma*, 126.
8. Ibid., 129. Later in life, Williams would write words that summed up his position concerning the condition of humanity in general: "Abstract yourselfe with a holy violence from the Dung heape of this Earth." Ibid., 130.
9. Quoted in ibid., 125.
10. Bremer recounts this story in more detail in Bremer, *Winthrop*, 251.
11. Morgan, *Puritan Dilemma*, 134.

12. Quoted in Norton, *Founding Mothers and Fathers*, 361.
13. Hutchinson had borne fourteen children; three had died.

    In one of his many later attacks on Hutchinson and her husband, Winthrop described Mr. Hutchinson as "a man of a very mild temper and weak parts, wholly guided by his wife," but this statement cannot be taken at face value, as it was simply another method of undermining Hutchinson's standing in the community. Morgan, *Puritan Dilemma*, 134.
14. Ibid.
15. Norton, *Founding Mothers and Fathers*, 361.
16. John Cotton and Zechariah Symmes, quoted in ibid.
17. Quoted in ibid., 364.
18. *Plymouth Colony Records*, quoted in Deetz and Deetz, *Times of Their Lives*, 153.
19. Norton, *Founding Mothers and Fathers*, 364.
20. Quoted in ibid.
21. The words *gossip* and *gossiping* were originally positive ones, derived from an eleventh-century term, *godsib*, that meant "godparent." But by the late sixteenth century, circumstances had changed and *gossip* had come to mean "a woman's female friends invited to be present at a birth" as well as a woman "who delights in idle talk; a newsmonger, a tattler." The latter definition had emerged from increased male anxiety about unfettered female talk. Any indication of a woman's overstepping her bounds, such as an "ungoverned tongue" or, for that matter, her husband's allowing her to get out of hand was judged with great severity. Norton, *Founding Mothers and Fathers*, 223; Kamensky, *Governing the Tongue: The Politics of Speech in Early New England*, chap. 1. Kamensky writes, "By reporting her husband's shortcomings to her 'Gossips,' a 'nimble-tongued Wife' effectively 'published' his failure for 'all the town' to hear. And 'publishing,' as every Englishwoman knew, was men's business. Men, cultural norms held, were speakers — 'publishers,' in period parlance. Obedient women were listeners" (21). See chapters 1 and 3 for a more complete discussion of the ramifications of a female's unfettered speech.
22. Kamensky, *Governing the Tongue*, 21.
23. For a more complete discussion of the ideas of the public and private roles of women in the seventeenth century and Anne Hutchinson's complicated relationship to these roles, see Norton, *Founding Mothers and Fathers*, 380–85. Also, Eve LaPlante writes, "[A]s a woman she [Hutchinson] had no public role. . . . As a woman she had no voice or vote" (*American Jezebel*, 12).
24. Morgan, *Puritan Dilemma*, 137.
25. Norton, *Founding Mothers and Fathers*, 362.

CHAPTER TWELVE: *Ipswich*

1. Although no one recorded exactly when the Dudleys and Bradstreets began their journey, November 1635 seems the most likely time, as it was the last month before the snows of winter would strike and it was before Anne had had her second baby.

2. Morison, *Builders*, 223.
3. Quoted in White, *Anne Bradstreet*, 130.
4. Letter from Mary Dudley to Mrs. John Winthrop, quoted in ibid., 132.
5. Quoted in Cronon, *Changes in the Land*, 49–50.
6. Bradstreet, "Contemplations," in *Works*, 205, lines 23, 16, 17, 19, 24, 25.
7. Ibid., lines 10–11.
8. Quoted in Morison, *Builders*, 223–24.
9. Later in life, she would give thanks for the privacy of the long night hours in a poem to Simon. See "Another," in *Works*, 227, line 2.
10. Morison, *Builders*, 218. This catechism was more properly known as *The Westminster Shorter Catechism*.
11. "The New England Primer," in McMichael, *Concise Anthology of American Literature*, 54–55.
12. Leighton, *Early American Gardens*, 127.
13. Ibid., 232, 235–37, 243–44, 246–47, 275–76, 287–88, 299, 301–2, 308.
14. One contemporary expert wrote, "We absolutely forbid its entrance" into salads, citing evidence that eating garlic was a punishment for those who had "commided the horrid'st Crimes." Ibid., 307, 267–68, 321, 336–38, 343–44, 376–77, 384, 385–86.
15. Ibid., 124–25.
16. "M. W.," *The Queen's Closet Opened. Incomparable Secrets in Physick, Chirurgery, Preserving, Candying, and Cookery* (London: Nathaniel Brook, 1656), quoted in Leighton, *Early American Gardens*, 133.
17. Leighton, *Early American Gardens*, 87–88.
18. Ibid., 101.
19. Ibid., 107.
20. Bradstreet, "Meditation 35," in *Works*, 278.
21. Ulrich, *Good Wives*, 51.
22. White, *Anne Bradstreet*, 131.
23. Later in life Anne would describe the "carping tongues" of those who thought "my hand a needle better fits" than "a poet's pen," in Bradstreet, "The Prologue," in *Works*, 16, lines 27–29.

CHAPTER THIRTEEN: *Such Things as Belong to Women*

1. Edward Johnson, quoted in Morison, *Builders*, 120.
2. Thomas Weld, quoted in Norton, *Founding Mothers and Fathers*, 370.
3. This idea comes from Mary Beth Norton's *Founding Mothers and Fathers*. See especially 222–39. Norton writes that it was "only birthing rooms" that "provided women with environments that consistently excluded men" (223).
4. Bradstreet, "A Letter to Her Husband," in *Works*, 226, line 14; "Another," in ibid., 227, lines 11–13.
5. Bradstreet, "Another," in *Works*, 227, line 2.
6. Woodbridge, "Epistle to the Reader," in *Works*, 3.
7. Quoted in Norton, *Founding Mothers and Fathers*, 368.
8. Ibid., 368, 365.
9. Ibid., 369.
10. Edward Johnson, quoted in ibid., 369.

11. Quoted in Morison, *Builders*, 239.

12. Ward wrote, "It is said, that Men ought to have Liberty of their Conscience, and that it is Persecution to debar them of it: I can rather stand amazed than reply to this: it is an astonishment to think that the braines of men should be parboyl'd in such impious ignorance." Ibid., 238.

13. Anne wrote about this struggle between the spirit and the desires of the flesh in her prose reflections as well as her poetry. The most famous example is "The Flesh and the Spirit," where Spirit describes how often she has allowed herself to be "a slave" to Flesh's "flattering shows." In *Works*, 215–218, lines 52, 51.

14. Quoted in Morison, *Builders*, 220–21, 219.

15. Ibid., 218.

16. Nathaniel Ward, "Introductory Verse" in Bradstreet, *Works*, 4.

17. Ward's *Body of Liberties* takes a step forward for the rights of women, protecting them from the abuse of their husbands. See Morison, *Builders*, 234. In addition to his *Simple Cobbler of Aggawam*, his rant against women and fashion contained an implicit plea for the education of women. In other words, according to Ward, those women who chased from one silly fashion to another did indeed have only "squirrel" brains. But he raised the hope that there were others who refrained from such frivolous behavior and who therefore had more substantial mental faculties.

18. Quoted in Morgan, *Puritan Dilemma*, 143.

19. Quoted in Norton, *Founding Mothers and Fathers*, 128. In 1648, Massachusetts Bay passed a law that assigned the death penalty for rebellious children. See ibid., 104.

20. Quoted in ibid., 74.

21. Quoted in Eve LaPlante, *American Jezebel*, 50.

22. Quoted in Norton, *Founding Mothers and Fathers*, 374.

23. Quoted in Morgan, *Puritan Dilemma*, 149.

24. Ibid.

25. For the perception that women could not be "public" individuals and that, therefore, the Hutchinson trial upset the colony's notions about "private" and "public" proceedings, see Norton, *Founding Mothers and Fathers*, especially chapter 8.

26. Quoted in Morgan, *Puritan Dilemma*, 149.

27. Ibid., 150.

28. Ibid., 151.

29. Quoted in Norton, *Founding Mothers and Fathers*, 387.

30. Morgan, *Puritan Dilemma*, 153.

31. Quoted in ibid., 154.

32. For a more extensive account of Hutchinson's trials, see Eve LaPlante's *American Jezebel*.

CHAPTER FOURTEEN: *Old England and New*

1. Bradstreet, "An Elegy upon That Honourable and Renowned Knight Sir Philip Sidney," in *Works*, 191, lines 80, 83.

2. Ibid., 191, line 84.

3. Bradstreet, "In Honour of Du Bartas, 1641," in ibid., 192–94, lines 4, 20, 32, 36, 49, 53, 94.

4. Bradstreet, "In Honour of That High and Mighty Princess Queen Elizabeth of Happy Memory," in ibid., 198, lines 100–5.

5. Ibid., 195–98, lines 124, 46, 48, 51, 78.

6. Ibid., lines 45, 113, 128, 127.

7. Bradstreet, "The Prologue," in ibid., 16, lines 27–28.

8. Woodbridge, "Epistle to the Reader," in ibid., 3.

9. See Ulrich, *Good Wives*, 146.

10. Quoted in Norton, *Founding Mothers and Fathers*, 395. Over time the story about Hutchinson's "monster" mushroomed into far-fetched tales that implicated all of her followers in her heresies. As late as 1667, long after all those involved were dead, one such version was recorded by an Englishman as part of his official report on the state of the colony. "Sir Henry Vane," he declared, "in 1637 went over as governor to N. England with 2 women, Mrs Dier [a famous supporter of Hutchinson] and Mrs Hutchinson . . . where he debauched both, and both were delivered of monsters." Norton, *Founding Mothers and Fathers*, 394–95.

11. Bradstreet, "Autobiography," in *Works*, 244.

12. *New England's First Fruits* (London, 1643), quoted in White, *Anne Bradstreet*, 156.

13. Bradstreet, "A Letter to Her Husband," in *Works*, 226, lines 20, 22.

14. Bradstreet, "Another II," in ibid., 229, lines 4, 17, 25–28.

15. Ulrich, *Good Wives*. Ulrich develops the term *deputy husband* throughout her book but provides the fullest explanation of the concept in chapter 2.

16. Norton, *Founding Mothers and Fathers*, 139–64. Norton's discussion of "fictive widows" — women empowered by their husbands to make legal decisions — suggests that these women were often perceived as a threat to men. See 162–80. For more on the status of widows, see Ulrich, *Good Wives*, 7, 38, 148, 249, and Norton, *Founding Mothers and Fathers*, 10, 139–64.

17. Quoted in Morgan, *Puritan Dilemma*, 171.

18. Quoted in Morison, *Builders*, 238.

19. Quoted in Green, *A Short History*, 501.

20. Morgan, *Puritan Dilemma*, 177.

21. Quoted in Green, *A Short History*, 530.

22. Ibid., 531.

23. John Milton, quoted in White, *Anne Bradstreet*, 102.

24. Bradstreet, "A Dialogue between Old England and New," in *Works*, 182, lines 96–103.

25. Ibid., 183, lines 131–37.

26. Ibid., 179, lines 138–40, 24.

27. Ibid., 186–88, lines 236–37, 270–72, 282–84.

28. Ibid., 184, lines 245, 246, 171–72, 187.

29. Nathaniel Ward, "Introductory Verse," in Bradstreet, *Works*, 4, line 18.

30. Anne wrote several poems to Dudley in which she expressed her admiration for him and the important role he had played in encouraging her

writing. See Bradstreet, "To the Memory of My Dear and Ever Honoured Father" and "To Her Most Honoured Father, Thomas Dudley Esq., These Most Humbly Presented," in *Works*, 201–3, 13. Ward's role is suggested by his contribution to the prefatory material of *The Tenth Muse*. Anne never made any reference to Simon as a reader of her work; he does not seem to have played an important role as her intellectual companion, at least according to the records that are left. Certainly Simon himself left no account of what he thought of his wife's poetry.

CHAPTER FIFTEEN: *Now Sister, Pray Proceed*

1. Ulrich, *Good Wives*, 3.
2. Bradstreet, "An Epitaph on My Dear and Ever-Honoured Mother," in *Works*, 204, lines 6, 8–9, 17–20.
3. Bradstreet, "Meditation 72," in ibid., 289–90.
4. She was the widow of one of his neighbors in Roxbury, Samuel Hackburne. See White, *Anne Bradstreet*, 219.
5. Thomas Dudley, quoted in Ulrich, *Good Wives*, 10.
6. Evidence of Anne's literary partnership with her father can be found in her poem, ""To Her Most Honoured Father." Referring to *The Quaternions* as her "four times four," she writes, "I bring my four times four, now meanly clad / To do their homage unto yours, full glad," in *Works*, 13, lines 14–15.
7. Bradstreet, "Before the Birth of One of Her Children," in ibid., 224, lines 9–10, 19–26.
8. Bradstreet, "In Reference to Her Children," in ibid., 234, lines 83–86, 91–94.
9. Bradstreet, "To Her Most Honoured Father," in ibid., 13, line 5.
10. Ibid., 13, line 18.
11. Bradstreet, "The Four Elements," in ibid., 18, lines 9–10, 13–17.
12. Bradstreet, "To Her Most Honoured Father," in ibid., 14, lines 37–43.
13. Bradstreet, "Fire," in ibid., 19, lines 50–53.
14. Bradstreet, "Water," lines 276–77; "Earth," lines 142–43; "Air," lines 402–4, in ibid., 25, 27, 29.
15. Hutchinson and her family had left Rhode Island, seeking an even greater purity in New York, or "New Netherland." In September 1643 Hutchinson was scalped, along with fifteen others — the perfect punishment for such a sinner, the Massachusetts magistrates felt — although the renegades in Rhode Island declared that this dreadful "effusion of blood" stemmed directly from the cruelty of the Bay colony court. Norton, *Founding Mothers and Fathers*, 396–97.
16. White, *Anne Bradstreet*, 191. White points out that Bradstreet paraphrases Crooke here. See Crooke's *Microcosmographia, or a Description of the Body of Man.*
17. Bradstreet, "Phlegm," in *Works*, 49, lines 556–61.
18. Bradstreet, "Choler," in ibid., 39, lines 41–43.
19. Bradstreet, "Phlegm," in ibid., 50, lines 596–97, 600–9.
20. Quoted in Morgan, *Puritan Dilemma*, 179.

CHAPTER SIXTEEN: *Foolish, Broken, Blemished Muse*

1. Quoted in Bailey, *Historical Sketches of Andover*, 27.
2. Massachusetts Colony Records, vol. 1, 141, quoted in White, *Anne Bradstreet*, 222.
3. Ibid., 223.
4. Quoted in Green, *A Short History*, 539.
5. Morison, *Builders*, 242.
6. This account came from a letter written by John's brother, Stephen. See White, *Anne Bradstreet*, 174.
7. MS transcript of the original records of the First Church in Boston, 1630–87, 24, collection of the Massachusetts Historical Society, Boston, quoted in ibid., 174.
8. Quoted in Ulrich, *Good Wives*, 112.
9. Quoted in White, *Anne Bradstreet*, 175.
10. Ibid.
11. MS transcript of the original records of the First Church in Boston, 1630–87, 25–26, quoted in White, *Anne Bradstreet*, 17.
12. Bradstreet, "Winter," in *Works*, 72, lines 257–64.
13. Quoted in White, *Anne Bradstreet*, 228.
14. Milton, "The Verse," in *Complete Poems*, 210.
15. Bradstreet, "The Four Monarchies," in *Works*, 172, lines 3412–17.
16. Ibid.
17. Ibid., 75, lines 72, 88; 160, lines 2967, 2985; 161, line 3031.
18. John Woodbridge, "To My Dear Sister, the Author of These Poems," in *Works*, 4, lines 7, 10; 5, lines 60, 66.
19. Bradstreet, "David's Lamentation for Saul and Jonathan II Sam. 1:19," in *Works*, 199–200.
20. Bradstreet, "The Four Monarchies," in ibid., 177, lines 3550–51.
21. Green, *A Short History*, 552.
22. Bradstreet, "The Four Monarchies," in *Works*, 177, lines 3555–56.

CHAPTER SEVENTEEN: *The Tenth Muse*

1. Bradstreet, "To Her Most Honoured Father," in *Works*, 13.
2. Bradstreet, "The Prologue," in ibid., 15, lines 3–8.
3. Ibid., 16, lines 29–30.
4. Ibid., lines 39–43.
5. We cannot be sure of the identities of all of them, since they signed their letters of approbation only with initials, the literary tradition of the era.
6. Nathaniel Ward cited this criticism of Anne in his "Introductory Verse," in *Works*, 4, line 12.
7. After 1650 Anne's poetry changes. Her work becomes more contemplative, more focused on her inner life as a Christian.
8. Her poem "Contemplations" is based on her meditative walks in the countryside (in ibid., 204–14). Also, she writes, "In secret places Thee I find / Where I do kneel or walk," in "In My Solitary Hours in My Dear Husband's Absence," in ibid., 267, lines 13–14.
9. Eyewitness account, quoted in Kishlansky, *Civilization and the West*, 499.

10. Ibid., 501.
11. Andrew Marvell, "An Horatian Ode upon Cromwell's Return from Ireland," in *The Complete Poems*, ed. Elizabeth Donno (New York: Penguin, 1979), 55, line 13.
12. Quoted in White, *Anne Bradstreet*, 248.
13. Bradstreet, "David's Lamentation," in *Works*, 199, lines 17, 19.
14. Ibid., 200, line 42.
15. Woodbridge, "Epistle to the Reader," in ibid., 3.
16. "In Praise of the Author, Mistress Anne Bradstreet," in ibid., 8.
17. Woodbridge, "To My Dear Sister," in ibid., 5, lines 19–21, 36–38.
18. Bradstreet, "The Author to Her Book," in ibid., 221, lines 11, 8.
19. Ibid., lines 1, 12–13.
20. Ibid., lines 14–19.
21. Ibid., line 9.
22. Hensley, introduction to *Works*, xxxiii; Probate Records, Northampton, Massachusetts, January 13, 1729/30; Thomas H. Johnson, "Edward Taylor: A Puritan 'Sacred Poet,'" *New England Quarterly* 10 (June 1937): 321.
23. Pattie Cowell writes that Bradstreet enjoyed a wide audience in New England. Cowell and Stanford, *Essays*, 270–79.
24. Quoted in Hensley, introduction to *Works*, xxxiii.
25. Woodbridge, "Epistle to the Reader," in ibid., 3.
26. Ibid. In the 1660s the English writer Aphra Behn would produce plays and earn her living working for the theater, but not until Mary Wollstonecraft in the eighteenth century did another Englishwoman write with the kind of intellectual capacity and encyclopedic breadth that distinguished Anne.
27. William London's trade list (1657), quoted in White, *Anne Bradstreet*, 271–72; quoted in Hensley, introduction to *Works*, xxxiii.
28. John Rogers, quoted in White, *Anne Bradstreet*, 363.
29. Cotton Mather, *Magnalia Christi Americana*, quoted in ibid., 362. Jeannine Hensley writes that the identity of the editor of the second edition of Anne's work is unclear, but she suggests that John Rogers is the most likely candidate. Hensley, introduction to *Works*, xxix.
30. Bradstreet, "To the Memory of My Dear and Ever Honoured Father," in ibid., 201, lines 8–10, 13–15.
31. Ibid., lines 17, 25.
32. Ibid., lines 28–33.
33. Bradstreet, "Childhood," in ibid., lines 76, 73, 75; "From Another Sore Fit"; "August 28, 1656," in ibid., 53, 248, 254.
34. Bradstreet, "As weary pilgrim now at rest," in ibid., 295, line 44.
35. Bradstreet, "Meditations When My Soul Hath Been Refreshed," in ibid., 250.
36. Bradstreet, "July 8th, 1656," in ibid., 252, lines 17, 19.
37. Bradstreet, "From Another Sore Fit," in ibid., 248, lines 1–4.
38. Bradstreet, "Childhood," in ibid., 52–55, lines 125, 128, 138.
39. Bradstreet, "Autobiography," in ibid., 240.
40. Ibid., 240, 243–44.
41. Ibid., 245.

CHAPTER EIGHTEEN: *Farewell Dear Child*

1. Bradstreet, "May 13, 1657," in *Works*, 256, lines 6–7.
2. Ibid., lines 16–17, 23.
3. Vital Records of Andover, Massachusetts, vol. 2, 62, quoted in White, *Anne Bradstreet*, 312.
4. Bradstreet, "May 13, 1657," in *Works*, 256, line 20.
5. Baym et al., *Norton Anthology of American Literature*, 5th ed., 284.
6. Ibid., 295.
7. Ibid., 284.
8. Bremer explains Simon's position as a moderate in *Puritan Experiment*, 144.
9. Ibid., 143, 152.
10. The will of Thomas Dudley, quoted in White, *Anne Bradstreet*, 296.
11. Green, *A Short History*, 589.
12. Bremer, *Puritan Experiment*, 155.
13. Ibid., 155–56.
14. Bradstreet, "In My Solitary Hours in My Dear Husband's Absence," in *Works*, 265, lines 6–7, 10–11.
15. Ibid., 267, lines 13–14.
16. Bradstreet, "Autobiography," in *Works*, 243.
17. Bradstreet, "Contemplations," in *Works*, 211–12, lines 190, 186, 169, 198, 200, 204.
18. Ibid., 213, lines 127, 129, 104, 205–11.
19. Ibid., lines 135, 139, 141, 219, 223, 225.
20. Ibid., 214, lines 219, 223, 225.
21. Scully Bradley, Richard Beatty, E. Hudson Long, and George Perkins, eds., *The American Tradition in Literature*, 4th ed. (New York: Grosset and Dunlop, 1974), 34.
22. Bradstreet, "The Flesh and the Spirit," in *Works*, 215, lines 10–13, 16–17.
23. Ibid., lines 80–85.
24. Bradstreet, "Meditation 68," in ibid., 288.
25. Bradstreet, "To the Memory of My Dear Daughter-in-Law, Mrs. Mercy Bradstreet Who Deceased Sept. 6, 1669, in the 28 Year of Her Life," in ibid., 238, line 21; "Upon My Son Samuel," in ibid., 258, line 3.
26. Woodbridge, "To My Dear Sister," in ibid., 5, line 43.
27. Bradstreet, "For My Dear Son Simon Bradstreet," in ibid., 271.
28. Bradstreet, "Meditation 10," "Meditation 39," "Meditation 38," in ibid., 273–74, 279.
29. Bradstreet, "Meditation 38," "Meditation 39," in ibid., 279.
30. Bradstreet, "Meditation 34," "Meditation 37," in ibid., 278.
31. Bradstreet, "Meditation 70," in ibid., 289.
32. Bradstreet, "In Memory of My Dear Grandchild Elizabeth Bradstreet," in ibid., 235, lines 6–12.
33. Bradstreet, "Meditation 14," "Meditation 50," in ibid., 274, 282.
34. Bradstreet, "In Memory of My Dear Grandchild Anne Bradstreet," in ibid., 236, lines 20, 16, 14.

35. Bradstreet, "Upon the Burning of Our House," in ibid., 292, lines 7, 9, 8, 12–14.
36. Ibid., lines 15–16, 17.
37. Ibid., lines 26–32, 20–21.
38. Bradstreet, "In Memory of My Dear Grandchild Anne Bradstreet," in ibid., 236, lines 14, 16.
39. Ibid., lines 8–17.
40. Ibid., lines 7, 20–21.
41. Bradstreet, "As weary pilgrim," in ibid., 294, lines 1–12.
42. Ibid., 294–95.
43. Bradstreet, "On My Dear Grandchild Simon Bradstreet," in ibid., 237, lines 5–6.
44. Ibid., lines 7–12.
45. Anne wrote a commemorative poem to Mercy, "To the Memory of My Dear Daughter-in-law, Mrs. Mercy Bradstreet Who Deceased Sept. 6, 1669, in the 28 Year of Her Life"; however, either she or the printer put the wrong date in the title by a year. Mercy died in 1670, not 1669.
46. Simon Bradstreet, quoted in White, *Anne Bradstreet*, 358.
47. Bradstreet, "Autobiography," in *Works*, 240.

EPILOGUE: *A Voice in the Wilderness*

1. Quoted in White, *Anne Bradstreet*, 359.
2. Ibid., 357.
3. Ibid.
4. Bailey, *Historical Sketches of Andover*, 130.
5. Berryman's first book of poems had been derided as imitative of the Irish poet Yeats, and as "derivative." In writing his next important work, "Homage to Mistress Bradstreet," he was looking for a distinctive "American" voice, one that could only be called original. Hence, Bradstreet, the first American poet, became the "muse" for his work.
6. Hensley, the editor of Bradstreet's complete works, has suggested that it is Rogers who was the editor of this edition. See Hensley, introduction to *Works*, xxix.
7. "Phlegm," in ibid., 48, lines 533–35.

Bibliography

Adams, James Truslow. *The Founding of New England.* Boston: Atlantic
    Monthly Press, 1921.
Aiken, Conrad. *American Poetry, 1671–1928: A Comprehensive Anthology.*
    New York, 1929.
Arch, Stephen Carl. *Authorizing the Past: The Rhetoric of History in
    Seventeenth-Century New England.* DeKalb: Northern Illinois Uni-
    versity Press, 1994.
Arpin, Gary, ed. *The Poetry of John Berryman.* New York: Kennikat Press,
    1978.
Axtell, James. *The European and the Indian: Essays in the Ethnohistory of Colonial
    North America.* Oxford: Oxford University Press, 1981.
Ayre, John, ed. *The Works of John Whitgift.* Cambridge: Cambridge University
    Press, 1851.
Bailey, Sarah Loring. *Historical Sketches of Andover.* Boston: Houghton Mifflin,
    1880. Reprint, Andover, MA: North Andover Historical Society, 1990.
Ball, Kenneth. "Puritan Humility in Anne Bradstreet's Poetry." *Cithara* 13
    (1973): 29–41.
Baudet, Henri. *Paradise on Earth: Some Thoughts on European Images of Non-
    European Man.* New Haven, CT: Yale University Press, 1965.
Bawer, Bruce. *The Middle Generation.* Hamden, CT: Archon Press, 1986.
Baxter, Richard. *Reliquiae Baxterianae,* edited by M. Sylvester. London, 1696.
———. *The Saints Everlasting Rest.* 9th ed. London, 1649/1650. 9th ed., rev.
    London: Tyton and Underhill, 1662.

Baym, Nina, et al., eds. *The Norton Anthology of American Literature*. 3rd ed. Vol. 1. New York: Norton, 1989.

———. *The Norton Anthology of American Literature*. 5th ed. Vol. 1. New York: Norton, 1998.

Bell, Daniel. "The 'Hegelian Secret': Civil Society and American Exceptionalism." In Shafer, *Is America Different?*

Benfy, Christopher. "The Woman in the Mirror: Randall Jarrell and John Berryman." In *Men Writing the Feminine: Literature, Theory, and the Question of Gender*, edited by Thais Morgan. Albany: State University of New York, 1994, 123–38.

Bennet, A. L. "The Principal Rhetorical Conventions in the Renaissance Personal Elegy." *Studies in Philology* 51 (1954): 107–26.

Bercovitch, Sacvan. *The American Jeremiad*. Madison: University of Wisconsin Press, 1978.

———. "The Image of America: From Hermeneutics to Symbolism." In *Early American Literature*, edited by Michael Gilmore. Englewood Cliffs, NJ: Prentice Hall, 1980.

———. *The Puritan Origins of the American Self*. New Haven, CT: Yale University Press, 1975.

———. *The Rites of Assent: Transformations in the Symbolic Construction of America*. New York: Routledge, 1993.

Berry, Boyd M. *Process of Speech: Puritan Religious Writing and Paradise Lost*. Baltimore: Johns Hopkins University Press, 1976.

Berryman, John. *The Dream Songs*. New York: Farrar, Straus and Giroux, 1969.

———. *The Freedom of the Poet*. New York: Farrar, Straus and Giroux, 1976.

———. *Homage to Mistress Bradstreet*. New York: Farrar, Straus and Cudahy, 1956.

———. *Love and Fame*. New York: Farrar, Straus and Giroux, 1970.

———. *Recovery*. New York: Farrar, Straus and Giroux, 1973.

Blake, Kathleen. "Edward Taylor's Protestant Poetic: Nontransubstantiating Metaphor." *American Literature* 43 (1971).

Bloom, Harold. *The Anxiety of Influence: A Theory of Poetry*. London: Oxford University Press, 1973.

Bloomfield, Morton. "The Elegy and the Elegiac Mode: Praise and Alienation." In *Renaissance Genres*, edited by Barbara Lewalski. Cambridge, MA: Harvard University Press, 1986.

Bossy, John. *Christianity in the West, 1400–1700*. Oxford: Oxford University Press, 1985.

Bozeman, Theodore D. *To Live Ancient Lives*. University of North Carolina Press, 1988.

Bradford, William. *Of Plymouth Plantation*. In Baym et al., *Norton Anthology of American Literature*.

Bradshaw, William. *English Puritanisme*. London, 1605.

Bradstreet, Anne. *The Works of Anne Bradstreet*. Edited by Jeanine Hensley. Cambridge, MA: Harvard University Press, 1967.

Bremer, Francis. *Congregational Communion: Clerical Friendship in the Anglo-American Puritan Community, 1610–1692*. Boston: Northeastern University Press, 1994.

———. *John Winthrop: America's Forgotten Founding Father*. New York: Oxford University Press, 2003.

———. *The Puritan Experiment: New England Society from Bradford to Edwards*. Hanover, NH: University Press of New England, 1995.

———, ed. *Puritanism: Transatlantic Perspectives on a Seventeenth-Century Anglo-American Faith*. Boston: Massachusetts Historical Society, 1993.

Breward, Ian. "The Significance of William Perkins." *Journal of Religious History* 4 (1966–67): 113–28.

———. "William Perkins and the Origins of Reformed Casuistry." *Evangelical Quarterly* 40 (1968): 3–20.

Brooks, Cleanth. *Historical Evidence and the Reading of Seventeenth-Century Poetry*. Columbia: University of Missouri Press, 1991.

Brown, Anne, and David Hall. "Family Strategies and Religious Practice: Baptism and the Lord's Supper in Early New England." In *Lived Religion in America*, edited by David Hall. Princeton, NJ: Princeton University Press, 1997.

Brown, John. *The English Puritans*. Cambridge: Cambridge University Press, 1910.

Brumm, Ursula. "Jonathan Edwards and Typology." In *Early American Literature*, edited by Michael Gilmore. Englewood Cliffs, NJ: Prentice Hall, 1980.

Buchanon, Jane. "Poetic Identity in the New World: Anne Bradstreet, Emily Dickinson, and Derek Walcott." Diss., Tufts, 1985. Ann Arbor: University of Michigan, 1986.

Bush, Douglas. *English Literature in the Earlier Seventeenth Century*. London: Oxford University Press, 1962.

Byington, Ezra. *The Puritan in England and New England*. Reprint, New York: Lenox Hill, 1972.

Calamy, Edward. *Memoirs of John Howe*. London, 1724.

Caldwell, Patricia. *The Puritan Conversion Narrative*. Cambridge: Cambridge University Press, 1983.

Calvin, John. *Commentary on the Epistles of Paul the Apostle to the Corinthians*. Translated by John Pringle. 2 vols. Edinburgh, 1848. Reprint, Grand Rapids, MI, 1955.

———. *Institutes*. Translated by T. Norton. London, 1561.

———. *Institutes of the Christian Religion*. Edited by John T. McNeill. Translated by Ford Lewis Battles. 2 vols. Philadelphia, 1961.

———. *On the Christian Faith: Selections from the Institutes, Commentaries, and Tracts*. Edited by John T. McNeill. New York: Liberal Arts Press, 1957.

Campbell, Mary. *The Witness and the Other World*. Ithaca, NY: Cornell University Press, 1988.

Canny, N., and A. Pagden, eds. *Colonial Identity in the Atlantic World, 1500–1800*. Princeton, NJ: Princeton University Press, 1987.

Canup, John. *Out of the Wilderness: The Emergence of an American Identity in Colonial New England.* Middletown, CT: Wesleyan University Press, 1990.

Carlson, Leland, and Albert Peel, eds. *Cartwrightiana.* London: Allen and Unwin, 1951.

Carroll, Peter. *Puritanism and the Wilderness.* New York: Columbia University Press, 1969.

Cartwright, Thomas. *A Commentary upon the Epistle of Sainte Paule Written to the Colossians.* London: Nicholas Okes, 1612.

———. *The Rest of the Second Replie of Thomas Cartwright.* London, 1577.

———. *The Second Replie of Thomas Cartwright.* London, 1577.

Chaplin, Joyce E. "Natural Philosophy and an Early Racial Idiom in North America: Comparing English and Indian Bodies." *William and Mary Quarterly* 54 (January 1997): 229–52.

Chiapelli, Fred, ed. *First Images of America: The Impact of the New World on the Old.* 2 vols. Berkeley: University of California Press, 1976.

Clark, Michael. "The Honeyed Knot of Puritan Aesthetics." In Peter White, *Puritan Poets and Poetics,* 67–83.

Cliffe, J. T. *Puritans in Conflict.* London: Routledge, 1988.

Cohen, Charles. *God's Caress: The Psychology of Puritan Religious Experience.* New York: Oxford University Press, 1986.

Colish, Marcia L. *The Mirror of Language: A Study in the Medieval Theory of Knowledge.* Lincoln: University of Nebraska Press, 1983, 7–54.

Collinson, Patrick. "The Beginnings of English Sabbatarianism." *Studies in Church History* 1 (1964): 207–21.

———. *The Birthpangs of Protestant England.* London: Palgrave Macmillan, 1988.

———. "A Comment: Concerning the Name Puritan." *Journal of Ecclesiastical History* 31 (1980).

———. *English Puritanism.* London: Historical Association, 1983.

Corns, Thomas. *Uncloistered Virtue: English Political Literature, 1640–1660.* Oxford: Clarendon Press, 1992.

Cowell, Pattie, and Ann Stanford, eds. *Critical Essays on Anne Bradstreet.* Boston: G. K. Hall, 1983.

Cragg, Gerald. *Puritanism in the Period of the Great Persecution, 1660–1688.* Cambridge: Cambridge University Press, 1957.

Cressy, David. *Coming Over: Migration and Communication between England and New England in the Seventeenth Century.* Cambridge: Cambridge University Press, 1987.

Crèvecoeur, Hector. *Letters from an American Farmer.* In Baym et al., *Norton Anthology of American Literature,* 557–82.

Cronon, William. *Changes in the Land: Indians, Colonists, and the Ecology of New England.* New York: HarperCollins, 1983.

Crouch, Joseph. *Puritan Art: An Inquiry into a Popular Fallacy.* London: Cassell, 1910.

Culverwell, Ezekiel. *The Way to a Blessed Estate in This Life.* Appended with separate pagination to *A Treatise of Faith.* London, 1622.

Cushman, Stephen. *Fictions of Form in American Poetry*. Princeton, NJ: Princeton University Press, 1993.

Daly, Robert. *God's Altar: The World and the Flesh in Puritan Poetry*. Berkeley: University of California Press, 1978.

———. "The Powers of Humility and the Presence of Readers in Anne Bradstreet and Phyllis Wheatley." *Studies in Puritan American Spirituality* (December 4, 1993): 1–24.

———. "Puritan Poetics." In *Early American Literature*, edited by Michael Gilmore. Englewood Cliffs, NJ: Prentice Hall, 1980.

Daniels, Bruce C. *Puritans at Play*. New York: St. Martin's Press, 1995.

Davis, John. *Heresy and Reformation in the South-East of England, 1520–1559*. Royal Historical Society Studies in History Series 34. London, 1983.

Deetz, James, and Patricia Deetz. "The Puritan Errand Re-viewed." *Journal of American Studies* 18, no. 3 (1984): 343–60.

———. *The Times of Their Lives*. New York: W. H. Freeman, 2000.

Delbanco, Andrew. *The Puritan Ordeal*. Cambridge, MA: Harvard University Press, 1989.

Dent, Arthur. *The Plaine Mans Path-Way to Heaven*. London, 1601.

Douglas, Ann. *The Feminization of American Culture*. New York: Anchor, 1977.

Dow, George Francis. *Everyday Life in the Massachusetts Bay Colony*. New York: Arno Press, 1977.

Du Bartas, Guillaume. *The Divine Weekes and Workes*. Translated by Joshua Sylvester. Vol. 1 of *The Complete Works of Joshua Sylvester*, edited by Alexander B. Grosart. New York: AMS Press, 1967.

Dudley, Thomas. "Deputy Governor Dudley's Letter to the Right Honorable, My Very Good Lady, the Lady Bridget, Countess of Lincoln." In Young, *Chronicles*.

Durston, Christopher. "'For the Better Humiliation of the People': Public Days of Fasting and Thanksgiving during the English Revolution." *Seventeenth Century* 7 (1992): 129–49.

Durston, Christopher, and Jacqueline Eales, eds. *The Culture of English Puritanism, 1560–1700*. New York: St. Martin's Press, 1996.

Eales, Jacqueline. "The Continuity of English Puritanism." In Durston and Eales, *Culture of English Puritanism*.

———. "Sir Robert Harley and the 'Character' of a Puritan." *British Library Journal* 15 (1989), 134–57.

Earle, Alice. *Child Life in Colonial Days*. 1899. Reprint, Stockbridge, MA: Berkshire House Publishers, 1993.

———. *Home Life in Colonial Days*. 1898. Reprint, Stockbridge, MA: Berkshire House Publishers, 1993.

Eberwein, Jane Donahue. "'No Rhet'ric We Expect': Argumentation in Bradstreet's 'The Prologue.'" In Cowell and Stanford, *Critical Essays*, 218–26.

———. "The 'Unrefined Ore' of Anne Bradstreet's Quaternions," in *Early American Literature* 9, no. 2 (1974).

Edwards, Jonathan. *Complete Works of Jonathan Edwards.* 4 vols. Reprint of Worcester edition. New York, n.d.

———. *Images or Shadows of Divine Things,* edited by Perry Miller. New Haven, CT: Yale University Press, 1948.

Eliot, T. S. *Selected Prose of T. S. Eliot.* New York: Farrar, Straus and Giroux, 1975.

Elliott, J. H. *The Old World and the New, 1492–1650.* Cambridge: Cambridge University Press, 1970.

———. "Renaissance Europe and America: A Blunted Impact?" In Chiapelli, *First Images of America,* 1:11–23.

Ellis, John Harvard. *Works of Anne Bradstreet in Prose and Verse.* Charlestown, MA: Abram E. Cutter, 1857. Reprint, New York: Peter Smith, 1932, 1962.

Emerson, Everett. *Puritanism in America, 1620–1750.* Boston: Twayne Publishers, 1977.

———, ed. *Letters from New England: The Massachusetts Bay Colony, 1629–1638.* Amherst: University of Massachusetts Press, 1976.

Emerson, Ralph Waldo. *The Portable Emerson.* New York: Viking Press, 1981.

Erdt, T. *Jonathan Edwards, Art, and the Sense of the Heart.* New Haven, CT: Yale University Press, 1980.

Falco, Raphael. *Conceived Presences: Literary Genealogy in Renaissance England.* Amherst: University of Massachusetts Press, 1994.

Felt, Joseph. *History of Ipswich, Essex, and Hamilton.* Ipswich, MA: Clamshell Press, 1966.

Fiering, N. *Jonathan Edwards' Moral Thought and Its British Context.* Cambridge: Cambridge University Press, 1981.

Ford, Karen. *The Poetics of Excess.* Jackson: University Press of Mississippi, 1997.

Forshall, Josiah, and Frederic Madden, eds. *The Holy Bible, Made from the Latin Vulgate by John Wycliffe and His Followers.* Oxford: Oxford University Press, 1850.

Fowler, Alistair. *Seventeenth-Century Verse.* Oxford: Oxford University Press, 1992.

Frere, W., and C. E. Douglas, eds. *Puritan Manifestoes: A Study of the Origin of the Puritan Revolt.* London: Church Historical Society, SPCK, 1954.

Frost, Carol. "Berryman at Thirty-eight: An Aesthetic Biography." *New England Review* 16, no. 3: 36–53.

Fussell, Edwin. *Lucifer in Harness.* Princeton, NJ: Princeton University Press, 1973.

Galinsky, Hans. "Exploring the 'Exploration Report' and Its Image of the Overseas World: Spanish, French and English Variants of a Common Form Type in Early American Literature." *Early American Literature* 12 (1977): 5–24.

Gelpi, Albert. *The Tenth Muse: The Psyche of the American Poet.* Cambridge: Cambridge University Press, 1991.

George, C. H. "Puritanism as History and Historiography." *Past and Present* 41 (1968).

Goodhue, Sarah. "A Valedictory and Monitory Writing." In *Ipswich in the Massachusetts Bay Colony, 1633–1700*, edited by Thomas F. Waters. Ipswich, MA: Ipswich Historical Society, 1905.

Goodwin, Thomas, Philip Nye, et al. *An Apologeticall Narration*. London, 1643.

Gouge, William. *Of Domesticall Duties*. London, 1622, 1626, 1634.

Green, J. R. *A Short History of the English People*. London: MacMillan, 1876.

Greenblatt, Stephen. *Renaissance Self-Fashioning*. Chicago: University of Chicago Press, 1980.

Greene, Jack P. *The Intellectual Construction of America*. Chapel Hill: University of North Carolina Press, 1993.

Greer, Germaine, Susan Hastings, Jeslyn Medoff, Melinda Sansone, eds. *Kissing the Rod: An Anthology of Seventeenth-Century Women's Verse*. New York: Farrar, Straus and Giroux, 1988.

Gura, Phillip. *A Glimpse of Sion's Glory: Puritan Radicalism in New England, 1620–1660*. Middletown, CT: Wesleyan University Press, 1984.

Haffenden, John. *John Berryman: A Critical Commentary*. New York: New York University Press, 1980.

Hakluyt, Richard. "Discourse on Western Planting." In *The Original Writings and Correspondence of the Two Richard Hakluyts*, edited by E. G. R. Taylor. 2 vols. London, 1935.

Hall, David. *The Antinomian Controversy, 1636–1638*. Middletown, CT: Wesleyan University Press, 1968.

———, ed. *Lived Religion in America: Toward a History of Practice*. Princeton, NJ: Princeton University Press, 1997.

———. "On Common Ground: The Coherence of American Puritan Studies." *William and Mary Quarterly* 44 (1987): 193–229.

———. "Religion and Society: Problems and Reconsiderations." In *Colonial British America*, edited by Jack P. Greene and J. R. Pole. Baltimore: Johns Hopkins University Press, 1984.

———. *Worlds of Wonder, Days of Judgment: Popular Religious Belief in Early New England*. Cambridge, MA: Harvard University Press, 1989.

Hallek, Fitz-Greene. "Connecticut." In *American Poetry*, edited by John Hollander. Vol. 1. New York: Library of America, 1993.

Halliday, E. M. *John Berryman and the Thirties: A Memoir*. Amherst: University of Massachusetts Press, 1987.

Halyburton, Thomas. *Memoirs of the Life*. 2nd ed. Edinburgh, 1715.

Hammatt, Abraham. *The Hammatt Papers: Early Inhabitants of Ipswich, Massachusetts, 1633–1700*. Baltimore: Genealogical Publishing, 1980.

Hammond, Jeffrey. "'Make Use of What I Leave in Love': Anne Bradstreet's Didactic Self." *Religion and Literature* 17 (1985): 11–26.

———. *Sinful Self, Saintly Self: The Puritan Experience of Poetry*. Athens: University of Georgia Press, 1993.

Harvey, Elizabeth D. *Ventriloquized Voices: Feminist Theory and English Renaissance Texts*. New York: Routledge, 1992.

Hawthorne, Nathaniel. *The Scarlet Letter*. New York: Bantam, 1989.

Heimert, Alan, and Andrew Delbanco, eds. *The Puritans in America: A Narrative Anthology*. Cambridge, MA: Harvard University Press, 1985.

Hendricks, Margo, and Patricia Parker, eds. *Women, "Race," and Writing in the Early Modern Period*. London: Routledge, 1994.

Heninger, S. K. *The Subtext of Form in the English Renaissance*. University Park: Pennsylvania State University Press, 1994.

Hensley, Jeannine, ed. Introduction to *The Works of Anne Bradstreet*. Cambridge, MA: Harvard University Press, 1967.

Heylyn, Peter. *Aerius Redivivius, or the History of the Presbyterians*. London, 1670.

Higginson, Francis. *New Englands Plantation*. 3rd ed. London, 1630. In *Massachusetts Historical Society Proceedings* 62 (1929).

Hill, Christopher. *Society and Puritanism in Pre-revolutionary England*. 2nd ed. New York: Schocken, 1967.

———. *The World Turned Upside Down: Radical Ideas during the English Revolution*. 1972. Reprint, New York: Penguin Books, 1991.

Hirsch, Edward. *How to Read a Poem*. Harcourt Brace, 1999.

Holder, Alan. "Anne Bradstreet Resurrected." *Concerning Poetry*, no. 2 (Spring 1969): 11–18.

Holifield, E. Brooks. *Era of Persuasion: American Thought and Culture, 1521–1680*. Boston: Twayne Publishers, 1989.

Hollander, John. *The Poetry of Everyday Life*. Ann Arbor: University of Michigan Press, 1998.

Hooker, Thomas. *The Soules Preparation for Christ, or a Treatise of Contrition*. London, 1632.

———. *Survey of the Summe of Church Discipline*. London, 1648.

Hulme, Peter. *Colonial Encounter: Europe and the Native Caribbean, 1492–1797*. London: Methuen, 1986.

Hunt, William. *The Puritan Moment: The Coming of Revolution in an English County*. Cambridge, MA: Harvard University Press, 1983.

Hutchinson, Thomas. *The Hutchinson Papers: A Collection of Original Papers Relative to the History of . . . Massachusetts*. 2 vols. Boston, 1865.

Irigary, Luce. "The Power of Discourse and the Subordination of the Feminine." In *This Sex Which Is Not One*, translated by Catherine Porter, 68–85. Ithaca, NY: Cornell University Press, 1985.

Irvin, William J. "Allegory and Typology 'Imbrace and Greet': Anne Bradstreet's 'Contemplations.'" *Early American Literature* 10 (1975): 30–56. Reprinted in Cowell and Stanford, *Critical Essays*, 174–89.

Jantz, Harold S. *The First Century of New England Verse*. New York: Russell and Russell, 1962.

Jardine, Alice. *Gynesis: Configurations of Women and Modernity*. Ithaca: Cornell University Press, 1985.

Jarrell, Randall. *The Complete Poems*. New York: Farrar, Straus and Giroux, 1969.

Johnson, Barbara. *A World of Difference*. Baltimore: Johns Hopkins University Press, 1987.

Jonson, Ben. *Works of Ben Jonson*. Edited by C. H. Herford and P. E. Simpson. 11 vols. Oxford, 1925–1952, VI.

Josselyn, John. *An Account of Two Voyages to New England*. London, 1672.

Kamensky, Jane. *Governing the Tongue: The Politics of Speech in Early New England*. New York: Oxford University Press, 1997.

Keats, John. *The Complete Poetry and Selected Prose of John Keats*. New York: Random House, 1951.

Keeble, N. H. *The Literary Culture of Nonconformity*. Athens: University of Georgia Press, 1987.

Keller, Evelyn Fox. *Reflections on Gender and Science*. New Haven: Yale University Press, 1985.

Kelly, Richard, ed. *We Dream of Honor: John Berryman's Letters to His Mother*. New York: Norton, 1988.

Kendall, Ritchie D. *The Drama of Dissent: The Radical Poetics of Nonconformity, 1380–1590*. Chapel Hill: University of North Carolina Press, 1986.

Kendrick, Christopher. *Milton: A Study in Ideology and Form*. New York: Methuen, 1986.

Kester, J. "Anne Bradstreet in England: A Bibliographical Note." *American Literature* 13 (March 1941).

Kibbey, Ann. *The Interpretation of Material Shapes in Puritanism*. Cambridge: Cambridge University Press, 1986.

Knapp, Peggy Ann. *The Style of John Wyclif's English Sermons*. The Hague: Mouton, 1977.

Knight, Janice. *Orthodoxies in Massachusetts*. Cambridge, MA: Harvard University Press, 1994.

Knott, John R. *The Sword of the Spirit*. Chicago: University of Chicago Press, 1980.

Kopacz, Paula. "'Simple I according to My Skill': Anne Bradstreet and the Problem of Feminist Aesthetics." *Kentucky Philological Review* (1988): 21–29.

———. "'To Finish What's Begun': Anne Bradstreet's Last Words." *Early American Literature* 23 (1988): 175–87.

Lake, Peter. "'A Charitable Christian Hatred': The Godly and Their Enemies in the 1630's." In Durston and Eales, *Culture of English Puritanism*.

———. "Defining Puritanism — Again?" In Bremer, *Puritanism*.

LaPlante, Eve. *American Jezebel: The Uncommon Life of Anne Hutchinson, the Woman Who Defied the Puritans*. San Francisco: HarperSanFrancisco, 2004.

Leighton, Ann. *Early American Gardens*. Amherst: University of Massachusetts Press, 1986.

Lepore, Jill. *The Name of War*. New York: Knopf, 1998.

Levin, Harry. *The Myth of the Golden Age in the Renaissance*. London: Oxford University Press, 1972.

Lewalski, Barbara Kiefer. *Protestant Poetics and the Seventeenth-Century Religious Lyric*. Princeton, NJ: Princeton University Press, 1979.

———. *Renaissance Genres: Essays on Theory, History, and Interpretation*. Cambridge: Harvard University Press, 1986.

———. *Writing Women in Jacobean England*. Cambridge, MA: Harvard University Press, 1993.

Linebarger, J. M. *John Berryman*. New York: Twayne Publishers, 1974.

Locke, John. "The Second Treatise on Government." In *Two Treatises,* edited by Peter Laslett, 2nd ed. Cambridge: Cambridge University Press, 1967.

Low, Anthony. *Love's Architecture: Devotional Modes in Seventeenth-Century English Poetry.* New York: New York University Press, 1978.

Lowell, James Russell. "Ode Recited at the Harvard Commencement, July 21, 1865." *American Poetry,* edited by John Hollander, vol. 1. New York: Library of America, 1993.

Lyon, Irving. *The Colonial Furniture of New England: A Study of the Domestic Furniture in Use in the Seventeenth and Eighteenth Centuries.* New York: E. P. Dutton, 1977.

Major, R. H., ed. *Selected Letters of Christopher Columbus.* London, 1897.

Margerum, Eileen. "Anne Bradstreet's Public Poetry and the Tradition of Humility." *Early American Literature* 12, no. 2 (Fall 1982): 152–60.

Mariani, Paul. *Dream Song: The Life of John Berryman.* New York: William Morrow, 1990.

Marshall, Stephen. *A Sermon of the Baptizing of Infants.* London, 1644.

Martin, Hugh. *Puritanism and Richard Baxter.* London: SCM Press, 1954.

Martin, Wendy. "Anne Bradstreet's Poetry: A Study of Subversive Piety." In *Shakespeare's Sisters: Feminist Essays on Women Poets,* edited by Sandra Gilbert and Susan Gubar. Bloomington: Indiana University Press, 1979.

Martz, Louis. *The Poetry of Meditation.* New Haven, CT: Yale University Press, 1962.

Mather, Cotton. *Magnalia Christi Americana.* 1702. 2nd American ed., edited by Thomas Robbins. Hartford, CT, 1853.

Mather, Samuel. *Figures and Types of the Old Testament.* 1705. Reprint, New York: Johnson, 1969.

Matthew, F. D., ed. *The English Works of Wyclif Hitherto Unprinted.* 2nd ed. Early English Text Society, O.S. 74, 1902. Reprint, Millwood, NY: Kraus Reprint Co., 1973.

Mawer, Randall. "'Farewel dear Babe': Bradstreet's Elegy for Elizabeth." *Early American Literature* 15 (1980): 29–41. Reprinted in Cowell and Stanford, *Critical Essays,* 205–17.

McGiffert, Michael, ed. *God's Plot: Puritan Spirituality in Thomas Shepard's Cambridge. The Paradoxes of Puritan Piety, being the Autobiography and Journal of Thomas Shepard.* Amherst: University of Massachusetts Press, 1972, 1994.

McMahon, Helen. "Anne Bradstreet, Jean Bertault, and Dr. Crooke." *Early American Newsletter* 3 (Fall 1968): 118–23. Reprinted in Cowell and Stanford, *Critical Essays.*

McMichael, George, et al., eds. *Concise Anthology of American Literature.* 2nd ed. New York: Macmillan, 1985.

Meserole, Harrison, ed. *American Poetry of the Seventeenth-Century.* University Park: Pennsylvania State University Press, 1985.

Miles, Josephine. *The Primary Language of Poetry in the 1640's.* Westport, CT: Greenwood Press, 1971. Reprint of 1948 edition by University of California Press.

Miller, Perry, ed. *The American Puritans: Their Prose and Poetry*. Garden City, NY: Doubleday, 1956.

———. "A Colonial Dialect." In *Early American Literature*, edited by Michael Gilmore. Englewood Cliffs, NJ: Prentice Hall, 1980.

———. *Jonathan Edwards*. New York: Doubleday, 1949.

———. *The New England Mind: The Seventeenth Century*. 1939. Reprint, Cambridge, MA: Harvard University Press, 1954.

———. *Orthodoxy in Massachusetts*. New York: Doubleday, 1933.

Miller, Perry, and Thomas H. Johnson, eds. *The Puritans: A Sourcebook of Their Writings*. New York: Harper, 1963.

Milton, John. *Complete Poems and Major Prose*. Edited by Merritt Hughes. Indianapolis, IN: Odyssey Press, 1957.

Montefiore, Jan. *Feminism and Poetry: Language, Experience, Identity in Women's Writing*. London: HarperCollins, 1994.

Morgan, Edmund. *The Puritan Dilemma: The Story of John Winthrop*. New York: Harper Collins, 1958.

———. *The Puritan Family*. New York: Harper and Row, 1944, 1966.

———. *Visible Saints: The History of a Puritan Idea*. New York: New York University Press, 1963.

Morgan, John. *Godly Learning: Puritan Attitudes towards Reason, Learning, and Education, 1560–1640*. Cambridge: Cambridge University Press, 1986.

Morison, Samuel Eliot. *Builders of the Bay Colony*. 1930. Boston: Houghton, 1958.

———. *The Founding of Harvard College*. Cambridge, MA: Harvard University Press, 1935. Reprint, 1965.

———. "Mistress Anne Bradstreet." In Cowell and Stanford, *Critical Essays*, 43–55.

———. *The Oxford History of the American People*. New York: Oxford University Press, 1965.

Moseley, James. *John Winthrop's World*. Madison: University of Wisconsin Press, 1992.

Murdoch, Kenneth. "The Colonial Experience in the Literature of the United States." In *Early American Literature*, edited by Michael Gilmore. Englewood Cliffs, NJ: Prentice Hall, 1980.

———. *Literature and Theology in Colonial New England*. Cambridge: Harvard University Press, 1949.

Nash, Roderick. *Wilderness and the American Mind*. New Haven: Yale University Press, 1967.

Nichols, Josias. *The Plea of the Innocent*. London, 1602.

Nicolay, Theresa Frieda. *Gender Roles, Literary Authority, and Three American Women Writers: Anne Bradstreet, Mercy Otis Warren, Margaret Fuller Ossoli*. New York: Peter Lang, 1995.

Norton, Charles Eliot. "The Poems of Mrs. Anne Bradstreet." In *The Poetry of Mrs. Anne Bradstreet Together with Her Prose Remains*, edited by Hopkins. New York: Duodecimos, 1897.

Norton, Mary Beth. *Founding Mothers and Fathers: Gendered Power and the Forming of American Society*. New York: Knopf, 1996.

Nuttall, Geoffrey. *The Holy Spirit in Puritan Faith and Experience*. Oxford: Basil Blackwell, 1946.

O'Gorman, Edmundo. *The Invention of America: An Inquiry into the Historical Nature of the New World and the Meaning of History*. Bloomington: University of Indiana Press, 1961.

Orsi, Robert. "Everyday Miracles: The Study of Lived Religion." In *Lived Religion in America*, edited by David Hall. Princeton, NJ: Princeton University Press, 1997.

O'Toole, Patricia. *Money and Morals in America*. New York: Clarkson Potter, 1998.

Parker, Henry. *A Discourse Concerning Puritans*. London, 1641.

Parrington, Vernon Louis. *Main Currents in American Thought*. Vol. 1. New York: Harcourt, Brace, and World, 1927.

Peel, Albert, ed. *The Seconde Parte of a Register*. Cambridge: Cambridge University Press, 1915.

Perkins, William. *Christian Oeconomie*. Translated by T. Pickering. London, 1609.

———. *The Works*. Cambridge, 1605.

Peterson, Mark. *The Price of Redemption: The Spiritual Economy of Puritan New England*. Stanford: Stanford University Press, 1997.

Pettit, Norman. *The Heart Prepared: Grace and Conversion in Puritan Spiritual Life*. New Haven, CT: Yale University Press, 1966.

Piercy, Josephine. *Anne Bradstreet*. New York: Twayne Publishers, 1965.

Pope, Alan. "Petrus Ramus and Michael Wigglesworth: The Logic of Poetic Structure." In Peter White, *Puritan Poets and Poetics*, 210–28.

Pope, Robert. *The Half-Way Covenant: Church Membership in Puritan New England*. Princeton, NJ: Princeton University Press, 1969.

Porterfield, Amanda. *Female Piety in Puritan New England*. New York: Oxford University Press, 1992.

Prynne, William. *A Quench Coal*. London, 1637.

Quarles, Francis. *The Complete Works in Prose and Verse of Francis Quarles*. Edited by Alexander B. Grosart. New York: AMS Press, 1967.

Quilligan, Maureen. *Milton's Spenser: The Politics of Reading*. Ithaca, NY: Cornell University Press, 1983.

Raleigh, Walter. *The Discoverie of the Large, Rich, and Bewtiful Empire of Guiana, with a Relation of the Great and Golden City of Manoa (Which the Spaniards Call El Dorado)*. 1596. Reprint, edited by Robert H. Schomberg, for Hakluyt Society, 1848. Reprint, New York: Lenox Hill, 1970.

Reinitz, Richard. "Perry Miller and Recent American Historiography." *Bulletin of the British Association for American Studies* (1964).

Requa, Kenneth. "Anne Bradstreet's Poetic Voices." Reprinted in Cowell and Stanford, *Critical Essays*, 150–65.

Richardson, Robert D., Jr. "The Puritan Poetry of Anne Bradstreet." In Cowell and Stanford, *Critical Essays*, 101–15.

Ricks, Christopher. *The Force of Poetry*. Oxford: Oxford University Press, 1984.

Roberts, John, ed. *New Perspectives on the Seventeenth-Century English Religious Lyric*. Columbia: University of Missouri Press, 1994.

Rogers, Daniel. "Matrimoniall Honor." London, 1642. In Haller and Haller, "The Puritan Art of Love." *Huntington Library Quarterly* 2 (January 1942): 245–46.

Rogers, Richard. *Certaine Sermons Preached and Penned by Richard Rogers.* London, 1612.

Rosenfield, Alvin H. "Anne Bradstreet's 'Contemplations': Patterns of Form and Meaning." *New England Quarterly* 43 (1970): 79–96. Reprinted in Cowell and Stanford, *Critical Essays.*

Rosenmeier, Rosamund. "'Divine Translation': A Contribution to the Study of Anne Bradstreet's Marriage Poems." *Early American Literature* 12 (1977): 121–35.

———. "The Wounds upon Bathsheba: Anne Bradstreet's Prophetic Art." In Peter White, *Puritan Poets and Poetics,* 129–46.

Rosenthal, M. L. *The New Poets: American and British Poetry since World War II.* New York: Oxford University Press, 1967.

Round, Philip. *By Nature and By Custom Cursed: Transatlantic Civil Discourse and New England Cultural Production, 1620–1660.* Hanover, NH: University Press of New England, 1999.

Rowe, Karen. "Prophetic Visions: Typology and Colonial American Poetry." In Peter White, *Puritan Poets and Poetics,* 47–66.

Rumsey, Peter L. *Acts of God and the People, 1620–1730.* Ann Arbor: University of Michigan Research Press, 1986.

Russell, Howard. *Indian New England before the Mayflower.* Hanover, NH: University Press of New England, 1980.

Ryan, Michael T. "Assimilating New Worlds in the Sixteenth and Seventeenth Centuries." *Comparative Studies in Society and History* 23 (1981).

Sacks, Peter. *The English Elegy: Studies in the Genre from Spenser to Yeats.* Baltimore: Johns Hopkins University Press, 1985.

Saltman, Helen. "'Contemplations': Anne Bradstreet's Spiritual Autobiography." In Cowell and Stanford, *Critical Essays.*

Scammell, G. V. "The New World and Europe in the Sixteenth Century." *Historical Journal* 12 (1969): 389–412.

Scheik, William. *Authority and Female Authorship.* Lexington: University Press of Kentucky, 1998.

———. *Design in Puritan American Literature.* Lexington: University Press of Kentucky, 1992.

———. "Tombless Virtue and Hidden Text: New England Puritan Funeral Elegies." In Peter White, *Puritan Poets and Poetics.*

———, ed. *Two Mather Biographies: "Life and Death" and "Parentator."* Bethlehem, PA: Lehigh University Press, 1989.

Schweitzer, Ivy. "Anne Bradstreet Wrestles with the Renaissance." *Early American Literature* 23 (1988): 291–312.

———. *The Work of Self-Representation: Lyric Poetry in Colonial New England.* Chapel Hill: University of North Carolina Press, 1991.

Seaver, Paul. *The Puritan Lectureships: The Politics of Religious Dissent.* Palo Alto, CA: Stanford University Press, 1970.

———. *Wallington's World: A Puritan Artisan in Seventeenth-Century London.* Palo Alto, CA: Stanford University Press, 1985.

Shafer, Byron. ed. *Is America Different? A New Look at American Exceptionalism.* Oxford: Oxford University Press, 1991.

Shapiro, Alan. *In Praise of the Impure: Poetry and the Ethical Imagination.* Evanston, IL: Northwestern University Press, 1993.

Sheils, W. J. "Puritans in the Diocese of Peterborough, 1558–1610." *Northants Record Society* 30 (1979): 2.

Showalter, Elaine. *Sister's Choice: Tradition and Change in American Women's Writing.* Oxford: Clarendon Press, 1991.

Shucard, Alan. *American Poetry: The Puritans through Walt Whitman.* Boston: Twayne Publishers, 1988.

Shurtleff, Nathaniel, ed. *Records of the Governor and Company of the Massachusetts Bay in New England,* Vol. IV — Part I, 1650–1660. Reprint, New York: AMS Press, 1968.

———. *Records of the Governor and Company of the Massachusetts Bay in New England, 1644–1657.* Vol. 3. Reprint, New York: AMS Press, 1968.

Sidney, Sir Philip. "An Apology for Poesy." In *The Norton Anthology of English Literature,* edited by M. H. Abrams et al. 4th ed. New York: Norton, 1979.

Skulsky, Harold. *Language Recreated: Seventeenth-Century Metaphorists and the Act of Metaphor.* Athens: University of Georgia Press, 1992.

Slavin, Arthur J. "The American Principle from More to Locke." In Chiapelli, *First Images of America,* 1:139–64.

Smith, Anthony. *Theories of Nationalism.* New York: Harper and Row, 1971.

Smith, John. *A Description of New England.* London: Humfrey Townes, 1616. In *Tracts and Other Papers,* edited by Peter Force. 2 vols. New York: Peter Smith, 1947.

———. *New England Trials.* London, 1622. In *Tracts and Other Papers,* edited by Peter Force. 2 vols. New York: Peter Smith, 1947.

Spencer, Luke. "Mistress Bradstreet and Mr. Berryman: The Ultimate Seduction." *American Literature* 66 (1994): 353–66.

Spengemann, William C. *A New World of Words: Redefining Early American Literature.* New Haven, CT: Yale University Press, 1994.

Spenser, Edmund. *Edmund Spenser's Poetry.* Edited by Hugh Maclean. New York: Norton, 1968.

Sprunger, Keith. *The Learned Doctor William Ames.* Urbana: University of Illinois Press, 1972.

Stachniewski, John. *The Persecutory Imagination: English Puritanism and the Literature of Religious Despair.* Oxford: Clarendon Press, 1991.

Stanford, Anne. "Anne Bradstreet: Dogmatist and Rebel." *New England Quarterly* 39 (September 1966).

———. *Anne Bradstreet: The Worldly Puritan.* New York: Burt Franklin, 1974.

Stavely, Keith. *Puritan Legacies: Paradise Lost and the New England Tradition, 1630–1890.* Ithaca, NY: Cornell University Press, 1987.

Stevens, Wallace. *The Collected Poems.* New York: Vintage Press, 1954.

Stone, Lawrence. *The Family, Sex, and Marriage in England, 1500–1800*. New York: Harper and Row, 1977.

Summers, Claude, and Ted-Larry Pebworth, eds. *"Bright Shootes of Everlastingnesse": The Seventeenth-Century Religious Lyric*. Columbia: University of Missouri Press, 1987.

Sweet, Timothy. "Gender, Genre, and Subjectivity in Anne Bradstreet's Early Elegies." *Early American Literature* 23 (1988): 152–74.

Sylvester, Joshua. *The Complete Works of Joshua Sylvester*. Edited by Alexander B. Grosart. 3 vols. New York: AMS Press, 1967.

Taylor, Thomas. *A Man in Christ, or A New Creature*. London, 1628.

Thomas, Harry, ed. *Berryman's Understanding: Reflections on the Poetry of John Berryman*. Boston: Northeastern University Press, 1988.

Tillyard, E. M. W. *The Elizabethan World Picture*. New York: Vintage Books, 1971.

Tocqueville, Alexis de. *Democracy in America*. 1831. New York: Signet Books, 1956.

Toon, P. *The Emergence of Hyper-Calvinism in English Nonconformity 1689–1765*. London, Olive Tree Press, 1967.

Tracy, P. *Jonathan Edwards, Pastor*. Madison: University of Wisconsin Press, 1980.

Trinterud, Leonard, ed. *Elizabethan Puritanism*. New York: Oxford University Press, 1971.

Tyler, Moses Coit. *History of American Literature, 1607–1765*. 1878. Reprint, Ithaca, NY: Cornell University Press, 1949.

Ulrich, Laurel Thatcher. *Good Wives: Image and Reality in the Lives of Women in Northern New England, 1650–1750*. 1980. Reprint, New York: Vintage, 1991.

———. *A Midwife's Tale: The Life of Martha Ballard Based on Her Diary, 1785–1812*. 1990. Reprint, New York: Vintage, 1991.

Vendler, Helen. *The Given and the Made*. Cambridge, MA: Harvard University Press, 1995.

———. *Part of Nature, Part of Us*. Cambridge, MA: Harvard University Press, 1980.

Virgoe, Roger, ed. *Illustrated Letters of the Paston Family: Private Life in the Fifteenth Century*. New York: Weidenfeld & Nicolson, 1989.

Walker, Cheryl. "Anne Bradstreet: A Woman Poet." In Cowell and Stanford, *Critical Essays*, 254–62.

Wall, Robert E. *Massachusetts Bay: The Crucial Decade, 1640–1650*. New Haven, CT: Yale University Press, 1972.

Waller, Gary. *The Sidney Family Romance*. Detroit: Wayne State University Press, 1993.

Waller, Jennifer. "'My Hand a Needle Better Fits': Anne Bradstreet and Women Poets in the Renaissance." *Dalhousie Review* 54 (1974): 436–49.

Wallerstein, Ruth. *Studies in Seventeenth-Century Poetics*. Madison: University of Wisconsin Press, 1950.

Ward, Samuel. *A Coal from the Altar to Kindle the Holy Fire of Zeal in a Sermon Preached at a General Visitation at Ipswich*. London, 1615.

Watters, David H. *"With Bodilie Eyes": Eschatological Themes in Puritan Literature and Gravestone Art.* Ann Arbor: University of Michigan Research Press, 1981.

Weber, Donald. "Historicizing the Errand." *American Literary History* 2, no. 1 (1990): 101–18.

White, Elizabeth Wade. *Anne Bradstreet: "The Tenth Muse."* New York: Oxford University Press, 1971.

White, Peter, ed. *Puritan Poets and Poetics: Seventeenth-Century American Poetry in Theory and Practice.* University Park: Pennsylvania State University Press, 1985.

Whittier, John Greenleaf. "Massachusetts to Virginia." In *Concise Anthology of American Literature,* edited by George McMichael. New York: Macmillan, 1985.

Widdowes, Giles. *The Schismatical Puritan.* Oxford, 1631.

Williams, Stanley. *The Beginnings of American Poetry, 1620–1855.* Uppsala, Sweden: Almquist and Wiksells, 1951.

Wilson, John. *Pulpit in Parliament: Puritanism during the English Civil Wars.* Princeton, NJ: Princeton University Press, 1969.

Winebrenner, Kimberly Cole. "Anne Bradstreet: The Development of a Puritan Voice." PhD Diss., Kent State University, 1991.

Winthrop, John. *The History of New England from 1630 to 1649.* Edited by James Savage. Vols. 1 and 2. New York: Arno Press, 1972.

———. *The Journal of John Winthrop, 1630–1649.* Abridged Edition. Edited by Richard S. Dunn and Laetitia Yeandle. Cambridge, MA: Harvard University Press, 1996.

Woodbridge, Linda. *Women and the English Renaissance: Literature and the Nature of Womankind, 1540–1640.* Chicago: University of Chicago Press, 1984.

Wright, Louis B. "The Purposeful Reading of Our Colonial Ancestors." *A Journal of English Literary History* 4, no. 2 (June 1937): 85–111.

Yin, Joanna Milbauer. "Regenerating the Argument: Representation of Women in Puritan Literature." PhD Diss., University of Hawaii, 1995. Ann Arbor, MI.

Young, Alexander, ed. *Chronicles of the First Planters of the Colony of Massachusetts Bay.* 2 vols. Boston: Little and Brown, 1846.

Zakai, Avihu. *Exile and Kingdom: History and Apocalypse in the Puritan Migration to America.* Cambridge: Cambridge University Press, 1992.

Ziff, Larzer. *The Career of John Cotton: Puritanism and the American Experience.* Princeton, NJ: Princeton University Press, 1962.

———, ed. *John Cotton on the Churches of New England.* Cambridge, MA: Harvard University Press, 1968.

Zuckerman, Michael. "Identity in British America: Unease in Eden." In *Colonial Identity in the Atlantic World, 1500–1800,* edited by N. Canny and A. Pagden. Princeton, NJ: Princeton University Press, 1987.

Index

adultery, Puritanism and, 47
Aiken, Conrad, 283
air. *See also* "The Four Elements"
  characterized as element, 221
Ambrose (ship), 83, 90, 116
  deaths aboard, 106, 299n31
Andover, Bradstreets' move to,
  226–229
Angel Gabriel (ship), 95
Anglicanism, Puritan dispute with,
  54–55
Antwerp, massacre of Protestants in,
  58
Arbella (ship), 83, 84. *See also* voyage to
  New World
  accommodations on, 90–91
"As weary pilgrim now at rest" (Bradstreet), 277–278
"The Author to Her Book" (Bradstreet), 251, 252
autobiography, Anne Bradstreet's,
  258–259

baptism of infants, 134
Bartholomew Fair (Jonson), 296n1
"Before the Birth of One of Her Chil-
  dren" (Bradstreet), 215
Behn, Aphra, 309n26
Berryman, John, "Homage to Mistress
  Bradstreet," 192, 284, 311n5
Blackstone, William, 113
blood, as bodily humor, 222
Body of Liberties (Ward), 201–202,
  305n17
Book of Martyrs (Foxe), 56, 293n4
Book of Sport (James I), 42
Boston (England), 21–22, 296n20
Boston (Mass.)
  as more "chosen," 183–184
  support of Anne Hutchinson, 187,
    190
  Winthrop's establishment of,
    113–114
Botolph's stone, 21
Bowtell, Stephen, 244
Bradstreet, Anne (daughters of Samuel
  and Mercy), 275, 276, 279–280
Bradstreet, Anne Dudley
  ambitions of, 129–130, 191–193
  Anne Hutchinson as worrisome
    "model" for, 177–180
  aptitude for poetry, 33–34, 35

Bradstreet, Anne Dudley (*continued*)
  attitude toward Catholicism, 58–59
  autobiography of, 258–259
  barrenness of, 117
  concerns regarding plagiarism,
    219–220, 236
  death of, 280–282
  desire to be remembered after
    death, 214–216
  early relationship with Simon,
    42–44
  education of, 32–33, 34–35, 36–37
  farewell poem, 277–278
  homes of, 123, 164, 166, 228
  house destroyed by fire, 275–276
  household responsibilities of,
    125–126, 131–133, 175, 200, 205
  illnesses of, 34–35, 48–50, 126–127,
    256, 257–258, 260
  importance of Du Bartas to, 33–34,
    193, 218, 219
  intellectual hunger of, 180–183
  marriage of, 50–51
  mastering writing literacy, 36–37
  meditations (*see* meditations, Anne
    Bradstreet's)
  move to Andover, 228–229
  move to Ipswich, 158–163, 303n1
  and oath of commitment, 110–112
  personal relationship with God, 50
  poems of (*see* poems, Anne Brad-
    street's)
  pregnancies of, 130–131, 159
  relationship with her father, 19, 36,
    209–210, 214, 306n30, 307n6
  relationship with John Woodbridge,
    237–238, 239–240, 271–272
  relationship with Nathaniel Ward,
    180–183, 209–210, 306n30
  reluctance to emigrate, 4–5, 61, 68,
    78, 108
  response to departure preparations,
    71–72
  sexual concerns of, 46–47, 51,
    292n2
  spiritual concerns of, 16–17, 19–20,
    24, 43, 197–198, 258–259
  struggle between flesh and spirit,
    180, 268–270, 284, 305n13
  testimonials and accolades to, 243,
    253–254
  weariness of, 256, 257–258

ABOUT THE AUTHOR

Charlotte Gordon has published two books of poetry, *When the Grateful Dead Came to St. Louis* and *Two Girls on a Raft*. She received an undergraduate degree in English and American Literature from Harvard University and a PhD from Boston University. She was a postdoctoral fellow at Boston University and has taught at many New England schools and colleges, including Boston University, Salem State College, The Glen Urquhart School, and The Waring School in Beverly, Massachusetts. She currently lives in Gloucester, Massachusetts.